Warrior Nations

Also by Roger L. Nichols

General Henry Atkinson: A Western Military Career (Norman, Okla., 1965)

(ed.) *The Missouri Expedition, 1818–1820: The Journal of Surgeon John Gale* (Norman, Okla., 1969)

(ed. with George R. Adams) *The American Indian: Past and Present* (Waltham, Mass., 1971; 6th ed., Norman, Okla., 2008)

(with Leonard Dinnerstein and David M. Reimers) *Natives and Strangers: Ethnic Groups and the Building of America* (New York, 1979)

(with Patrick L. Halley) *Stephen Long and American Frontier Exploration* (Newark, Del., 1980)

(ed.) *Arizona Directory of Historians and Historical Organizations* (Tucson, 1985)

(ed.) *American Frontier and Western Issues: A Historiographical Review* (Westport, Conn., 1986)

Black Hawk and the Warrior's Path (Arlington Heights, Ill., 1992)

Indians in the United States and Canada: A Comparative History (Lincoln, Nebr., 1998)

(ed.) *Black Hawk's Autobiography* (Ames, Iowa, 1999)

American Indians in U.S. History (Norman, Okla., 2003)

Warrior Nations

The United States and Indian Peoples

ROGER L. NICHOLS

University of Oklahoma Press : Norman

This book is published with the generous assistance of the McCasland Foundation, Duncan, Oklahoma.

Library of Congress Cataloging-in-Publication Data

Nichols, Roger L.
   Warrior nations : the United States and Indian peoples / Roger L. Nichols.
      pages cm
   Summary: "The author's purpose is to provide a broader analytical framework with which to study Native American wars. The endeavors to ascertain how it was that Natives and American settlers came to chose the military option as a way of dealing with one another during the century after the American Revolution. The other presents the work using a chronologically ordered series of chapter-length case studies, each devoted to a specific "Indian war." "—Provided by publisher.
   Includes bibliographical references and index.
   ISBN 978-0-8061-4382-8 (pbk.)
   1. Indians of North America—Wars.   I. Title.
   E81.N53 2013
   970.004'97—dc23   2013009233

The paper in this book meets the guidelines for permanence and durability of the Committee on Production Guidelines for Book Longevity of the Council on Library Resources, Inc. ∞

For
Sandi, Brittini, Asheli, and Kassidi
Welcome to the family

Contents

List of Maps

MAPS

Preface

This book grew out of my long-held interest in American pioneer settlement activities and the relationships between the settlers and the American Indian communities that already occupied the land sought so eagerly by the invaders. For years historians have so emphasized the military side of these events that it is now much easier than before to find detailed accounts of the incidents, battles, and campaigns or the chiefs, generals, and politicians involved in them. Yet it seemed to me that only a few of the really first-rate accounts addressed the nonmilitary aspects of the story—in particular, the causes that brought on violent conflict. This is not a formal military history, though at times campaigning gets some attention. Rather, it is a general work that offers a broad comparative framework demonstrating the wide variety of ideas, policies, and actions that led to the Indian wars examined here.

With that objective in mind, I devote each chapter in this book to a different U.S.-Indian war. Each case study emphasizes the local situation and the deeds of particular people that helped start hostilities. By design the chapters all follow a similar format in order to facilitate comparison. This makes it possible to demonstrate what the groups in each situation shared with other Native and white people and what elements made their circumstances distinct. To do that, every chapter opens with an incident or series of events that led directly to open violence. Then it backtracks to describe the Native situation briefly and moves to a narration of the events that shifted from confrontation to open warfare. Each of these conflicts shared similar causes with some of the others but also had distinctive elements. Often Indian war narratives focus primarily on national policies or on disputes between the federal authorities, civilian or military, and the tribes. Certainly such disputes occurred repeatedly, but an emphasis on U.S. actions obscures the divisions among peoples on both sides. It may overlook the complexities of tribal, band, and village societies and may neglect tribal attachments to traditional homelands, even though these often proved central to the events. At the same time a history from a purely U.S. perspective implicitly assumes that the national administration, Congress, the Office of Indian Affairs, the army, and the local civilian population all acted on similar motivations and objectives when dealing with Native peoples.

The following chapters demonstrate conclusively that such a view does little to help readers understand the two most important elements in how and why the wars began. One was the ongoing invasion of North America, from the seventeenth through the nineteenth century, by millions of people. Whether peaceful or not, this long-term movement of population brought members of two distinct cultures into close contact. As thousands of pioneers forced their way west, they found little to admire in the indigenous societies they encountered. Instead they considered Indians dirty savages who blocked their chances for economic success. The deep fear of their tribal neighbors that frontier citizens had has colored American thinking to the present. The repeated use of "Indian Country" as a label for enemy-held territory in wars from Vietnam to Afghanistan and the code name "Geronimo" attached to Osama Bin Laden by the Navy Seals who killed him illustrate this.

The actions of the Native people provide the second factor necessary to understanding these events. To them, the invaders represented a threat to their land and lives, and so they took both offensive and defensive actions to ensure their own well-being. They also followed social and military customs that terrified their pioneer neighbors. The clearly incompatible social, economic, and political differences that separated the villagers from the Anglo-Americans guaranteed friction, misunderstandings, disputes, and violence between the two groups. It is difficult to reach any other conclusion than that warfare could not have been avoided even if all interracial dealings had been honest and fair, or even if the federal system for dealing with tribal peoples had worked flawlessly.

Any scholarly book benefits from help from colleagues and other scholars in raising issues, addressing research questions, and sharing and ideas. Over the years archivists, university librarians, and state historical society staff members have all willingly made documents and books available. In particular, staff at the Library of Congress, the Wisconsin Historical Society, the Arizona Historical Society, and the University of Arizona libraries have all assisted in many ways. Professional colleagues Gary Anderson, Bruce Dinges, Michael Green, and Armand LaPotin each read at least one chapter and helped steer me toward needed material and away from wrongheaded assumptions. Here in the University of Arizona History Department, Katrina Jagodinsky and the First Friday Readers Group read a draft of the introduction and offered insightful suggestions about it. I am grateful for all of this effective help and the improvements that each contributed to the final version of this project.

Individuals on the staff of the University of Oklahoma Press always help to make "book production" pleasant and as hassle free as possible. Particular thanks are due to Alessandra Jacobi Tamulevich, Acquisitions Editor for American Indian and Latin American studies, and to Emmy Ezzell, Assistant Director and Production Manager, and her staff. A special thanks to Tom Jonas for turning my notes into coherent maps for this book.

As always, Marilyn read the chapter drafts carefully, and her comments helped focus my ideas and clarify the prose. Whatever errors of fact or judgment remain I have made despite these often penetrating critiques.

Tucson, Arizona
January 2013

Introduction

War and violence may fascinate or repel Americans, but examples of conflict litter the pages of our history. In fact, one might paraphrase H. Rap Brown's famous statement from the 1960s that war is as American as cherry pie. This is no idle claim. Without question, an honest look at the nation's past fully supports this accusation. From the earliest days of settlement the invading Europeans in the British colonies fought against both international competitors and their Indian neighbors. These clashes included at least the Anglo-Powhatan War, 1622; the Pequot War, 1637; the second Anglo-Powhatan War, 1644; King Philip's War, 1675–76; Bacon's Rebellion, 1676; King William's War, 1689–97; Queen Anne's War, 1702–13; the Tuscarora War, 1711–12; King George's War, 1744–48; the Cherokee War, 1759–61; the French and Indian War, 1756–63; Lord Dunmore's War, 1774; and the American Revolution. Even this extended list of colonial-era conflicts overlooks the raiding and minor local hostilities that failed to gain space in the narratives of the early national experience.

Attaining independence brought no change as the United States continued to follow the same violent and bloody path. It has conducted foreign wars in every generation from the war against the Barbary pirates in 1801–1805 through the combat in Afghanistan in the twenty-first century, as well as "more than 40" wars against the Indians.[1] These recurring

1

conflicts prompted at least three authors to describe American foreign policy as carrying out "Perpetual War for Perpetual Peace" and helped create a virtual culture of war in our society.[2] For example, three of the most important secular holidays—Memorial Day, the Fourth of July, and Veterans' Day—all commemorate past military actions. Many popular historic monuments such as the Gettysburg Battlefield, the Little Bighorn Battlefield, and the Vietnam Memorial reflect this same focus. In addition, the government uses military terms to mobilize support for domestic programs such as the wars on poverty, on drugs, and on terror.

Many Indians lived in highly militarized societies too. The young men in almost every village had the arms and experience to provide a fighting force that could act as colonial minutemen or frontier volunteer militia did in white society. Through a variety of public ceremonies and tribal warrior groups Indians recognized and honored military skills as much as the invaders did. Students of tribal experiences need little reminding of the central roles that raiding and warfare played in Native villages.[3] Daring and competence in wartime led to personal recognition and respect, and few social curbs discouraged hostile actions. Young men received approval and status when they demonstrated bravery in battle or skill in raiding. From long before the earliest days of colonial settlement, Indians had attacked each other at least as often as they later battled against whites. To the list of conflicts above, one can add intertribal wars involving the Iroquois-Hurons, Cherokees-Creeks, Savannahs-Westos, Tuscaroras-Savannahs, Sauks-Osages, Sioux-Pawnees, Utes-Navajos, Apaches-O'odhams, and others.

Often these conflicts differed from fighting against the Europeans because they tended to be small in scale and the indigenous weapons lacked the devastating power of firearms. Most of the early intertribal violence did not reach the level of total war that became the norm by the late eighteenth century because the village societies would not accept the number of casualties that this would bring. Nevertheless, their frequent participation in raids and other hostilities had prepared the Indians to defend themselves, attack outsiders, seize new territories, and take captives for ransom, slavery, or incorporation into their societies long before Europeans arrived. Certainly by the nineteenth century those experiences equipped the villagers with the skills and tactics needed when they encountered the invading whites. This is presented clearly in the extensive scholarship on intertribal warfare by a host of authors, including Wayne Lee, John Grenier, Pekka Hämäläinen, Ned Blackhawk, and Colin Calloway, to mention just a few.[4]

Peace remained elusive when the two militarily experienced societies met. It should come as no surprise that the U.S. Bureau of the Census (reporting on the same data that it thought showed the end of the frontier) noted in 1894 that the nation had waged over forty wars against tribal groups since Independence. The report's authors estimated that at least 30,000 tribal members had died in the fighting. They pointed out that Indians tended to "conceal, where possible, their actual loss in battle and carry their killed and wounded off," so the number should be increased by at least another 15,000 fatalities. In addition, they estimated that individual pioneers had killed another 8,500 Native people. Their analysis concluded that at least 53,500 Indians had died as the direct result of American military action and violence toward the tribes.[5] These figures ignored the additional lives lost because of malnutrition, forced population moves, and diseases that carried off many of the survivors. Even if the officials undercounted the fatalities, the figures seem particularly significant because they came from mostly faceless bureaucrats who crunched the numbers gathered during the census, rather than from some muckraking campaign to criticize the federal government.

Assuming that the clerks reviewed the data correctly, one Indian war occurred for every three years of America's national existence between George Washington's presidency and the head count just over a hundred years later. Violent conflicts with the indigenous people broke out in other settler societies such as Australia and Canada, but neither of those countries experienced the amount of fighting that took place in the United States.[6] Apparently the situation in America allowed or encouraged more interracial conflict than elsewhere at the same time. For years American scholars have offered a variety of reasons for how and why these conflicts began. Some depict the federal government as being totally to blame, either by design or through ineptitude. David Nichols, for example, blames a corrupt political system, while Thom Hatch depicts frontier leaders as trying to use wars for personal advancement.[7] Activist writers such as Thomas DiLorenzo, David E. Stannard, Russell Thornton, and the now discredited Ward Churchill go far beyond these views. Using terms like "genocide," "holocaust," or both in their titles and analyses, they depict U.S. authorities as violent invaders who seized the land and its resources while they destroyed the tribes.[8]

Others disagree (some sharply) about any concerted effort to destroy Indians physically. For example, despite his clearly stated pro-Indian feelings, anthropologist James Clifton denies that U.S. leaders had any such intent. In fact, he states boldly: "In the over 200 years it has existed as a nation, no U.S. administration from George Washington to Ronald Reagan has ever approved, tolerated, or abetted a policy aimed at the deliberate, systematic extermination of Indians."[9] While technically true, this comment ignores the fact that in the long run the actions or inaction of federal officials brought destruction to thousands of Native people as the nation expanded to the Pacific coast. Certainly the United States took tribal lands and resources and destroyed cultures, but the evidence clearly demonstrates that the government had no program for the purpose of physically destroying tribal people.

Gary Anderson offers a third interpretation of American dealings with Native people that falls between extermination and having no deliberate plan to harm Indian society. Using post-1990 definitions he presents whites' actions toward tribal people as resulting in "deliberate ethnic cleansing," at least in Texas. According to Anderson, the state leaders wanted tribal land, so they encouraged or allowed the Texas Rangers and other frontiersmen to use violence to drive the Indian groups out of the state.[10] This happened in other regions too. Bands of pioneers or frontier militiamen assaulted Indian villages to murder, rob, or capture the Native people. Federal officials could not or would not prevent these raids, which were often meant to drive tribal groups from their land.

In contrast to the pioneers' violence, federal programs from the 1790s into the twentieth century sought the same results through more peaceable means. For nearly a century the government concluded treaties that it hoped gave protection, payments, and help to the tribes. Despite what those agreements promised, federal officials faced repeated opposition from American citizens. As early as 1796 George Washington complained to secretary of war Timothy Pickering that "scarcely any thing short of a Chinese wall, or a line of troops, will restrain Land jobbers, and the encroachment of settlers upon the Indian territory." That difficulty did not shake officials' determination to acculturate the Native peoples.[11] They used schools, churches, and farms and later reservations (at least in theory) to prepare Indians for entry into the majority society, but without most of their land. Because most of the villagers preferred their own culture, those programs usually failed except in stripping away most of the tribal lands.

When war between the United States and the Indians began, local issues rather than national policies often triggered the fighting. While the invasion of tribal territory by aggressive Americans was a central element in beginning the conflicts, this study shows that Indian actions and customs also played large roles. Often they led to culturally approved retaliation that contributed directly to starting later hostilities. Other factors stand out as well. The pioneers' utter contempt for tribal people and their way of life became another important cause for war. A range of incidents that escalated from personal insults to beatings, robberies, rapes, and murders of their families and friends by pioneers caused bitter resentment among the villagers and often led to murderous incidents that contributed directly to starting large-scale hostilities. At times the government's dithering and inattention encouraged rather than prevented such violence. It is possible that the villagers saw the government's lack of effective means or will to punish those responsible as an encouragement for white aggression. Examples of white atrocities against Native groups and of Indian complaints about unjust treatment certainly appear in virtually every account of frontier settlement. Studies by Albert Hurtado, Karl Jacoby, and Gary Anderson all offer graphic accounts that depict nineteenth-century pioneer or civilian "wars of extermination" against the Indians.[12]

The repeated frontier violence between whites and Indians both resulted from and led to increased fear, suspicion, and hatred between the two peoples. Long before American Independence the hostilities had devolved into all-out race war.[13] In fact, because ever-growing numbers of whites moved into the newly opened areas, the interracial bitterness rarely faded.[14] While the weak new government hoped to keep peace with the Native groups, it signaled its determination to establish control and authority over people living beyond the Appalachians. Despite having just escaped what the patriots saw as the burdens of colonialism, American leaders quickly developed their own versions of it. In 1787, as delegates struggled to write the new constitution at Philadelphia, the Confederation Congress enacted the Northwest Ordinance, which laid down the rules for establishing new territories in the west. That document created a colonial system to govern its citizens as it encouraged them to move into newly opened regions still occupied by many indigenous groups.[15]

The determination to control affairs in frontier areas affected the thinking about Indian relations too. Because of their victory over England, leaders of the early republic reasoned that they held the same legal rights to the land claimed earlier by the British. Under that theory the government owned all the land, while the tribes could use their home territory until they sold it to the United States or lost it in war. For the next century federal policies stood on that basis. From the start national leaders talked and acted as if they wanted to include Indians as a part of American society. As early as the 1790s agents such as Benjamin Hawkins pushed a full-fledged acculturation program. A few years later, as president, Thomas Jefferson encouraged Indians to become farmers and stop hunting so that the United States could get additional tribal land. By the War of 1812 the government had begun to fund Christian groups as they organized churches, built schools, and operated model farms to further this program of land thievery presented as social incorporation. The evidence suggests that few citizens shared or accepted this goal. Rather, the hatred and racism that had characterized relations between pioneers and Indians during the colonial era remained. In addition, in the few instances where the villagers successfully adapted white farming practices, their pioneer neighbors became jealous and worried that they could never obtain the lands being occupied by tribal farmers and herders.

Many Americans rejected any effort to bring Indians into the general society, and government officials responded at least in part to their views. While some early federal policies sought acculturation, later government actions produced a sort of schizophrenia as Americans worked to "other" Native peoples and to acculturate them at the same time. The most obvious example of treating them as perpetual outsiders came after the early 1830s when Chief Justice John Marshall labeled them "domestic dependent nations." The informal and then forced removal of eastern tribes to land beyond the Mississippi River that followed his ruling as well as the continued refusal of whites to tolerate Indians in their society illustrated this duality. Western reservations that segregated the tribes after 1850 continued this confusion. Working through one of these conflicting approaches, in every case the United States acted to end tribal independence and remove any chance for the indigenous people to have control over their own lives. Some leaders apparently assumed that they could implement national policies without violence. For example, in 1849 Senator Jefferson Davis supported the transfer of the Office of Indian Affairs from the War Department to the newly created Interior Department. Peace rather than war had become "the ordinary condition" of relations with the tribes, he argued, so it made sense to let civilians oversee tribal relations.[16] Despite that optimism, another senator charged that "mismanagement, bad faith, fraud, speculation, and downright robbery" characterized government actions as federal officials tried to implement their goals.[17] The degradation of tribal environments, aggressive and greedy white pioneers, traders, and Indian leaders, poor translations, and even just plain bad luck further complicated matters, kept relations volatile, and ensured continued intermittent violence.

Much of the literature that discusses these issues either depicts Indians as victims or focuses heavily on the formal military actions in each conflict. Scholars have chronicled specific wars, written biographies of tribal leaders and army officers, and traced Indian-newcomer violence as part of individual tribal or regional and state histories. Hundreds of books and articles about these wars line the shelves of libraries, historical societies, and private collections of military history. Much of this work is excellent, combining thorough research with thoughtful writing. Even studies that locate a single conflict within a broad national setting, however, rarely draw parallels linking their subject to other hostilities. Certainly some scholarship on Native-newcomer violence has offered the analytical framework needed to understand the hostilities between the Indians and the United States. For example, scholars such as Robert M. Utley, Bruce Vandervort, and Robert Wooster have analyzed regional, national, and comparative international conflicts between indigenous people and invaders and placed them within coherent patterns of frontier conquest.[18]

This book ties America's wars against the Indians directly to the continuing demands for tribal land and resources that grew out of national territorial expansion. But its goal is to move beyond the existing frameworks of battle and campaign narratives, government corruption and incompetence, and tribal victimization. Building on the existing studies of each war, the study places the conflicts on what at first appear to be two parallel tracks. First it demonstrates how each one shared broad general causes with many other Indian wars. Then the narrative moves on to analyze the specific decisions made in Indian villages as well as actions taken by local whites and government officials that led to particular incidents that in turn escalated into open violence. When considered together, the shared and particular elements in each situation help keep the analysis centered on both Indian initiatives and local pioneer actions. Often those explain more about the causes of war than do the bureaucratic or military actions.

From the start national policies toward Native peoples and the demands of an ever-expanding white population set the parameters for Indian-white relations. The white population swelled from a mere 3.9 million recorded in the 1790 census to 62.9 million a century later. As part of this nearly explosive growth hundreds of thousands of pioneers demanded federal actions that threatened tribal independence and actual survival. This kept the invaders and the Indians uneasy, perhaps fearful, about their neighbors. While individual whites may have seen some elements of Indian culture as worth copying, as Philip Deloria has shown, the majority of those living nearest the Native groups thought otherwise.[19] They assumed the superiority of American ideas such as private property, hierarchical government, and individual participation in a capitalistic economy. Those practices underlay national efforts to overcome the perceived shortcomings of tribal life. They provided a framework for the changing system of ill-conceived and poorly administered federal Indian policies that suffered from corruption, greed, hatred, ignorance, and occasional military overreaction.

The wars examined here demonstrate clearly that when violence began Native Americans fought the United States for more reasons than self-defense. Some incidents resulted from tribal leaders' determination to retain their local independence and village cultures, when federal officials insisted that they accept new and foreign practices. Clearly, most Native leadership practices differed vastly from those accepted in white society. Among the Indians, village and band headmen shared authority with hunting and war leaders as well as shamans, and firmly rooted tribal customs often prevented them from agreeing on a single course of action. The chiefs' inability to keep peace with rival tribes or to ensure compliance with signed treaties, for example, led to repeated friction within their home villages as well as with other nearby tribes, pioneer communities, and American authorities.

Indian leaders almost universally rejected the assumption by federal officers that all members of a tribe had to follow treaty provisions when only some of the village leaders or band chiefs had signed the treaty. Such agreements often called on local headmen to end the basic cultural practice of clan revenge, which they lacked authority to do. As a result, when Americans ignored or rejected that reality and tried to force the chiefs' to stop the young men from carrying out their duties, they angered the villagers, who saw this as just another instance of unacceptable white meddling in their lives. Obviously, some Indian practices and actions created uncertainty and resentment within the nearby white communities. In each of the wars analyzed here, a combination of irreconcilable customs and social practices and deep ethnocentrism on both sides provided the context for violence within the ongoing American invasion of the land.

Many of the forty conflicts that the census office noted might be seen as incidents or tragic events rather than wars, but not the eight discussed here. Their duration provided one way to distinguished between an incident or fight that lasted only a day or two and a war. In each case the hostilities occurred during a period from a few weeks to several years. These examples all include the use of federal troops in the campaign. Unlike many local incidents, these all received national attention. Some readers might have preferred having different wars included here, but these eight met my criteria as well or better than any other list that might be proposed. As a group they illustrate the variety of circumstances as well as the long-established patterns that led to hostilities during most of the century-long time span. They demonstrate Native-newcomer issues in many of the distinctive regions of the country. Most of them include at least one novel or nearly unmatched cause. While sharing many elements that brought violence, each of these tribal conflicts had distinctive local issues, as the following preview of these wars demonstrates.

The Ohio Valley conflict represents open American diplomatic and military aggression as well as foreign (British) intervention. To the south the Red Stick War illustrates bitter internal divisions surrounding religious revival and cultural changes. The Arikara War in Dakota includes the fusion of pressures brought by the fur trade and ongoing bitter intertribal conflicts. The Black Hawk War shares many particular issues with the others, but it resulted from a probably fraudulent treaty, bitterly divided village leadership, and accidental fighting. The Minnesota Sioux War depicts the impact of the Indians' economic collapse and the actions of clearly dishonest and grasping white traders and local politicians. The Cheyenne Arapaho War in Colorado came from the disruption of essential buffalo hunting by whites migrating west, the political aspirations of Colorado leaders, and, at least as important, the lack of federal supervision during the Civil War. In the Southwest the Apache conflict evolved out of long-standing violence between those people and outsiders: Spain, Mexico, and the United States. The Nez Perce War reflects Native attempts to remain separate from invading miners and land-hungry farmers. In all but the Arikara War and Apache War, white demands for land proved central. At the same time, existing divisions among both whites and Indians limited chances to resolve fundamental issues between the two groups.

In the wars examined here the indigenous people shared some experiences with other Native groups. At one time or another contact with the newcomers brought epidemic disease, wholesale population loss, and major disruption of village life. Pioneer encroachments into tribal territory or onto Native lands undoubtedly led to both immediate and long-term interracial stress. Whether because of the reduction of game, the seizure of good land, the invasion and desecration of sacred spaces, personal misunderstandings, or local violence, relations between Anglo-Americans and Indian Americans deteriorated every time. In each case divided leadership on both sides added to the confusion. Willful ethnocentric actions created their own sets of issues. American insistence on ending Indian independence coupled with the equally strong determination of tribal leaders to retain it and violent acts by individual villagers brought interracial conflict. Neither village chiefs nor pioneer community leaders could restrain their own people from committing random hostile acts, which further strained relations. In each instance presented here, some combination of these elements led to war.

The analysis of these conflicts demonstrates the vast gulf between national policy objectives and the results of their implementation. When the government sought to incorporate tribal groups into the general society, its programs failed because neither whites nor tribal people wanted that outcome. Unlike many immigrants who sought to become part of American society, most Indians had no desire to change their lives drastically. Certainly they incorporated European and Anglo-American goods and practices that made their lives easier or more pleasant, but they rejected becoming mere copies of the invaders. During the century examined here Indian chiefs faced enormous challenges posed by the ever-expanding American society. As leaders of small, divided societies, they had no chance to retain their independence or traditional economic practices. Their ultrademocratic social customs both encouraged young men to carry out risky and violent activities and limited the chiefs' authority to stop that conduct. Individual traditional leaders exercised almost complete autonomy, so they often ignored treaties that they had opposed. That infuriated U.S. officials who had negotiated those documents.

At the same time, U.S. officials found it almost impossible to implement their often contradictory policies aimed at Native Americans. When dealing with most tribes, they remained ignorant of, rejected, or ignored the deeply held Indian beliefs about local band independence. They had no intention of negotiating with each small group when they could pressure a few chiefs to accept their demands. This tactic limited the number and expense of council meetings but more importantly provided an excuse for harsh actions toward groups whose leaders refused or avoided signing treaties that ceded their tradition homelands and surrendered their local independence. At the same time American citizens disregarded laws and treaties just as young Indian men ignored their leaders' wishes. Those actions created tension, frustration, and violence on both sides. The power relationships between the two societies heavily favored the United States. Federal officials bore the responsibility for curbing illegal and hostile actions by frontier whites but repeatedly failed to do so.

It is my contention that a variety of acts and ideas erupted to start these wars. First, the ethnocentric and racist ideas of the invading American pioneers led to belligerent and persistent anti-Indian actions and attitudes. Second, white newcomers made unending demands that the United States acquire tribal lands. Third, the government showed an inability or unwillingness to prevent or punish pioneer anti-Indian violence. Fourth, the highly militarized nature of village society and the related ceremonies honored successful martial actions. Fifth, tribal customs required young Indian men to protect their clan and avenge injuries to its members by outsiders. Sixth, the Indians were determined to keep their traditional lands, culture, and tribal independence. Together these elements played central roles in helping to cause almost all of the wars examined here.

CHAPTER 1

The Ohio Valley War, 1786–1795

In mid-September 1786 Colonel Benjamin Logan led an 800-man force of Kentucky militiamen north into Shawnee country, hoping to avenge the continuing Indian raids on pioneer settlements. Moving up the Miami River in western Ohio, on October 6 Logan's men attacked the village of Mackachack, home of Moluntha, a leading Shawnee peace chief. Although many of the villagers fled, he remained and called for others to surrender. With a ritual pipe in hand, he led his wives and children to meet the Kentuckians. One officer, Captain Hugh McGary, demanded to know if Moluntha had been at the 1782 Battle of Blue Licks, where the officer had led Kentucky militiamen into a crushing defeat. When the chief (who understood little English) nodded, McGary murdered him with an axe. Then the attackers swept farther into Shawnee country. Moving quickly, they destroyed eight villages and hundreds of acres of crops ready for harvest. Satisfied with their work, the troops pronounced the raid a great success and, loaded with everything they could steal plus twenty-eight women and children as prisoners and eleven Indian scalps, returned south to Kentucky.[1] Contrary to expectation, Logan's raid failed to end the fighting. Instead the troops' actions persuaded any Shawnees who had still hoped to avoid war to join their hostile kin and defend themselves from the invading Americans.

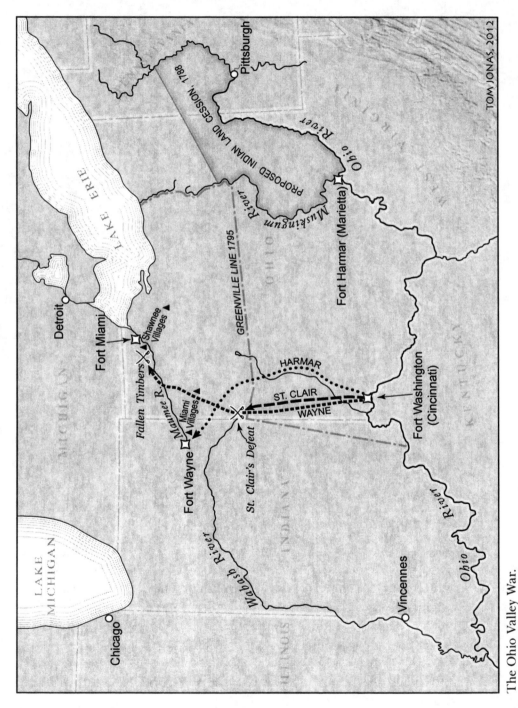

The Ohio Valley War.

14

The attacks led directly to the nation's first major conflict with its tribal neighbors. It began without planning or forethought but resulted from complex and numerous causes that stretched back an entire generation. While only one other of these eight Indian wars included even modest elements of foreign involvement, the Indian-British alliance that had developed during the War for Independence and continued through the War of 1812 not only proved important but set this conflict apart from the others in this study. Invasions of Indian country by land-hungry pioneers occurred repeatedly, but not all of the other conflicts included the recurrent cycle that this one did of raids and atrocities by both sides that stretched back nearly four decades. Hasty, ill-planned demands for land by the weak U.S. government following Independence also played a major role. In fact diplomatic belligerence and military aggression characterized most American action in this era. That approach persuaded many of the Indians who had joined the British during the War for Independence to remain hostile or at least suspicious of the United States. Expecting to keep their independence and deflect American land-grabbing, they developed multitribal confederacies and sought renewed support from English officials in Canada. The Indians' open enmity made this situation different from most others as well. Without doubt the Ohio Valley Indian War of 1786–95 provided one of the most direct multitribal challenges to U.S. expansion. It disrupted or halted pioneer settlement, included one of the worst military defeats in American history, and forced the federal government to reshape its policies and tactics for later dealings with the Native peoples.

This outbreak should not have surprised many people at the time. Sporadic violence in the region between the Great Lakes and the Ohio River occurred repeatedly at least as early as the 1750s during the Seven Years', or French and Indian, War. Then most tribes in that area had supported their French trading partners against the encroaching English; when Britain won that war they shifted their stance to grudging neutrality. By the 1770s pioneers pushed west into southern Ohio from Fort Pitt at present Pittsburgh and others entered central Kentucky via the Cumberland Gap from the southeast. Tribal leaders recognized the arrogant Americans as the biggest threat to their independence and adapted two related tactics to counter this invasion. First, they worked to build a multitribal confederacy; second, they sought renewed help from British officials in

Canada. While the American colonists struggled to gain independence, the Indians used both diplomacy and repeated military action to retain theirs. As early as Pontiac's War in 1763 and continuing sporadically into the 1780s tribal raiding and war parties crisscrossed western Pennsylvania, central Kentucky, and the upper Ohio Valley to repel or destroy the invading whites. Those actions often succeeded during the War for Independence, but they left deep-seated bitterness on both sides and increased the already widespread anti-Indian hatred.[2]

In 1783 the Treaty of Paris recognized the United States of America as newly independent. Although the agreement signaled that fighting against the British had ended, it ignored the ongoing conflict with the Indians beyond the Appalachians. In fact the pact said nothing about the tribes at all. As recently as a year before the peace treaty had been signed, several tribes had crushed frontier militia armies in both Ohio and Kentucky. Now those groups who had fought against the colonists faced American retribution without any open support from their former British allies. Neutral tribes and even some who had helped the rebels fared little better during the chaotic years immediately after the war. The intermittent raids and retaliatory forays by pioneers and Indians alike kept frontier settlements and tribal villages in turmoil. In fact those incidents put the United States and the villagers on a collision course.[3]

Flush from their defeat of the British, the victorious Americans wasted little time in extracting land from their tribal neighbors. In October 1784 U.S. commissioners rejected Iroquois claims that the Ohio River separated Indian land from that of the new republic. Instead of the usual diplomatic give-and-take that characterized most Indian councils, the federal negotiators announced that the Iroquois tribes had forfeited any right to bargain. Instead they told their astonished listeners that "you are mistaken in supposing that . . . you are become a free and independent nation, and may make what terms you please. It is not so. You are a subdued people."[4] Then they browbeat the chiefs into signing away much of their land in the 1784 Treaty of Fort Stanwix. A year later at Fort McIntosh the commissioners used the same tactics to awe Delaware, Wyandot, and Chippewa chiefs into surrendering much of southern Ohio by telling them that the United States had taken the land through its military victory. Next they persuaded a few Shawnee leaders to parley and repeated the earlier assertion that the British had given the Indians' land to the

Americans. Despite the chiefs' repeated objections, they gave in and signed the 1786 Treaty of Fort Finney.[5]

While the boastful American negotiators acted as if the United States had defeated the western tribes, Ohio Valley Indian leaders thought otherwise. They had no intention of surrendering their homelands meekly to the advancing "Big Knives." Instead, beginning in 1783, they met repeatedly at Sandusky, Detroit, their own villages, or frontier British outposts as they tried to organize a confederacy to defend themselves against the United States. These efforts to use united leadership against the American negotiators' tactic of acquiring land from one tribe at a time provide a causal factor not often present in most later Indian wars. U.S. officials often sought to divide leaders in a single Native community by pitting one group of chiefs against another. The participants in these meetings varied and almost never included all of the chiefs from any single Indian group. Often the delegations represented individual villages instead, because their varying circumstances shaped the chiefs' attitudes toward peace or war differently. Communities nearest the marauding pioneers might accept some white demands for land, while those living at what seemed a safe distance from the raids could ignore the pioneers or even call for retaliatory attacks. Usually the civil chiefs sought negotiations while the military leaders wanted to resist U.S. demands that they sign treaties ceding some of their land.[6] This continuing struggle for dominance between the civil chiefs and the war leaders kept some groups divided much of the time.

Despite their divisions, in 1786 Indian leaders meeting in a council at Detroit repudiated the three earlier treaties and insisted that the Ohio River remain the border with the United States. Joseph Brant, a Mohawk leader who had served as an officer in the British army during the Revolution, often took the lead even though he did not live in the disputed area. He tried to persuade representatives from other tribes that the land belonged to all of them and urged them to reject any proposals for cessions by any single group. Instead he insisted that all treaty talks should include representatives from the whole confederacy. Many of his listeners agreed, and in December 1786 Brant sent an address to Congress that included those ideas. It repudiated the earlier land cessions, demanded a renegotiation of the borders, and asked Congress to stop "your surveyors and other people from coming upon our side [of] the Ohio River."[7]

Although they disagreed with each other bitterly, both the United States government and the frontier inhabitants rejected any such limit. While the pioneers continued to encroach on tribal land and attack Native American villages, inaction by the cash-strapped Congress made keeping them out of the Indian country almost impossible. Rather than consider rolling back the border, Congress had already passed the Land Ordinance of 1785 to encourage settlement in the disputed area north of the Ohio River. That law established a system for the survey and sale of land to the pioneers in areas that the Indians considered to be still part of their home territory.[8] By the summer of 1786 survey crews had begun running their lines across what became known as the first Seven Ranges in the southeastern corner of present Ohio. While they struggled to haul their instruments through the forests, the trickle of pioneers into the area beyond Fort Pitt at present Pittsburgh became a torrent. This flood of settlers into their country enraged the Indians, who hurried to launch new attacks on the intruding whites. The resulting incidents fed directly into existing white hatred and fear of the Indians and their determination to destroy the area tribes.

Still on the verge of bankruptcy, Congress paid little attention to growing western violence and the pioneers' complaints. Instead it encouraged more frontier settlement, hoping to increase revenue from land sales by enacting the Northwest Ordinance of 1787, which laid out the pattern for creating new territories and eventual states. During their deliberations, the authors of the new law responded to the chaos in the Ohio Valley with little more than platitudes. As a result the document stated: "The utmost good faith shall always be observed towards the Indians." Article 3 stated that "their lands and property shall never be taken from them without their consent . . . unless in just and lawful wars authorized by Congress."[9] American leaders somehow hoped to stimulate migration west without increasing violence there. Whatever role the new ordinance played in encouraging the pioneer movement, by June 1788 the commander at Fort Harmar near present-day Marietta, Ohio, reported counting 631 boats carrying 12,205 people down the Ohio River.[10]

With this many pioneers seeking new land in what remained Indian country, George Washington's administration (which took office in late 1789) inherited a situation that modern scholars would label "total war." The combatants on either side rarely had any understanding of what motivated their enemies or sympathy for the tactics that they used. Indian custom demanded that relatives or friends seek revenge when outsiders killed or injured family or clan members. If tribal raiders successfully retaliated against pioneer atrocities, the frontier population labeled the events "massacres," and the deaths of whites in battle with the tribes became "murders" rather than casualties. During the 1780s the white border population thought of their opponents as hopeless savages and publicly called for their destruction. By then the violence had devolved into an undeclared race war in which people on both sides frequently tortured, scalped, mutilated, and slaughtered noncombatants. At times those actions became the norm.[11]

Meanwhile, the two ordinances set the pattern for how Americans would acquire and move onto tribal lands that the new federal government followed for another century. Because of the continuing hostilities in the Ohio River Valley, Congress ordered Arthur St. Clair, first governor of the newly created Northwest Territory, to reopen negotiations over the disputed treaties. By this time even the most obtuse officials realized that the government had to shift from its earlier policy of claiming Indian land by conquest based on the 1783 peace treaty with Britain. To do that St. Clair received $26,000 to purchase the area in question. His instructions did not authorize him to return any land to the tribes, however, or to admit any wrongdoing by earlier American negotiators. The process started badly when the governor chose Fort Harmar rather than a neutral site for the negotiations. In response Mohawk leader Joseph Brant urged a full boycott, but some of the other chiefs ignored his call. Delays by both sides pushed negotiations into December 1788, when several hundred Iroquois, Delawares, Potawatomis, and Wyandots arrived at Fort Harmar. During the meetings that followed both sides restated their earlier positions. First the governor read parts of a proposed new treaty. Then Indian leaders repeated their earlier insistence on having an Ohio River border.[12]

St. Clair had orders to reject Indian demands for any change to the border, so he fell back on the earlier American claims of having conquered the tribes. He contended that the defeated British had ceded the villagers' land to the United States. Then he brazenly asserted that the agreements negotiated at Forts Stanwix, McIntosh, and Finney had proved the new republic's goodwill. According to the governor, charity not vengeance had motivated the congressional negotiators' dealings with the tribes. Only the Americans' generosity allowed the tribes to retain some land rather than having to surrender all of it. Claiming to be acting in the same spirit, the governor offered modest payments to seal the earlier treaty agreements. In his effort to make another one-sided treaty acceptable, St. Clair promised to include a statement of the Indians' right to continue hunting on the lands surrendered in the earlier agreements. Of course, he neglected to tell his listeners that they would lose that right once the government sold the land and settlement began. All of his posturing ignored the tribal leaders' repeated calls for the invading whites to withdraw south and east of the Ohio River. Yet after more discussion the chiefs signed the new agreements. The governor boasted that the northwest Indian "confederacy is broken, and . . . Brant has lost his influence."[13]

That optimistic message repeated St. Clair's claim of having to beat down the chiefs' objections and ignored their obvious dissatisfaction. Yet he failed to note that the leading Shawnee and Miami leaders had boycotted the negotiations, so the resulting treaties had little chance to bring peace. In fact, along with many of the Delaware villagers, these two groups remained in open warfare with pioneers from the Virginia, Kentucky, and eastern Ohio settlements. The new terms did nothing to change that situation. Rather than quiet the frontier, the agreement achieved little. By summer 1789 observers claimed to have seen large amounts of powder and lead supplied by British traders at the village of Shawnee chief Blue Jacket and the homes of other war leaders. Some frontier officials still hoped that the continuing negotiations and the exchange of captives might bring peace. They overlooked the chiefs' repeated demands that the Americans "settle all these misunderstandings, and touch not our lands."[14] The United States had no intention of doing that and as a result could not end the Indian attacks on pioneers moving down the Ohio River. In fact long-time trader and British agent Alexander McKee reported that young men from three or four tribes had taken part in the raids along the river and that the Shawnees, in particular, "declare themselves at war with the Americans."[15]

When George Washington became president that same year, he inherited the bitter fighting between whites and Indians in the Ohio country that showed no signs of ending. The villagers refused to accept the

American invasion of their homeland, and U.S. authorities would not or could not prevent the growth of settlements in the Northwest Territory. Repeated pioneer attacks on Indian villages brought a new round of retaliatory raids, so the new administration faced an immediate crisis. It had to satisfy the pioneers' demands that it punish the area tribes and open the land for their continuing occupation. Given the nation's empty treasury, secretary of war Henry Knox had to find some other way to gain peace without launching a costly invasion. He urged the administration to develop a "conciliatory system" for satisfying the tribes to avoid actions resulting in "blood and injustice which would stain the character of the nation." If that failed and a major war broke out, he estimated that the United States would have to raise an army of 2,500 men at a cost of at least $200,000, an amount far beyond its ability to pay.[16]

Even if the government had wanted immediate peace, continued raiding by pioneers and Indians along the Ohio River and in Kentucky persuaded national officials that they had to act forcibly. Yet in 1789 the army included only 762 officers and men, hardly a force large enough to bring peace.[17] The next year a reluctant Congress enlarged the army to just over 1,200 officers and men, still far short of the numbers and support needed for an effective campaign. When Governor St. Clair reported that military force offered the only way to achieve peace, President Washington asked Congress to call out the militia. At the same time he cautioned the governor to use force only if he failed to persuade the Indians to accept peace. St. Clair ignored Washington's goal of peaceful negotiations during a meeting with Indian representatives at Vincennes in western Indiana. There, instead of offering conciliation, he repeated earlier threats and challenged village leaders, saying: "I do now make you the offer of peace; accept it or reject it as you please."[18]

Clearly the governor had lost patience with diplomacy and made little effort to reduce the Indians' rage over the continuing invasion of their country. Partly this resulted from his own bellicose statements; but even when he tried to be diplomatic his message often failed to reach the desired leaders. For example, in late April 1790 he sent Antoine Gamelin as an emissary to the Miami Indian villages in present Indiana. When some of the villagers objected to St. Clair's threats, and seemed ready to kill the messenger, Gamelin delivered only a few of the governor's demands. Despite that, Shawnee leader Blue Jacket complained that they had received many communications from the Americans but that "not one is alike," because "we suppose they intend to deceive us."[19] The chief decided not to reply, because he suspected that the peace offer from the United States only masked the government's plan to take more Indian lands. He told Gamelin that the Indians wanted to get advice from their British allies at Detroit. Wary frontier officials considered this answer to be just another excuse to prepare for renewed attacks, and in May 1790 Major John Hamtramck, commander at Fort Knox near Vincennes, reported that "a war seems inevitable."[20]

By then St. Clair, Henry Knox, and the president agreed that they could not avoid war. In June 1790 the secretary of war wrote: "No other remedy remains but to extirpate utterly if possible the said banditti," as he called the hostile Indians.[21] Now federal tactics shifted from negotiations to war. General Josiah Harmar received orders to lead the campaign using mostly militia units from Pennsylvania and Kentucky, the very men who had raided the Indian villages repeatedly for years. Gathering and equipping his force, a logistical nightmare, took months; but by September 1790 Harmar had just over 1,400 men, including about 300 U.S. regular troops. Although this army appeared ready, it lacked cohesion. Disputes over who should command the militia units disrupted matters, as did the inexperienced pioneer soldiers' contempt for the regular army officers and refusal to obey their orders.[22]

With the nation poised to open its first formal war against the Indians, the close British ties to the northern tribes stood out clearly. Worried that an invasion of the Ohio Valley might further complicate the difficult relations between the United States and Britain, Secretary of War Knox instructed Governor St. Clair to notify the British garrison commander at Detroit of the coming offensive. Apparently the administration hoped that it could avoid starting an accidental war with England by sharing that information. St. Clair's letter to Major Patrick Murray at Detroit explained that the campaign had "the sole design of humbling and chastising some of the savage tribes whose depredations are become intolerable" to the frontier settlers.[23] Clearly the government wanted to make certain that the British realized that U.S. actions posed no threat to them. If the villagers had not already heard about the coming expedition from the Americans by then, they soon learned of it from British officials. Unlike most other Indian wars, in this one the tribes received information and direct foreign encouragement, which many pioneers assumed to have been the case all along.

Once the campaign got started, the difficulties of commanding an ill-equipped and poorly led militia army became painfully obvious. The troops lacked uniform weapons, enough horses, and any willingness to follow orders. Along the march men wandered off to hunt, to shoot at an occasional Indian, and to loot when they found abandoned lodges. By October 18, when Harmar's army reached the deserted Miami towns, the Indians had retreated. The men had to be satisfied with burning lodges and crops and gathering whatever the villagers had left behind. Angry at not being able to kill any of their enemies, several militia officers begged for a chance to pursue them. In their first operation on October 19 Colonel John Hardin led a 200-man force into an ambush. As his militiamen fled they shouted to the regular troops, "For God's Sake retreat—You will Be all killed—there is Indians enough to Eat you all up."[24] As Harmar started his men back south the next day, he sent another detachment back to the same village, apparently hoping to surprise the returning Indians. Instead the warriors attacked; the militia panicked again, leaving the small detachment of regular troops to be overrun and destroyed. This second defeat so demoralized the army that the troops retreated south to Fort Washington in a near panic.[25]

Fortunately for the pioneer army, Native shamans interpreted a lunar eclipse on the night of Harmar's defeat as a negative omen, so many of the Indians stopped fighting. With their force splintered tribal leaders could not make any serious effort to attack the fleeing whites.[26] Shawnee leader Blue Jacket later complained angrily that after the shamans' message "we were obligated to suffer the Americans to retreat without further molestation" even though they had fled "in great confusion."[27] When Harmar's battered army straggled back to its base camp, the results became obvious. The 1,400 invading troops had suffered more than 180 men killed or missing as well as losing at least a third of their horses, many weapons, and large amounts of other supplies. Rather than defeating the villagers, inflicting heavy casualties, or damaging their crops and villages, the campaign had the opposite effect: it encouraged the victors. Calls for resistance spread to some of the neutral groups. The defeat brought repeated complaints about Harmar's leadership from the Kentucky militia officers and men, although their cowardice had assured the

Indian victories. Facing mounting criticism over his leadership, Washington's displeasure, and a formal inquiry into his conduct, the general ended his military career some months later.[28]

While certainly happy about having repulsed the American attack, some tribal leaders realized that they needed continuing help from the British. So a multitribal delegation traveled to Detroit with British Indian agent Alexander McKee asking for military supplies and for aid in rebuilding their destroyed villages. With McKee as his translator, Shawnee leader Blue Jacket lobbied hard. He reminded his listeners that his people had fought alongside the English against the Americans. Now, he continued, the situation had changed and the tribes needed help from the English. First he asked for soldiers and for the traders to bring weapons and ammunition. Then he warned that without outside support many of the Indians could no longer resist the Big Knives (as the Indians there called the Americans) and some of the villagers would have to retreat west beyond the Mississippi, which would further disrupt the fur trade. Even if that happened, however, he assured his listeners that the Shawnees would remain "to meet . . . an enemy who came . . . with a premeditated design to root us out of our land."[29]

This direct appeal for help brought difficult choices for the British. Often the men who had direct contacts with the Indians wanted to help them, but higher-level officials had orders to preserve peace. After hearing his guests' pleas for active support, Major John Smith, commander at Detroit, had few options. He lacked authority to pledge any substantial help, so he could offer little more than encouragement. Sir Guy Carleton (Lord Dorchester), then the top official in Quebec, advised Smith to give the Indians enough ammunition so that they could defend themselves if necessary. He cautioned that "we are at peace with the United States and wish to remain so."[30] Unless the Americans actually attacked one of the British military posts along the border, the major should tell the Indians to avoid any provocative actions. When the chiefs understood that they could expect no men and not much material either, they took McKee's advice and moved their villages north up the Maumee River farther away from the pioneer raiding parties and closer to their British suppliers. Despite widespread American certainty that high-ranking officials in Canada had incited the tribes to attack the pioneers, that did not occur. Instead, fearing an American move to capture Detroit and added pressure for the British to abandon the Northwest Posts, Lord Dorchester offered to mediate the ongoing border dispute.[31]

Despite that effort, British agents Alexander McKee and Matthew Elliott repeatedly ignored their orders and continued to encourage the villagers in Ohio and Indiana to resist the expanding frontier population. As soon as the chiefs left the Detroit meeting, McKee sent the American renegade Simon Girty to the Miami villages to urge renewed attacks on the pioneers. There the war leaders decided to raid two settlements on opposite sides of the Ohio. In January 1791 a small Indian force moved down the Muskingum River toward Marietta in southeastern Ohio. They attacked the Big Bottom settlement, killing all but the five prisoners that they took before returning home. A week later a second group of nearly two hundred Shawnee men moved down the Miami River farther west toward the small settlements north of Cincinnati. There Blue Jacket led the raiders against the nearly fifty pioneers and soldiers at Dunlop's Station. They surrounded the little outpost and kept up their attack for more than twenty-four hours. Just when it seemed that the defenders might have to surrender, a relief party arrived and the Indians left.[32]

Two months later, in March 1791, another multitribal war party assaulted a small regular army detachment and numerous civilians as they traveled together on the Ohio River. As about half of the group walked along the Kentucky side of the river, Indians ambushed them, inflicted heavy casualties, and scattered the rest. For the next week other attackers captured, tortured, and killed several dozen more whites who ventured farther downstream. These acts demonstrated the Indians' resolve to defend their homeland. They also suggest that British frontier agent Alexander McKee, who handed out presents and some supplies to leaders of at least twelve Indian groups, had plenty of local influence.[33] These new raids after Harmar's crushing defeat signaled the tribal leaders' resolve to protect their homelands. At the same time they strengthened American officials' determination to launch another campaign against the tribes in Ohio and Indiana.

In part that campaign was a response to pioneer outrage: the citizens in Ohio and Kentucky insisted that the government help them destroy the Indians, who had become even more belligerent. Rufus Putnam reported from Marietta that the Indians "were much elated with there [sic] success" and threatened to drive all of the settlers from the area by the end of the next summer.[34] Complaints also flooded in from Kentucky, where some leaders had talked earlier about secession from the United States. Whether this was serious or merely a ploy to get more help from federal authorities, news of those rumors and the continuing frontier warfare now received full attention. President Washington called on Congress to help the administration punish the aggressive tribes of the Ohio Valley frontier. Shortly after news of Harmar's defeat reached the East, in January 1791, Secretary of War Knox asked for funds to pay the costs of another "indispensable" expedition against the Indians.[35]

Congress provided the money that the administration had requested, and soon Governor St. Clair received an appointment as a major general and orders to organize and lead the new invasion. While he had actively sought the commission, St. Clair found that becoming a general was far easier than creating and equipping a frontier army. His orders included having to send out calls for peace negotiations; but instead of waiting for the chiefs to respond, he ordered Kentucky militia general Charles Scott to attack the smaller Wea villages along the Wabash River. While a multi-tribal army of over one thousand men waited for the smaller militia force at Kekionga (the Shawnee town on the Miami River), the whites slipped west, destroying several nearly undefended villages. The attackers captured more than forty women and children and brought them back to Fort Washington near Cincinnati as hostages. If force would not bring the villagers to the negotiating table, perhaps having their family members held captive would.[36]

News of this new white incursion infuriated the Indians. They had not expected the Kentuckians to outflank them and strike so far to the west. Having trouble just feeding so many warriors at one time, the leaders asked McKee for more food and ammunition. During the spring and summer of 1791 British authorities hoped to mediate the war for their own commercial advantage and to help their Indian trading partners as well. McKee continued to encourage and supply the warriors as they moved south to attack the pioneers and asked them to propose a new boundary. When they chose the Muskingum River in eastern Ohio, the agent forwarded this news to his superiors. On September 2, 1791, while St. Clair's army continued its preparations for the fall campaign, British minister George Hammond offered to lead peace negotiations between the Indians and the United States. This came too late because by then the

Americans had no intention of returning any land in eastern Ohio or halting their forthcoming invasion of Indian country.[37]

Having taken most of the summer to gather, equip, and try to train the mostly militia force that he commanded, St. Clair finally started the troops north in August 1791. This time the army made no effort to conceal its movements, as it marched a few miles and then halted to build small stockades to store additional supplies and weapons. With their general suffering from colic, asthma, and gout, the troops carried him on a litter hung between two horses. The army struggled through rain, cold, and mud farther into Indian country, taking until November 1791 to advance almost one hundred miles from Fort Washington at Cincinnati, where the campaign had begun. On the afternoon of November 3 St. Clair halted his troops for the night. Although he was criticized at the time and later by scholars for poor preparations, his local security measures included some reasonable precautions.[38]

Whatever view one holds about St. Clair's generalship, when more than a thousand Indians stormed into the camp at dawn the next morning they caught the sleepy soldiers almost completely by surprise. As had happened among Harmar's troops a year earlier, many of the militiamen broke ranks, fleeing through the defensive lines just ahead of their Indian attackers. Apparently told to focus their attack on the U.S. artillerymen and the officers, the warriors poured heavy fire into the surrounded soldiers. The tactic worked: St. Clair's army collapsed. Leaving the artillery, hundreds of weapons, and many of the most seriously wounded behind, the general led his shattered force south to Fort Washington. When the shock of battle faded, the count of dead and wounded was staggering. The army had lost nearly 950 officers, men, teamsters, and other camp followers. In fact fewer than 500 of the nearly 1,400 men in St. Clair's army reached Fort Washington uninjured. Once again a campaign that aimed to defeat the Indians, pacify the frontier, and open new lands north of the Ohio River had failed utterly. Rather than subduing the villagers, this second crushing defeat of the Americans encouraged them and increased their determination to resist the Big Knives.[39]

News of the disaster swept east quickly, and by late December 1791 Secretary of War Knox reported that the administration assumed that it could not avoid continuing the war because the Indians rejected any negotiations. After the Indians had crushed St. Clair's troops, "the pride of victory among them is too strong at present for them to receive offers of peace on reasonable terms," he reported.[40] That prompted him to submit Washington's proposal to establish a new national army (rather than depending on unpredictable state militiamen) to Congress. Following heated debate, in March 1792 it approved the new regiments and appropriated the necessary funds. A month later, after considerable head scratching, the president offered Anthony Wayne a commission as a major general and gave him command of the army-to-be. Expecting a delay before Wayne's force came together, other frontier militia units raided Miami and Piankeshaw towns in May and June that year.[41]

Meanwhile, in an August 1792 meeting at Vincennes, the American spokesman Rufus Putnam agreed to return the Indian captives, but not much else. Tribal leaders failed to comment about these contradictory actions but continued to debate their next moves. They lacked enough food to supply their men for long, so small groups of warriors drifted off to hunt while others returned to their homes. At the same time village spokesmen held yet another council where they debated whether to continue the war or stop fighting and negotiate with the Americans. As had happened earlier, divisions among the civil chiefs and war leaders within some groups and between the various tribes prevented any consensus. When the meeting ended, the participants left without reaching any agreement except to reconvene for new talks the next spring.[42]

At that point, having no idea of the Indians' views or the U.S. decision in favor of war, British officials in London decided that it was time for them to take action. In March 1792 foreign secretary Lord William Grenville sent his plan for ending the war to George Hammond, British minister to the United States. He proposed that the Muskingum River border that the Indians had demanded a year earlier should be one of the bases for negotiations and that Great Britain should continue to hold Detroit. This proposal had no chance for acceptance by American leaders. Certainly the victorious Indians had little reason to welcome this offer by the untrustworthy English. For the United States to accept that border would have meant accepting St. Clair's defeat, rolling back American settlement north of the Ohio River, and recognizing a neutral Indian barrier region between Canada and the United States. Hammond assumed that the new federal government would reject the scheme out of hand and therefore never presented it to his diplomatic counterparts.[43]

Still hoping to avoid expensive renewed warfare, the federal government tried to reopen negotiations. Using Samuel Kirkland, missionary to the Iroquois, as his messenger, Secretary Knox invited Mohawk leader Joseph Brant to visit Philadelphia for new talks. In June 1792 American officials tried bribery, but Brant rejected the presents. Instead he told his hosts that any effort to enforce the boundary laid out in the 1789 Treaty of Fort Harmar would bring renewed fighting, something that they chose to ignore. That same year Knox sent several other men to the Auglaize villages in northwest Ohio as spies, but the Indians killed nearly all of them. Despite that failure the government extended its peace-with-spying moves west to the villagers on the Wabash River and sent Captain Hendricks (Hendrick Aupaumut, an acculturated, Christian Stockbridge Indian) to speak in favor of peace. At the multitribal council meeting that summer Alexander McKee denounced Hendricks as an American spy, and the initiative failed.[44]

By the next October, in 1792, just less than a year after St. Clair's defeat, the Indians had shifted their location again. During the preceding years, raids by the Big Knives had damaged or destroyed many of the villages in southern and central Ohio and Indiana. So the tribes continued to move north, farther from the pioneers. That autumn they built more settlements along the Auglaize River and at its confluence with the Maumee some fifty miles southwest of Lake Erie about one hundred miles south of Detroit. Captain Pipe's Delaware village relocated there, as did the villages of several Miami bands. Speaking from this new, safer location, some of the leaders withdrew their proposal for a Muskingum River border and returned to the earlier demand that the Ohio River constitute the boundary, an idea long rejected by the United State. Despite this, or perhaps because he either had no knowledge of the change or refused to consider it, Henry Knox announced in 1793 that the United States would reopen negotiations with the western tribes.[45]

Whatever the Indians and their British patrons expected to result from the upcoming treaty talks, American leaders had few illusions. Thomas Jefferson later wrote that the government agreed to the meetings "to prove to our citizens that peace was unattainable."[46] Shortly after the negotiations began it became clear that the conflicting goals of each side ensured that renewed fighting lay ahead. The United States assumed that a peace without military victory would not last, so the government continued planning for war while its representatives talked peace. The villagers hoped to convince the Americans to accept their shadowy multi-tribal confederacy as their central negotiating power. Unfortunately the confederacy represented neither internal nor intertribal unity. Instead the Indians faced bitter divisions over what to do, as the western tribes and the Six Nations Iroquois supported differing proposals. After delays and heated debate among tribal leaders, the Indians' effort to reach any agreement on the terms to present to the Americans collapsed. That gave U.S. negotiators another chance to have their demands met by continuing to use their past tactic of dealing with one tribe at a time.[47]

During the summer and autumn of 1792 the Indians, the British, and the Americans all continued their efforts to influence the confederacy meetings. Tribal delegations from Canada, New York, Missouri, Tennessee, Michigan, and Wisconsin came to the Auglaize villages for consultations. Because of food shortages, lack of good housing, and the repeated absences of some local leaders the visiting delegations often remained only a few days or weeks before returning home. After repeated meetings by small groups of chiefs, the planned grand council began late in September. Representatives of at least eighteen groups gathered to consider how they should deal with their white neighbors. Shawnee, Miami, and Delaware chiefs including Blue Jacket, Little Turtle, and Buckongahelas persuaded most of the council to support their demands for the 1768 Ohio River border established in the Treaty of Fort Stanwix. This brought a confrontation with Mohawk spokesman Joseph Brant, who continued to support the Muskingum River border in southeastern Ohio as the only possible way to keep peace. He reminded his listeners that an Ohio River border would force the evacuation of all the American settlements that stretched along that river in southern Ohio and present Indiana, something that the United States several times had refused to consider.[48]

That same year, while the Indian village leaders at the Auglaize settlement debated how to deal with the Americans, farther west at Vincennes Rufus Putnam met Peoria, Kaskaskia, and Potawatomi chiefs who hoped to ransom their women and children who had been taken captive by Kentucky raiders. They signed a peace treaty there, and several Indian leaders even agreed to travel east to Philadelphia for more negotiations with the government. However, as often happened when delegations of Indians visited eastern cities, many of them contracted smallpox and died before they could return home. Making their losses even more futile, the Senate rejected Putnam's treaty, so the negotiations that summer brought lasting peace no closer.[49] In fact they probably did just the opposite. The more peaceful Wabash Valley tribes who formed part of the confederacy's western flank split from it, while militant villagers continued to take part in the confederacy meetings.

The western chiefs' independent action provided only one example of the continuing and bitter divisions that existed within the confederacy. Joseph Brant, representing the distant Iroquois, provided another. He called for the Muskingum River boundary, while leaders from the Ohio and Indiana villages and the United States all rejected this plan. Shawnee, Miami, and Delaware leaders took the most openly anti-American stand, because pioneers and militia units had attacked their villages far more often than those of other tribes. Their efforts to blunt or reject any compromise over the Ohio River border angered and frightened other members of the confederacy. At least in part some of this opposition to the Shawnees grew out of jealousy, because the Maumee River villagers had come to dominate the consultations. Others such as Delaware leader Buckongahelas objected to the continuing influence of British agent Alexander McKee and his maneuverings during confederacy deliberations. Tribes such as the Potawatomis, who lived far from the dangerous Big Knives, sided with Brant and their British suppliers, who urged continuing negotiations rather than war. As a result of these persistent divisions, any chance for unity had collapsed by late 1792. The Indians could only hope that the British would help them if the Americans invaded again.[50]

With the talks stalemated, village chiefs who rejected demands for the Ohio River line led their people away from what they saw as an area of sure conflict. In Canada, British lieutenant governor John Simcoe continued to ignore the confederacy's divisions and urged his subordinates to support Joseph Brant's ideas. That order had little impact. The local villagers rejected it, and American leaders seem to have held little hope for a peaceful settlement at another council planned for 1793 on the lower Sandusky River.[51] The government briefly considered accepting a few of the Indians' demands and actually returning a little of the land taken by earlier treaties. By then, however, it had sold much of the area in question to would-be settlers, so giving it back to the Indians was not a realistic option.

While American negotiators waited to meet the Ohio Indians in June 1793, tribal leaders met again for more discussions. By this time a major disagreement had entirely split the confederacy. Brant, representing the Six Nations, Ottawas, Chippewas, and Potawatomis, wanted to avoid war. So he proposed that the tribes accept the boundary as set out in the 1789 Treaty of Fort Harmar. That agreement had recognized some tribal claims to land ownership and offered modest payments for earlier land surrenders in much of present Ohio in the 1784, 1785, and 1786 treaties. Brant's offer overlooked the repeated objections to those earlier land cessions by the western tribes of the confederacy, including the Shawnees, Miamis, Wyandots, and Delawares. In fact their position had hardened: once again they demanded that the Ohio River be the border and that the United States remove its citizens from all Indian lands or face renewed war. This stand would make it impossible for the American commissioners to craft a treaty acceptable to either their own superiors or the more militant tribal leaders in their upcoming meeting.[52]

In mid-July 1793 the U.S. negotiators headed west, hoping to visit Detroit, but the British said no. Instead the diplomats halted at the mouth of the Detroit River and waited there for word that the village leaders had finished their discussions and would join them. Late that month the Indians met the commissioners. Soon after the talks opened on July 30 the chiefs insisted on the Ohio River border. Discouraged, the American negotiators replied that they could not accept that boundary. Instead they suggested the previously rejected 1789 Fort Harmar Treaty line again. Alexander McKee reported that he had worked for peace but that the Indians had rejected his advice. Existing scholarship suggests otherwise.[53] By then news of the Creeks and Cherokees fighting against the Americans in the South and of the new conflict between Britain and France apparently stiffened tribal leaders' resistance too. The Indians and the Big Knives hated each other. Both wanted the land and its resources, so they had little hope for a lasting peace.

While the Indian and American negotiators failed to agree on a border, General Wayne moved his troops north until they halted within seventy-five miles of McKee's Maumee River outpost. Later that winter, in February 1794, Lord Dorchester (the governor general of Canada) rekindled Indian expectations for continuing British help in dealing with the

Americans. Speaking to a delegation from the Seven Nations in Canada, he did everything but promise open military cooperation against the United States. His motivations remain unclear, but he reportedly told the Indians that "I shall not be surprised if we are at war with them [the United States] in the course of the present year; and if so, a Line must then be drawn by the Warriors." He went on to say that British patience with U.S. actions toward the Indians was "almost exhausted and seemed to forecast war between the two countries."[54] Then he ordered Lieutenant Governor Simcoe to strengthen the defenses for Detroit.

Following those orders, Simcoe arrived in April 1794. He immediately began construction of Fort Miami southwest of Lake Erie in present Ohio and garrisoned it with British regular troops to protect against a feared attack by General Wayne. Whatever impact his superior's rash speech may have had among the Indians, Simcoe's actions gave proof of British determination to remain in the area. He gave orders to rebuild other nearby forts that had been abandoned since 1783 and made plans to use the militia to defend Detroit. Within weeks Indian agents Alexander McKee and Matthew Elliott traveled from one village to another, promising arms, munitions, and even troop support. In the latter stages of this conflict the local British officials from Governor Simcoe down to McKee and Elliott far exceeded their orders in terms of retaining Indian support. In fact their actions often had just the opposite effect of what was expected in London. Praise of these officials for their "very prudent and pacific" actions at the time suggests that their superiors had little if any idea of the actual situation south of Detroit that summer.[55]

Confident of increasing British help, some tribal leaders encouraged renewed attacks and launched successful raids on pioneers living within twenty-five miles of Cincinnati. Others began to gather at the Glaize as they prepared to face Wayne's troops.[56] In midsummer 1794 the Indian leaders compelled the French and English traders and other whites who lived and worked in or near their villages to join their force against the hated Americans. On June 29 the nearly fifteen hundred men surprised and destroyed an army supply train on its way to Fort Recovery and then attacked the outpost itself. Their assault failed because they had no weapons to breach the fort's heavy log walls, and both sides suffered heavy losses during the fight. The Indians withdrew. Without a dependable food supply or enough powder and shot needed for both hunting and fighting, some of the warriors returned to their home villages, reducing the number of men left to oppose General Wayne.[57]

The last major battle of the war occurred in late August. General Wayne moved his troops north toward the Indian gathering at the Glaize, and the tribal forces gathered to oppose him while Canadian workers labored to strengthen Fort Miami in case of an American attack. At the last minute the American commander sent a message to village leaders urging them to ignore the British advice and to meet for more negotiations, but the Indians rejected his effort. Instead they prepared to fight by fasting to strengthen their medicine and purify themselves spiritually in preparation for battle. On August 19 approximately thirteen hundred warriors moved into the fallen timbers, an area of trees downed earlier by storms. There they met Wayne's attack on August 20 but had to retreat. The American force scattered the defenders, and the Indians withdrew downstream to Fort Miami hoping that the British would help or at least shelter them. Refusing to do either, the post commander ordered his men to close the gates, so the warriors had little choice but to flee. An observer reported that "this one thing did more towards making peace betwixt the Indians and the Americans than any one thing, because for weeks . . . the Indians had been promised aid and protection by the British."[58]

With General Wayne's troops camped in the middle of tribal lands in northern Indiana, the major fighting stopped, although a few minor raids continued into the late autumn. The disheartened village leaders had few options. While a few bands migrated west into Spanish territory beyond the Mississippi, most of the others seem to have recognized that they could expect little further help from the British and reluctantly agreed to seek peace. When chiefs asked about peace terms in November 1794, Wayne insisted that they had to accept the provisions of the 1789 Treaty of Fort Harmar. That agreement had set the boundary of Indian land at the Muskingum River in southeastern Ohio. At the same time, Wayne treated the visiting delegations generously, handing out blankets, paper "commissions" to some of the war chiefs, and later even a discreet bribe to Shawnee leader Blue Jacket. The general agreed to exchange prisoners with a party of the still hostile Miamis and encouraged American and French traders to tie the Great Lakes tribes into the expanding

American regional economy. Then he set June 15, 1795, as the day for the treaty negotiations to begin.[59]

Few Indians traveled to Greenville in the spring of 1795 because many of them faced starvation. The Americans had destroyed their crops during and after the fighting. Others had long distances to travel, and some dreaded the upcoming meetings. So it took until late July for all of the scattered bands to gather at the council grounds. Facing General Wayne's troops, they listened to the Americans' demands and accepted peace. First the treaty stripped away nearly all of their land in Ohio and part of eastern Indiana. Because of that, some would move west into Spanish territory across the Mississippi River or north into Canada. Those who remained had to agree to share a much reduced area. Next the United States established sites for future army posts and forced the Indians to cede land for routes between them. In return the negotiators promised to give the tribes trade items worth $10,000 each year. Once the chiefs signed the document, the negotiators promised to return all of the Indians still being held as captives. When only the Miami leader Little Turtle objected to some of the terms, Wayne silenced him. On August 3, 1795, tribal leaders put their marks on the paper. The Big Knives had won the war.[60]

General Wayne's army brought peace to the Ohio Valley, but only temporarily. News of his victory set events in motion that would lead to renewed fighting less than a generation later. Pioneers now rushed to settle on former Indian lands. They came so quickly that in 1792 Kentucky entered the Union as the first state beyond the Appalachians. The 1800 census showed over forty-five thousand people living in the Northwest Territory, many of them occupying land ceded at Greenville. Ohio became a state three years later, and the government established Indiana Territory. Following President Thomas Jefferson's directive, its new governor William Henry Harrison began acquiring more Indian land almost immediately. Using a combination of guile, bribes, and threats, he extracted some 45 million acres in Indiana, Illinois, and Wisconsin. Those cessions and recurring pioneer encroachments on their remaining lands persuaded some tribal leaders to reopen contacts with Canadian officials. At the same time a Shawnee shaman, Tenskwatawa, announced a new message from the Master of Life and called on his listeners to break off their dealings with the whites. Soon he attracted hundreds of followers, and in 1809 his brother Tecumseh tried to create a multitribe confederacy similar to that of the 1790s to end the land cessions. The Shawnee brothers' efforts persuaded many Indians living south of the Great Lakes to fight alongside British troops during the War of 1812 in another losing effort to retain both their independence and their tribal lands.[61]

CHAPTER 2

The Red Stick War, 1813–1814

In early July 1813 Red Stick leader Peter McQueen led a delegation of 280 Creeks to Pensacola, where they conferred with Spanish governor Don Mateo González Manrique. In the early stages of what became a violent Indian civil war, the visitors presented their desperate need for weapons and ammunition to him. On their way to the city, they had raided and burned several large farms belonging to some of their tribal opponents. The survivors reported the attacks and warned the governor that they would use any weapons that he supplied to the war parties to strike the frontier settlers, not just other Creeks. Despite that threat the governor gave his visitors a little food and ammunition. Hoping to avoid an ambush by tribal enemies on their way home, McQueen split his men into several smaller groups. His misgivings proved correct: soon afterward a detachment of some 150 territorial militiamen and 30 Creeks intercepted one of the pack trains.

On July 27, 1813, at Burnt Corn Spring in Alabama a small group of frontier militiamen and some Creeks attacked one of the Red Stick groups. The dozen or so Indians fled into a nearby swamp, so their enemies turned to looting their abandoned pack animals. When they saw this, the outnumbered warriors fought back. The renewed gunfire attracted other Red Sticks; together they routed the pioneers, who "were panic struck and made a quick and rapid retreat."[1] For the Creeks their

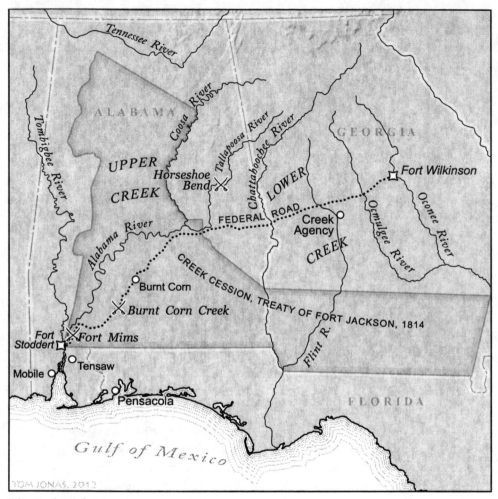

The Red Stick War.
© 2013 University of Oklahoma Press, Norman.

relatively easy victory reinforced Tecumseh's prophecy of triumphs over the whites made during his 1811 visit. Of more immediate significance, the militiamen's botched attack and the unexpected Indian victory helped to escalate what had begun as a bitter civil war among the Muskogean people of Alabama into the Creek or Red Stick War, a major frontier conflict with the United States.

This conflict shared many of the usual causes leading to frontier violence, but the war that erupted had distinct elements as well. Certainly the Creeks lacked the long history of hostility toward the Americans that some of the Ohio Valley tribes had. Yet the continuing demands of Georgia officials for land cessions in the years immediately after American Independence created some tensions and violence. The other Native groups considered here all surrendered land to the United States but not to individual states. At least for a time, however, Creek leaders did that and also became players in disputes between the federal and state governments. During their lengthy role in the fur and hide trade the villagers had welcomed, or at least accepted, frequent intermarriage between traders and other frontier whites and tribal women. Occasionally that brought some tensions within the mixed-race families between having to meet village and family and clan obligations and the outsiders' non-Indian economic and social desires. Continuing American efforts to acculturate the Creeks also distinguished their situation from that of all of the others in this study except the Dakota people in Minnesota. Working hard to blunt those pressures on their society, Creek shamans launched an aggressive religious renewal movement that became a central element in their conflict with the United States.[2]

The actions of two individuals modified or affected long-standing Creek village practices and helped create the situation leading to the Red Stick War. The Creek leader Alexander McGillivray and Benjamin Hawkins, the U.S. agent to the Muskogees, both worked to reduce village autonomy, strengthen the Creek National Council, then use that body to pursue their own objectives. Tecumseh, a Shawnee diplomat and military leader from Indiana, had a different goal when he visited the southern tribes and called for multitribal unity to opposite the Americans. He used fears of unusual natural phenomenon (such as an 1811 comet) effectively to recruit supporters. His visit and calls for war against the United States fed into a new set of anti-American religious teachings that rejected the white path. The shamans who headed this movement focused their doctrine on creating an Indian alternative to the whites' demands, which they saw as a threat to their land and way of life, Their followers called themselves the Red Sticks, taking the name of the colored sticks sent from one village to another as a call to war. At the same time the United States slipped into the War of 1812. The presence of Spanish officials and

British business leaders in the Gulf coastal region complicated Indian-white relations there. These circumstances created unusually deep and bitter disagreements that fractured Creek society so badly that the Indians often battled each other as they fought against the frontier armies that marched through their country.[3]

The Muskogean society that existed in present Georgia and Alabama by the 1780s included nearly twenty thousand people who lived in at least fifty villages. These communities developed over generations as groups of Yuchi, Natchez, Alabama, and Shawnee people migrated into the region. Gradually they established villages within what became the Creek Confederacy. Held together by language and shared social customs, the resulting society appeared solid, even thriving to some outsiders. But the acceptance of refugees and other neighbors into their society for generations had created lingering divisions among the villagers. It also helped diffuse authority and tended to limit government beyond the immediate town except for consultation, so authority remained in the hands of community elders and the local clans. Without an existing chieftainship, a loose general confederacy of villages developed and continued in place until the era of American Independence. By that time the earlier strong local autonomy began to erode as some leaders came to feel that unity in the face of the advancing Georgians had become essential.[4]

During the mid-eighteenth century the English had labeled the two clusters of Muskogean villages the Upper and Lower Creeks (who lived closest to the early Georgia settlements). Yet when James Oglethorpe negotiated the Treaty of Coweta with the Creek headmen in 1739, that geographic separation had no impact. In a stunning diplomatic victory, the chiefs included a provision saying that all of their "lands are held by the Creek Nation as Tenants in Common."[5] The Indian leaders therefore assumed that none of it could be sold except through an action of the National Council. Clearly they hoped to prevent individual village leaders from ceding land used by other Muskogees. Despite that, between the end of the French and Indian War in 1763 and the end of the War for Independence twenty years later, pro- and anti-American groups seem to have formed within the Creek Confederacy. But decisions such as those by several Lower Creek leaders to sign three treaties that ceded a large amount of tribal land to the Georgians more often resulted from close trade ties than from political ones.[6]

Traditionally Muskogean society had widely accepted social and economic rankings. By the beginning of the nineteenth century traders had married into prominent families for decades. Often they, their children, or traditional village leaders stood at the top of the Native society. Many of them had well-established farms and plantations that mirrored those of successful southern planters at the time. Often worked by black slaves, these farms had sizable herds of animals as well as fenced and well-tended fields that produced large crops for trade. In the chaotic years during and immediately after American Independence these men retained their village clan membership, but some adopted many of the white economic practices, as happened in the Tensaw district. That action separated some of them from their less acculturated Muskogean relatives, particularly if they played down or ignored clan obligations within their home villages. When that happened it helped create bitter divisions that had begun to tear Creek society apart by 1811.[7]

One early step in that process came from the actions of the Scotch-Creek Alexander McGillivray. Alexander was born in Creek country in 1750; his father, Lachlan, had brought him to the family plantation in Georgia when he was six and a few years later sent him to be educated in Charleston. There Alexander received training in plantation management. His family ties helped him make connections with several British trading companies, and after the Revolution he returned to his mother's people. Along with several other young Creeks, Alexander, now in his mid-twenties, settled on land in the Tensaw area and began farming. Through his mother he held membership in the Wind Clan, which shaped his identity and actions. Yet his attitudes also reflected the developing frontier white society nearly as much as the practices of his Indian neighbors and relatives.[8]

At least one analysis of McGillivray's action incorrectly depicts young Alexander as "deeply alienated from most Creek traditions and from the vast majority of the Creek people."[9] Certainly that appears on the surface to have been the case. McGillivray built and operated a plantation worked by sixty slaves. His substantial home built of squared logs bore little resemblance to the wattle-and-daub dwellings of many other Creeks. He hired a white man named William Walker as overseer of the slaves and several others to tend his large herds of horses, cattle, and hogs. In addition, McGillivray's lifestyle often seemed unconnected to village life. He wore white man's clothes and had none of the tattoos borne by many Muskogee hunters. In fact he ignored hunting and never received any recognition as a warrior either. When most Creek men left their villages each fall to hunt, he spent several months away from home visiting the Spanish.[10] Yet through his clan membership McGillivray attracted many followers in the Muskogee villages, while he weakened his health and shortened his life working for Creek autonomy.

Despite his distinctly "non-Creek" lifestyle, McGillivray seized a position of leadership quickly and soon gained the title of "most beloved man." Representing the British among the Creeks during the Revolution, he had provided trade goods and presents to the villagers, thus gaining their support during the war. More significantly, when that conflict ended the British surrendered their claims to the trans-Appalachian region to the United States in the 1783 Treaty of Paris. That encouraged Georgia authorities to extract a land cession from a few Lower Creek chiefs the same year in the Treaty of Augusta, and McGillivray moved quickly to thwart further cessions. He initiated contacts with the Spanish and a year later persuaded them to open diplomatic and trade relations with the tribe through the Treaty of Pensacola. In 1785 he explained this as an effort to remain "independent of the American states . . . & to preserve our Lands."[11] Here his actions resembled those of tribal leaders in the Ohio country, except that the British had far more influence there than did the Spanish among the Creeks in the South.

That agreement provided at least some counterweight to the expansive Georgia pioneers, and McGillivray's actions as the Spanish commissary to the Creeks a few months later allowed him to supply arms and ammunition to the villages. At the same time he became a secret partner in the British trading firm Panton, Leslie and Company and helped them keep their suppliers in the Indian trade. During the mid-1780s that connection enabled him to dominate much of the local economic activity. His ability to give or hold back desired trade items gave him considerable power to attract support from many of the other villagers. At least as important, by 1792 the salaries that McGillivray received from both Spain and the United States enabled him to act as a traditional village leader. He could give presents to those who accepted his ideas, provide for his family and relatives, and help needy villagers too. Each of those actions strengthened his role as a traditional Creek leader.[12]

In spite of his personal wealth McGillivray accepted his Wind Clan membership fully and used it to cement his relationships with many of the villagers. His personal ties to the British firm Panton, Leslie, and Company gained early support from the pro-British Upper Creek leaders. When he moved to extend his power beyond that base, the chiefs among the Lower Creeks with close ties to American traders immediately objected. Even though his actions may have sharpened intratribal tensions, those strains grew out of earlier disputes, not just opposition to him. As a Beloved Man or advisor he lacked the status of the *mico*s (chiefs) and drew continuing opposition from two prominent leaders, Hoboithle Mico (Tame King) and Eneah Mico (Fat King). During the Revolution these men had led pro-American groups while McGillivray had served as a British agent, so they rejected his leadership.[13]

Other factors played an important part in the dispute. Traditionally the peace chiefs directed village affairs except during wartime, when they stepped aside and the war leaders took control. Theoretically they should have reasserted their authority when the fighting ended in 1783, but the continuing volatile relations with Georgia delayed this. Instead the warriors retained their powers, and McGillivray worked through them frequently. He reinforced his influence by giving large amounts of guns and ammunition to those who agreed with him. As Spanish commissary officer he issued papers to village leaders that allowed them to get the weapons they wanted. Whenever possible he blocked shipments of those items to his tribal opponents. This proved effective in retaining support from the warriors' councils, but it continued to anger some of the others. To some Creeks McGillivray's actions may have seemed more European than Indian. Yet he identified himself as a Creek nationalist and based his opposition to the Georgians' repeated demands for more land cessions firmly on that.[14]

At this point the inability of the U.S. government to exercise its authority over Indian affairs under article 9 of the Articles of Confederation became a central issue. With the federal authorities taking no action, disputes over further land surrenders at the eastern edges of Creek country sharpened the disputes within the Creek Confederacy. At least some of the tension arose because chiefs from the Lower Creek villages in Georgia sold some of their land to that state. For example, in 1783 Hoboithle Mico (a Tallassee) and Eneah Mico (a Yuchi or Hitchiti) signed the

Treaty of Augusta surrendering land in central Georgia. When the National Council heard of the land sale it objected bitterly and sent men
who destroyed Hoboithle Mico's house, burned his cornfield, and killed
his livestock.[15] That failed to end the dispute, and two years later the
same headmen accepted another treaty at Galphinton ceding still more
Creek territory. When the Georgians threatened these chiefs with a large
militia force in 1786, they agreed to yet another cession at Shoulderbone
Creek. That agreement ratified their earlier treaties. The new pact outraged McGillivray, who told the Georgians that if they wanted the land
they should "come and take it."[16]

McGillivray's moves to create unity among the scattered and nearly independent villagers introduced a new element into Muskogean life—the
use of centrally directed force to achieve goals of the Creek Confederacy.
His efforts went far beyond traditional persuasion, social pressure, and
banishment. Recognizing the severity of the threats posed by Georgia,
the United States, and even Spain, McGillivray tried to strengthen the
National Council as a counterweight to village autonomy. When it became
clear that his control of the flow of Spanish goods into the villages had
failed to achieve that, he recruited warriors from his Wind Clan to "persuade" his opponents to cooperate. If they complained about his armed
"deputies," he defended the practice as necessary self-protection from
attacks by angry whites. In his view tribal survival demanded that Creek
leaders dispense with lengthy debates and divided councils. McGillivray
thought that they should use the National Council to oppose American
encroachments and reject any more land cessions. For a time his efforts
to develop a more centralized tribal authority succeeded.[17]

Throughout this era illegal white squatters moved onto tribal land,
stole Indian livestock, and brought repeated violence to Creek country.
McGillivray's efforts to deal with those issues succeeded when the National Council responded decisively to Georgia officials as they began to
set up new counties on formerly tribal land. This encouraged Creek warriors to join Cherokee raiders to drive the settlers out of areas claimed by
both tribes. By 1789 their successful raids had forced the invaders to call
for negotiations, and the new U.S. government sent commissioners south
to meet tribal representatives. When the Americans demanded that the
Indians accept Georgia's claims and surrender all of the disputed territory, Creek leaders stormed out of the meeting. An angry McGillivray

wrote: "by G——I would not have such a Treaty cram'd down my throat."[18] Some months after this failure to gain land and peace, President George Washington invited Creek negotiators to New York for talks, and the delegates spent much of the summer of 1790 there. The resulting Treaty of New York promised the tribe federal protection from further aggression by Georgia politicians and pioneers and solidified McGillivray's leadership within the tribe, at least until his death in 1793.[19] At the same time, however, that agreement deepened the fissures among the villagers, laid the foundation for some of the bitter divisions that followed, and set a pattern for increasing federal intervention in tribal life.

That intervention began in 1796, just three years after McGillivray's death, when Benjamin Hawkins arrived on the scene. Newly appointed as the U.S. temporary agent for Indian affairs south of the Ohio River, he represented what came to be called the "Indian Civilization Program." His goal was to implement total acculturation among the Creeks. In many ways he failed to achieve that, but his presence and specific actions further split Muskogean society. Once Hawkins recognized the rivalries and divisions among the Indians, he encouraged those trying to strengthen the National Council. In some ways his success in doing that built directly on McGillivray's earlier efforts. Yet his objectives differed radically. The Beloved Man had sought to create a strong central authority to help defend Creek lands and independence. The agent wanted to use the National Council to do just the opposite. He sought to break down tribal strength and force acceptance of his program of Americanization within the tribe.[20]

As a federal official Hawkins approached these goals with missionary-like zeal. Nearly all his efforts focused on persuading the Creeks to accept his plans for their acculturation. At first he traveled through Indian country, meeting village leaders and trying to convince them to adopt American-style sedentary agriculture. This early effort failed despite his enthusiasm. In 1797 he reported that the Indians told him that his plan "did not comport with the ways of the red people, who were determined to preserve the ways of their ancestors." Several years later a disappointed Hawkins acknowledged the continuing strong resistance to his plans. He noted "the difficulty of changing the old habits of indolence, and sitting daily in the [town] squares" practiced by the villagers.[21] At the same time he established a plantation with an orchard, large, well-fenced fields, a

vegetable garden, and herds of domestic livestock, intended to serve as a
model of American economic development. His efforts seem to have encouraged a few already partially acculturated Creek families to follow his
example. At that point he had made little impact on the traditionalists,
his obvious target.

Eventually the plantation and agency added sawmills and gristmills as
well as a blacksmith shop for making farm tools and repairing equipment
for the Indians. The agent's headquarters offered other inducements to
find a place in the growing regional market economy. Workers there
taught Creek women to spin and weave and purchased hickory nut oil,
crops, dairy products, and fowl from them. In this way Hawkins encouraged the women to think about earning money instead of just meeting
basic family needs. For the men he pointed to the success of their wealthy
neighbors, who had large herds of cattle and operated their farms and
plantations as profit-making businesses. That part of his program failed:
although those farmers dominated the local economy, some of their actions remained outside traditional Creek social and economic practices.[22]
At that point many of the Muskogee men began raising livestock, because
hunting failed to produce as many hides needed to pay the traders as it
had in earlier decades. They left gardening to the women and to non-
Indian men.

Hawkins's effort to bring basic changes in Creek gender roles generated a lot of opposition. As in many other Indian societies, the women
in Muskogee villages planted the crops, raised the children, and tended
their homes, while the men dealt with diplomacy, trade, and warfare.
Hunting for the fur and hide trade had taken them away from the villages for months each year for decades. Even though they accepted some
of the agent's suggestions and did much less hunting, they did not become farmers. That would have forced them to adopt the women's tasks
of food production and undercut the women's central economic roles in
family and village life. While the agent hoped that patriarchy would become the new order, Creeks of both genders rejected this (although a few
of the wealthy families had already accepted some of the changes).[23]

The growing influence of the planters in Muskogee society illustrated
the widening class and social divisions among the villagers. A modest number of the wealthy operated plantations with slave labor and raised large
herds of horses and cattle for commercial markets. The increased number

of fenced fields, locked doors, and branded cattle demonstrated the spreading acceptance of personal property. That in turn struck directly at Creek belief systems that encouraged sharing of wealth and reciprocity in gift giving as social virtues, even clan duties. Thus villagers who acquired personal wealth and private property placed themselves outside long-accepted practices that had avoided widespread social and economic distinctions in the villages.[24] Certainly a gap separated rich and poor, but it widened noticeably during Hawkins's time as agent. When the Creek civil war erupted, members of the two classes often fought on opposite sides.

Benjamin Hawkins's impact on Creek life and society extended far beyond the changes already noted. In order to accomplish his hoped-for transformation of Muskogee life, he had to undermine or get around clan responsibility and village authorities. So he turned his attention to wealthy leaders and the National Council. Under Alexander McGillivray that body sporadically had served as a centralizing force, but Hawkins saw it as a possible engine for change. The agent met with the chiefs annually and, at least according to his own reports, dominated the proceedings.[25] He claimed to have achieved unprecedented influence and reported that the National Council allowed him to use U.S. troops if needed to assist Creek enforcers with their duties.

The first significant example of Hawkins's influence came in 1801 when a National Council patrol of seventy-two men, sent at his request, arrested some Creeks who had raided south into Spanish Florida. The leader of the captives bore the brunt of the punishment. After having his ears cropped and his back whipped, he watched while the patrol destroyed his property.[26] As a Creek, McGillivray had used his Wind Clan deputies to enforce council decisions, but Hawkins was a clear outsider. The agent's persistent effort to strengthen and then dominate the National Council brought him personal power and suggests that some tribal leaders may have accepted American ideas about how effective power should work. Still, his actions struck at the base of clan responsibility and local village autonomy, which did not go unnoticed. This gave Creeks who opposed the foreign ideas and practices coming to dominate their lives one more reason to object.

Hawkins's influence and the growing dominance of the National Council caused repeated dissatisfaction. When members of the council agreed to the Treaty of Fort Wilkinson in 1802, they ignored objections from their Seminole neighbors that it ceded some of that tribe's best hunting grounds. They also disregarded complaints from young warriors who opposed any cession to the Americans. Today their reasons seem clear. The treaty offered cash to "the chiefs who administer the government."[27] Nineteen of them got personal payments as well as access to $10,000 worth of presents when they signed the document. Three years later similar undisguised bribery succeeded again as tribal leaders accepted the Treaty of Washington in 1805. That included a provision for cutting a four-foot-wide "horse path" from Hawkins's agency south and west to Mobile for mail delivery. For their agreement the signers each received cash payments or permits to operate ferries, inns, or stages along what became the new federal road.[28] Eventually several men, outraged by what they saw as corruption surrounding the treaties, assassinated Hopoy Mico, then speaker of the National Council.

As part of his routine administration of Creek-U.S. affairs, Benjamin Hawkins used funds from the treaty payments to reward those who cooperated with his program. He purchased items such as fence rails, pork, and beef at times when hunters had no food but also made gifts to the chiefs and headmen to get or keep their support. While these actions followed the traditional pattern for village chiefs, his casual use of "bribes" fed into the growing breakdown of the older clan and leadership practices of recycling food and other goods in each village. Although his actions contributed to that process, Hawkins began noting examples of the cultural breakdown. He described one Creek leader as "avaricious," a second as "intent on his own gain, regardless of the public," and others who sought office so that they could "embezzle their stipend."[29] Apparently his "civilization program" had taken root, although perhaps in ways that he had not anticipated.

Although he served as U.S. agent to the Creeks, Hawkins went far beyond his self-chosen role as the purveyor of American culture. Whether as a treaty negotiator or merely as a spokesman for the federal government, he relayed its demands to the tribe repeatedly. Yet despite his influence with members of the National Council, tribal leaders did not always rubber-stamp his proposals. For example, in 1811 he received orders to get Creek acceptance of another federal route across their territory. This was to be an actual road, not just a narrow path for post riders carrying the mail. When completed it would connect settlements in

Tennessee with those around Mobile. The first time Hawkins presented the idea, Hoboithle Mico rejected the request emphatically: "You ask for a path and I say no. . . . I hope it will never be mentioned again."[30]

Under federal pressure to get Creek agreement, the agent reintroduced the subject on September 11 at the next National Council meeting. He told its members that American pioneers needed roads to get their crops to market in Mobile and that the U.S. troops would use them whenever it became necessary. Rejecting his demands, the council members refused to act. Upper Creek village leaders feared that their frontier neighbors would cause trouble and wanted to avoid conflict by keeping them off tribal lands entirely. When the councilors ignored his demands and took no action on his proposal, Hawkins turned to bribery again. This time he offered cash payments to some village chiefs and promised others tools and the right to collect tolls on the new road. The dispute ended when the councilors agreed to accept the new road.[31]

By 1811 Hawkins had lived and worked among the Creeks for fifteen years. During that time he encouraged the Indians to accept fundamental changes in nearly all phases of their lives. His "civilization program" called for the villagers to remake themselves and their society. Gender roles had to be changed drastically, with the women moving inside their homes and abandoning farm labor to the men. At the same time his plan called for the males to shift their work from hunting, trading, and livestock raising to small-scale agriculture. Such changes would move the tribal economic practices closer to those of the successful Indian planters and ranchers that Hawkins admired and used as his examples of personal success. He also pushed village chiefs to strengthen the power of the National Council and then to use it to enforce conformity within the tribe. In doing this he helped to weaken clan ties and their role in mediating disputes. His success added to growing anti-American feelings.

The chiefs recognized this. During the September 1811 National Council meeting the agent's insistence that the Indians accept a road across their land had heightened resistance to his acculturation efforts. During that meeting the Shawnee diplomat and war leader Tecumseh arrived, leading a delegation of northern Indians as part of his effort to gain support for a multitribal alliance against the United States. While he had received some support from scattered individuals among the Choctaw and Chickasaw villagers, the Shawnee leader's words struck a more responsive chord at the Creek National Council meeting. An effective showman and persuasive speaker, Tecumseh introduced new public dances that focused attention on the colorful and impressive "uniforms" of his companions. He visited for some days and assured Hawkins that he favored peace. Once the agent left for home the Shawnee diplomat reminded his listeners of how much land they had lost to the advancing whites. He urged them to protect their independence by joining the northern tribes to create a multitribal resistance to the United States.[32]

To gain broader acceptance of his political and diplomatic message, Tecumseh introduced the religious ideas of his brother, the Shawnee prophet Tenskwatawa. He encouraged tribes to reduce contact and trade with the Americans and replace their older religious practices and leaders with his teachings. Tenskwatawa called for Indians to reject nearly all of the whites' technology and return to their traditional ways of life. To do that meant that they needed to destroy tools and manufactured items such as plows, looms, and spinning wheels, to kill domestic livestock, and to sever their ties to white traders. Some Creeks welcomed the Shawnee warrior's message for many reasons. Hoboithle Mico, the civil chief of the Upper Creek town of Tallassee, had a particular grievance because the new federal road would cut directly through the territory of his community. Josiah Francis, a leading shaman, and Peter McQueen, a wealthy planter from the same village, both joined efforts to oppose any further Americanization of Creek life. Leaders of some of the Alabama villages who chafed at the National Council's willingness to follow the urgings of agent Hawkins also found the Shawnee visitor's arguments persuasive.[33]

Tecumseh's visit had more success among the Creeks than among any of the other major southern tribes. Their growing resistance to Hawkins's "civilization program" and ongoing violent incidents with the encroaching pioneers made them particularly receptive to his ideas. Tecumseh used long-standing Shawnee and Creek friendship and his personal connection through his mother's family to gain a hearing. If those relationships failed to attract support, he used the villagers' ideas about natural omens as carriers of special truths as well. Earlier that summer and autumn a major comet had appeared, and his hosts had all seen it in the night sky by the time of his visit. Tecumseh's name "Shooting Star" allowed him to point to this natural wonder as a spiritual sign that gave extra weight to his message. The comet began to fade as soon as he left to return to Indiana and disappeared in another month. Yet all of the Indians had seen the comet, and apparently some of the Creeks recognized it as an omen telling them to accept their visitors' anti-American ideas.[34]

Only a few months after Tecumseh returned north, a series of devastating earthquakes began. The epicenter of the main quake on December 16, 1811, lay near New Madrid in southeastern Missouri, but violent tremors reached all the way to New England. Subsequent major quakes occurred on January 23 and again on March 15, 1812, with repeated minor aftershocks that followed for months. According to one contemporary account, the city of Louisville, Kentucky, counted 1,874 aftershocks. While the quakes disturbed people from the Mississippi Valley as far east as the Atlantic coast, many of the southeastern Indians considered this another sign or omen of the spirits' displeasure. The Creeks had at least one other explanation. Just a few months earlier Tecumseh had cautioned that the Great Spirit wanted them to refuse more land cessions and to discard white ways and goods. Rumors that the Shawnee spokesman had threatened to stamp the ground in order to destroy the houses in one of the villages that rejected his call to action circulated widely. Another story told of his threat to climb a mountain: at the top he would clap his hands and stamp his feet until the earth shook.[35]

Tecumseh's message struck a responsive chord, and some Creeks looked to the spirit world for answers. At that point Captain Sam Isaacs, an Upper Muskogean shaman, reported having a vision and receiving new religious teachings from a giant serpent that had caused some of the quakes. Other shamans appeared too, but their specific religious ideas remain unclear. Yet they shared a determination to wipe away all traces of Hawkins's "civilization plan." Some called for the villagers to change their diet from domestic animals to wild game and from corn and other farm crops to nuts and berries. Unfortunately those who switched back to traditional foods faced unexpected suffering from hunger, malnutrition, and even starvation during the war that followed. At this point the religious leaders took the red sticks (painted war clubs) as their symbol. Going beyond these efforts to "cleanse" their own villages, some of their followers moved quickly to direct action. They began attacking travelers on the federal road from Georgia, and in March and April 1812 they killed two single men and two pioneer families as well.[36]

These acts signaled the first step toward an open confrontation between the Red Sticks on one side and Hawkins and the National Council
on the other. The agent demanded that the chiefs live up to the terms of
the earlier Treaty of New York and punish the murderers. So they sent
police, who killed eight Muskogee men and flogged seven others.[37] That
incident brought increasing violence within the confederacy because
the police had shot one of the fugitives seeking refuge in Hoboithle
Mico's village while he sat in the chief's chair in the town square. Enraged Red Stick leaders used this open breach of Creek practices of sanc-
tuary and clan responsibility sanctioned by the National Council as evidence that their society needed to return to its traditional social values.
For some months open violence between the two sides subsided, but the
bitterness resulting from these incidents remained strong and "led directly to civil war."[38]

In June 1812 the United States declared war on Britain, a conflict that
would affect nearly every aspect of Creek life for the next several years.
Early the next spring Little Warrior led a party of Creeks back south after a visit with Tenskwatawa in the Ohio country. Having seen the Indians there fighting as British allies and hearing that their own confederacy
had gone to war with the Americans, the travelers attacked and destroyed
a small pioneer settlement near the mouth of the Ohio River. When they
got home Little Warrior described the incident proudly. Rather than receiving the praise he expected, he was shocked to be "severely repri-
manded by the rest of the Chiefs and ordered immediately to leave the
council house."[39] Benjamin Hawkins reacted angrily to news of Little
Warrior's action and persuaded the National Council to punish him and
the rest of the attackers. So in April 1813 it overrode clan practices again
and sent a force of over one hundred men to kill Little Warrior and his
companions. They slaughtered all but one, who fled; so they executed his
aunt in his place.[40]

This act destroyed whatever tribal unity remained, and by the summer
of 1813 civil war racked the Creek Confederacy. New Red Stick prophets
who accepted Tecumseh's ideas demanded that their followers should
"[k]ill the old Chiefs,[who were] friends to peace."[41] They destroyed Captain Isaac's home and killed some of his followers because they had murdered Little Warrior and his men. At first glance it appears that the
conflict pitted those who had profited most from Hawkins's acculturation

plan—the successful stock raisers, plantation owners, and small businessmen—against those who feared the ongoing changes in their society and economic life. While this is true, much of the violence came in response to actions of the National Council that seemed to work with the Americans against the Muskogean villagers. Some prominent and wealthy Creeks became active leaders in this nativist rebellion. For example, Peter McQueen, Josiah Francis, and William Weatherford all joined the traditionalists led by Hoboithle Mico and High Head Jim in the conflict. Existing records mention actions taken by others but often identify them only as prophets. As a result they lack the names of many individuals who rebelled against the National Council, its leadership, and Benjamin Hawkins's obvious influence in some of the villages.[42]

As the internal Creek quarrels intensified during 1812–13, the conflict between the United States and Britain focused on events in the North. Yet the pioneers and politicians alike feared that the Spanish officials and British traders both would encourage the Indians to attack the southern frontier settlements. Certainly Gulf coast Spanish officials saw the Creeks as a buffer against the advancing Americans, but they lacked either the manpower or resources to offer much help. In fact they faced American filibusterers who invaded east Florida in the so-called Patriot War there.[43] Several British trading firms had munitions and other items that the Indians needed, but they judged the situation in economic rather than military terms, so these items needed to be purchased. Whatever fears the U.S. government and Georgia authorities had about foreign intervention in the southeast to help the Indians there proved mostly unfounded. Unlike events in the Ohio Valley a generation earlier, neither foreign power had any significant role in the Red Stick War. The British took far too long in organizing their efforts along the Gulf coast, while the Spanish lacked manpower, money, and actual supplies to help the Creeks in any important way.[44]

Nevertheless, in the summer of 1813 Spanish authorities invited Red Stick leaders to confer with them at Pensacola. Uncertain what to expect, the Indians hoped that their trading partners would give them the firearms they needed so desperately. But the local officials expected to discuss long-term strategy, not provide supplies and weapons. When the talks ended, the Indians returned home without the hoped-for guns. Most of the Red Stick men had only war clubs or bows and arrows, so a

few weeks later Peter McQueen led a group of three hundred warriors to
Pensacola in another effort to get better weapons. Their arrival frightened the governor, who had barely enough troops to defend the city.
Although he provided his guests with about a thousand pounds of gun-
powder, lead, food, and blankets, the Indians got no new guns. They had
to return home without the items that they needed most. As they headed
north, the white militia from southern Mississippi Territory and some
Creeks allied with them attacked several of the small pack trains at Burnt
Corn Creek, fanning the smoldering embers of the Red Stick rebellion
into open civil war and conflict with the United States.[45]

Infuriated by the frontier militia and Creek ambush in July, Red Stick
leaders gathered almost a thousand men from more than a dozen towns
and led them south to attack the plantations and farms of the Tensaw
area. This outburst arose out of tensions between the acculturated Creek
leaders and those who rejected the "civilization" plan. On August 30 a
Red Stick force of nearly 750 men launched a frontal assault on Fort
Mims. The fort, which covered almost an acre, consisted of log buildings
surrounded by a palisade and housed hundreds of pioneers and Creeks
from the Tensaw area plantations, as well as slaves and free blacks. Unfortunately for the defenders, the stockade builders had cut the gun ports
about four feet above the ground. In theory the defenders could use
these to repel attackers, but in fact the Red Sticks fired through the open-
ings too.[46] Before the assault the Alabama prophet Paddy Walsh had assured the Creek attackers protection from the defenders' bullets, but this
promise failed. The warriors poured into the fort, taking over several of
the buildings and fighting a bitter hand-to-hand battle that lasted much
of the day. By evening when the shooting ended, Fort Mims lay in smoldering ruins. The Red Sticks had killed 250 people, taken 100 prisoners,
carried off another 243 slaves, burned the buildings, and then left to
mourn their own heavy losses.[47]

Exaggerated tales of butchery raced through the Mississippi-Alabama
backcountry as war parties of emboldened Red Sticks attacked the farms,
plantations, and ranches of their wealthy neighbors and white pioneers.
Mississippi Territory, Georgia, Tennessee, and the United States all prepared to crush the attackers as bitter fighting swept across southern frontier
regions. In 1814 three militia armies invaded the Creek homeland seeking vengeance. General Andrew Jackson proved most successful as he led

Tennessee militia units into what is now northern Alabama. During the winter of 1813–14 American forces destroyed many of the Upper Creek towns and killed more than 1,500 Red Stick fighters. At Tohopika or Horseshoe Bend on March 27 Jackson's force of militiamen, aided by Cherokees and some Creeks, destroyed at least 800 of the 1,000 Red Sticks and captured 350 Creek women and children. This defeat ended most of the fighting by the Upper Creek villagers.

By then the invading Americans had gained total victory. They killed at least 1,800 Red Stick men and several hundred more women and children. The troops attacked and destroyed almost fifty Upper Creek towns while they burned crops and killed the livestock. Just a few weeks after Horseshoe Bend U.S. officials declared the war over. General Thomas Pinckney promised to protect the land claimed by Creeks who had served as allies during the fighting. Andrew Jackson ignored that pledge when he forced the chiefs to sign the August 9, 1814, Treaty of Fort Jackson. That pact took much of the land belonging to the Lower Creek villages, many of whom had fought alongside Jackson during the war. In fact nearly 8 million of the 14 million acres that he extracted from the Indians belonged to villagers who had remained neutral or had allied themselves with the United States. Jackson's high-handed dealings enraged many of the Indians. Two thousand former Red Sticks and their supporters fled south into Spanish-held Florida. These bitterly anti-American refugees and large numbers of escaped slaves from Georgia built new villages or joined the Seminoles. Together they kept the border region tense until General Jackson invaded Florida in 1817 during the First Seminole War. With the fighting in Alabama over, most of the anti-American Indians gone, and millions of acres of rich land beckoning, thousands of pioneers flooded into Creek country. By 1820 at least 85,000 whites and another 42,000 slaves occupied the former Indian land.[48]

When the Red Stick War erupted in 1813 it shared many causes with other Indian-white conflicts. Nearby pioneers repeatedly trespassed and squatted on tribal land. Their presence, frequent thefts, and violent incursions brought determined retaliation by warriors bound by the rules of clan vengeance as well as raids by some villagers who saw the pioneers as a source for loot. Those two sets of actions kept the region in turmoil for years. As in the Ohio Valley example, repeated raiding by both sides kept tensions high and made long-term peace unlikely. In each war examined here divisions in Native society prevented tribal leaders from unified action when they dealt with outsiders. Peace chiefs and war leaders sought different methods to settle local disputes. At the same time shamans offered religious ideas that called for drastic changes in daily life for many tribal members. Chiefs in different villages chose a variety of approaches based on their locations, trading connections, and earlier experiences.

This war also had causes that distinguished it from other Indian-white conflicts. The Creek experience of having to deal with Georgia state officials rather than with federal negotiators put them outside the normal diplomatic framework. Immediately after Independence during the 1780s the new federal government struggled to assert its authority over Indian affairs. The nagging Ohio Valley violence forced it to ignore the Creeks' situation, so the villagers had little choice but to deal with their avaricious neighbors. Like the northern tribes they had a foreign border and outside traders, but neither played a central role for the Creeks. While all tribes had social and economic divisions, those in the Creek Confederacy appear to have been more disruptive to their society than most. At the same time the Muskogean experience differed from that of the other tribes because the villagers had a National Council that might have served as a central authority in their resistance to growing white demands. At first glance it appears as if the Creeks became more firmly united rather than splintering into divided and bickering groups, as often happened elsewhere. But eventually they split into two distinct groups with drastically differing goals. In their case sharp cultural, economic, and religious divisions and a highly charged nativist revitalization movement brought about civil war. Because American militiamen joined with Creeks to attack the Red Stick warriors in an ongoing civil war, violence spread to the white population as well. Clearly this conflict had origins far beyond mere white-Indian jousting over the land and its resources.

CHAPTER 3

The Arikara War, 1823

On May 30, 1823, William Ashley halted his two keelboats carrying seventy trappers and some French boatmen at the Arikara villages on the Missouri River in present South Dakota. Fur traders considered these Indians the most unpredictable and potentially dangerous of the groups living near that stream, but the trappers needed another forty horses to take west. The next morning they bargained for horses, but the results satisfied neither the Indians nor their visitors. By nightfall Ashley decided to continue upriver and try to get the rest of the horses from the next group of villages. In the morning a strong headwind made it impossible to move farther up the river, so they remained another day. Early the next morning, June 2, the Arikaras attacked. Indian gunfire killed or wounded many of the newly purchased horses and the forty trappers huddled on the unprotected beach. When the firing ended, Ashley led his party of badly shaken trappers back downriver. Along the way some of the men stopped to wait for reinforcements while the rest fled back to St. Louis, ending the worst disaster for Americans in fur trading history.[1]

Little known outside the northern plains region, this brief incident and the campaign that followed became the first American Indian war beyond the Mississippi River. As such it ushered in more than sixty years of interracial violence in the West. These events differed from the earlier nineteenth-century Indian wars already examined here. While they

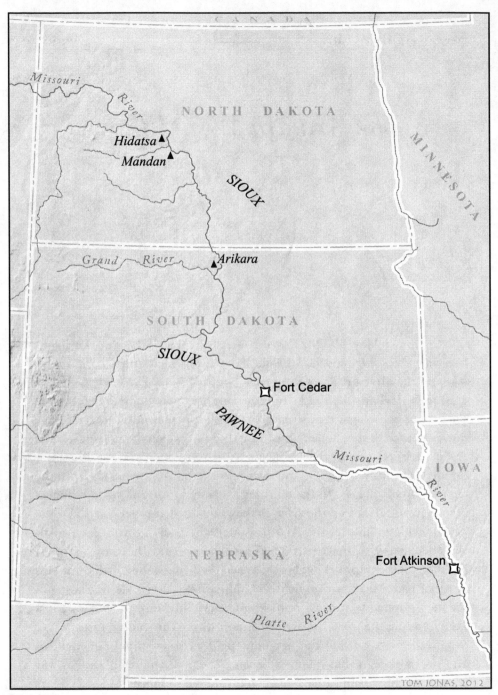

The Arikara War.
© 2013 University of Oklahoma Press, Norman.

resulted from a complicated variety of issues, the situation lacked hordes of greedy pioneers, scheming treaty negotiators, and precious resources creating demands that the tribe be pushed aside. In fact, it took another half-century before large numbers of Anglo-Americans appeared on the scene. This conflict had nothing to do with land grabbing. Instead it resulted from Indian customs, economic and social stresses from the fur trade, and intertribal competition and warfare among the villagers living in the Missouri River Valley. Thoughtless acts by individual white traders also complicated the fragile peace. Ignorance and simple bad luck resulting from actions by U.S. representatives complicated the situation, while an openly illegal act by the top American official there added to regional instability. These elements also had primary roles as causes for the fighting. This war differed from the others in one other important way. The Indians won!

When war broke out in 1823, the Arikara tribe included about two thousand people living in two villages near the confluence of the Grand and Missouri Rivers in present South Dakota. Descendants of people belonging to the Central Plains tradition that developed in Kansas, Nebraska, and western Iowa, they first appeared as hunting groups and gradually developed an economy that combined hunting, gathering, and agriculture. As farmers they lived in unfortified villages that stood along the banks of the small streams in that region.[2] A Caddoan group related to the Pawnees in Nebraska, the villagers migrated east into the Missouri Valley by the sixteenth century if not before. Eventually they moved into eastern Nebraska and north along the Missouri River into the area between the Bad and Cheyenne Rivers in present South Dakota.

The Arikara villages occupied sites that offered plenty of water, fuel, and timber near the mouths of streams flowing into the Missouri. Those features also made them attractive targets for raiding groups. In 1748 when the first Europeans arrived, they reported that the frequent attacks had led the Arikaras and their village neighbors, the Mandans and Hidatsas, to fortify their communities. By then these defenses consisted of log palisades "as thick as one's leg" standing at least five feet high. Often the villagers dug a ditch outside of the wall and packed earth against the logs for further protection. Within the walls the Arikaras built round earthen lodges nearly thirty feet in diameter with roofs up to fifteen feet high at their center.[3]

With a good location and surplus crops, these farmers traded and sometimes fought with other villagers and the newly mounted tribes of the plains. By the mid-eighteenth century their communities had become one of several regional trade centers in the area. Along with the Mandan and Hidatsa villagers living north of them along the Missouri in North Dakota, they exchanged their surplus corn and other foodstuffs for meat, hides, and leather with Sioux, Cheyennes, Crows, and others. Once horses and European trade items reached the region from the north and east, the villagers added them to their trade stock. These items increased the attractiveness of their goods for the hunting peoples of the region, so the Arikaras profited from their role as middlemen in a vast commercial trade network that stretched from Canada south and west to Santa Fe and from Iowa and Minnesota west to the Rocky Mountains or even beyond.[4]

Not long after manufactured goods reached the upper Missouri, individual Europeans followed. The French opened contacts in the region as early as 1738 when Pierre La Verendrye visited. Fifty years later representatives of the Hudson's Bay Company and the Montreal-based Northwest Company competed across much of the West. By the 1790s both groups had employees working among the village tribes along the Missouri.[5] News of these activities quickly reached the new Spanish governor, Luis Hector Carondelet, who issued a charter to the Missouri Company, a group of St. Louis merchants, in 1793. That group sent thirty-four men in four large boats loaded with trade goods up the river in 1795, hoping that they could get all the way to the Pacific. Although they failed, their actions encouraged other small groups of St. Louis investors to send wares up the Missouri.[6]

In the next decade small numbers of French, English, and St. Louis–based traders traveled through the area seeking furs and hides. When the Meriwether Lewis and William Clark Expedition began its trek up the Missouri in 1804, the general patterns of Indian-white relations had been established. The intruding Sioux wanted to control trade in the area, so the armed warriors treated traders roughly when they encountered them along the river. Although Lewis and Clark pushed past the attempted blockade, others faced the possibility of later attacks or pillaging. All of the tribes in the region wanted to get European items, often without paying much for them. This led to a cycle in which Indians

halted the traders and demanded goods. As they tried to profit and avoid
danger at the same time, the white traders often promised to return with
more items or to establish permanent trading posts, even if they had no
intention of doing so.[7]

This trading system brought both wealth and difficulties to the Arikaras. Certainly they benefited from the exchanges of guns, horses, and
foodstuffs. At the same time those profits disrupted existing social patterns among the villagers. Traditionally chiefs or other leaders had directed dealings with outsiders. They kept their influence by distributing
some of the new wealth to others in the village. The recipients in turn
tended to support the chiefs who had given them food and clothing. This
gradually changed as successful hunters began to sell their furs and skins
directly to visiting Indians and Europeans. As they gained new property
and status economic differences widened. That circumstance bypassed
the existing village practices of having the chiefs share some of the wealth.
The shift in earlier trade patterns not only threatened the chiefs' authority but became an increasingly divisive issue within the villages, as it had
among the Creeks a generation earlier.[8]

While these local social and economic issues began to transform Arikara life, more disruptive events devastated the village societies. Not long
after the first European traders arrived, smallpox tore through the towns,
repeatedly spreading throughout the Missouri Valley and out onto the
northern plains. The historical record on the epidemics remains unclear,
but certainly these white diseases forever changed life for these sedentary
Indians in the Dakotas. As smallpox and other contagions swept through
their communities, terrified villagers turned to their shamans, but their
cures offered little help. Instead the epidemics devastated the Indians,
and entire communities disappeared. Their villages, clans, and families
fell apart as people fled the pox.[9]

Near the end of the eighteenth century the results became clear. In
1795 the French trader Jean-Baptiste Truteau noted that "in ancient
times the Ricara nation was very large; it counted thirty-two populous
villages." Because of the smallpox epidemics, "a few families only from
each of the villages, escaped; these united and formed the two villages
now here."[10] Less than a decade later, when Lewis and Clark visited the
tribe in 1804, they reported that the people lived in three villages and
that they represented survivors from at least eighteen separate towns.

Apparently more band leaders and chiefs than other villagers lived through the epidemics: Pierre-Antoine Tabeau, their translator, told the explorers that more than forty-two chiefs lived in the three villages. He claimed that this caused repeated difficulty because each of these men "wishes at least to have followers and tolerates no form of dependence" on others.[11]

If Tabeau reported the number of chiefs correctly, the Arikara people had a somewhat uncommon problem. Rather than lacking leaders, they had too many. That made reaching agreements on major decisions difficult and at times impossible. According to several traders, the chiefs often squabbled, and their actions caused frequent trouble with both their economic competitors and their partners. Tabeau claimed that the splintered Arikara leadership brought instability and repeated conflicts within the towns. He probably complained about the chiefs' frequent quarrels over how to treat outsiders because he thought that they hurt his trading efforts. In any case, to outsiders the Arikaras appeared unwilling or unable to reach any long-term peace with the Mandan and Hidatsa villagers who lived farther upstream in North Dakota. Rather than uniting to defend themselves from the increasingly frequent Sioux attacks, these competing village societies argued and repeatedly fought each other. That meant that the three agricultural peoples almost never managed to cooperate in the face of increasingly hostile treatment by their Teton trading partners then living to the south.[12]

This encouraged their Sioux customers to become ever more demanding and aggressive and reduced chances for lasting peace in the region. Moving into and beyond the Missouri Valley by the end of the eighteenth century, the Sioux had traded with the Arikaras and Mandans for both food and European goods for years. By 1800 or shortly after that they managed to get white merchants to open a trading post for them south of the Arikara towns. That freed them from their dependence on the trading villages for the manufactured goods that they sought. Now they needed only food items (such as corn and vegetables) and horses. The combination of increasing Sioux numbers and their shrinking dependence on Native farmers also led directly to their increased violence toward the village Indians and white traders along the Missouri.

The well-armed, mounted, and numerous Teton Sioux sought to dominate the region by limiting or even prohibiting the movement of traders bringing goods to the tribes living farther upriver, whom they now saw as rivals rather than partners. Traveling up the Missouri River less than a year before Lewis and Clark, Thomas Selkirk noted that the Sioux "pursue[d] a system of preventing trade to all [Indian] nations up the Upper Missouri."[13] When dealing with the Arikaras in particular, they became increasingly aggressive and demanding. Often when they came to trade they just took what they wanted. Rather than paying the amounts of skins or meat that the Arikaras asked for, they gave the villagers whatever they pleased. The Sioux demonstrated their contempt by robbing the cornfields, letting their horses eat or trample Arikara vegetable gardens, insulting or beating the women when they objected, and trying to steal the villagers' horses.[14] Tabeau noted that they treated the Arikaras as if they were "a certain kind of serf, who cultivates for them and who, as they say, takes, for them, the place of women."[15]

While the Tetons' actions made life difficult for the Arikaras, their physical environment proved significant too. Repeated floods inundated and sometimes destroyed their crops planted on the river-bottom land. If they located their fields atop the bluffs and away from flood danger, they faced repeated drought. Depleted soil and grasshopper infestations made successful farming difficult in either location. They needed wood for their shelters, the palisades that surrounded the villages, and their heating and cooking, so they had to relocate their towns when they used up the nearby timber. If these factors had not persuaded them to move repeatedly, the recurring smallpox epidemics did. In just under thirty years from 1795 to 1823 they lived in three different sets of villages along the Missouri River in South Dakota.[16]

As in other instances studied here, Indian social customs also helped create uncertainty and frequent violence. Young men had several ways to gain status and notoriety in the community. Success in their limited summer buffalo hunts brought some attention. As the Sioux threat increased, however, the villagers almost abandoned their summer hunt. Instead they depended on getting their meat and hides from their dangerous neighbors rather than risking being attacked by them while searching for buffalo on the plains. This inability to hunt limited their chances to demonstrate personal bravery in either horse thievery or warfare. They avoided the Sioux and raided the less dangerous Mandans or Hidatsas instead. When the victims retaliated, this kept a cycle of raids and counterraids going for years. Because the village chiefs had little authority to limit or end the raiding, no one restrained the young men. Village customs encouraged them to demonstrate their skills as warriors, so the violence continued.[17]

Raiding and horse-stealing in each tribal society not only encouraged retaliation by the victims but also had other negative results. For example, if an Arikara raiding party failed to get the horses or other things it sought, the men faced ridicule when they returned home. Rather than endure the shame of returning to the village empty-handed they would "'cast their robes' . . . and vow to kill the first person they meet, provided he be not of their own nation."[18] This practice encouraged random attacks on anyone they met after taking that vow. To outsiders, killing peaceful neighbors or visiting traders seemed random and senseless and gave the Arikaras the reputation of being more unpredictable and dangerous than the other villagers in the region.

Certainly other tribes attacked their neighbors as well as Europeans and Americans traveling in their territory. Yet the Arikara town dwellers did other things that helped them to acquire this reputation. Like the Blackfeet of the northern Rocky Mountains, they had only a modest role in the bustling fur trade. Because they lived in an area with few beavers and had nearly abandoned buffalo hunting, they had almost no packs of hides or buffalo robes to exchange. That meant only modest profits, if any, for their traders, so the fur men tried to avoid keeping a permanent trading post open there. While the white traders who ventured into Indian country at the beginning of the nineteenth century saw the unprofitable villagers as dirty and disagreeable, they seem to have considered the mounted hunters of the plains noble by comparison. The lack of economic success appears to have prompted these frustrated, lonely men to report mostly negative ideas about their hosts.[19]

By the opening of the nineteenth century these social, economic, and cultural forces had created a situation that included an uneasy peace as well as bitter intertribal rivalries, recurring raids, and low-level intertribal warfare. The traders' descriptions of danger and uncertainty had some basis in fact. By the time Americans and others from St. Louis reached their villages, the Arikara, Mandan, and Hidatsa peoples faced increasing competition among fur traders, the ever-growing power of their Teton Sioux neighbors that disrupted long established economic patterns, and an ever-declining role in the river trade itself.

Americans entered the picture in March 1804 when Meriwether Lewis participated in the transfer of Louisiana from Spain to France and then the next day to the United States. For the next twenty years U.S.-based traders and their political representatives claimed to see evidence of British traders and agents behind every bush, but none existed. In fact complaints about British influence over the tribes near the Canadian border continued at least until 1825, when an army expedition into the region reported that the British had not been in the area for a generation.[20] Yet those concerns about having to deal with competition from the north seemed to have no impact on the St. Louis merchants. As the fur companies sent their employees up the Missouri River, the traders rarely recognized or made a serious effort to understand the bitter rivalries among the Indians. Often the whites' actions helped keep the region in turmoil.

At the same time actions by representatives of the federal government added to the instability if only by accident. For example, in 1804 the Lewis and Clark Expedition brought Americans into direct contact with the Arikaras. After they pushed up the Missouri past the Teton Sioux's attempted blockade, the explorers received a warm welcome from the villagers. In October that year the Arikaras had three towns near the mouth of the Grand River in present South Dakota. The explorers spent five days moving from one town to another. During their stay Sergeant John Ordway reported that the Indians "were all friendly and Glad to See us."[21] While enjoying this hospitality, Lewis and Clark strove to follow President Jefferson's instructions for dealing with the tribal peoples along their route. So they smoked, ate, and drank with leaders in each of the three towns and then delivered the president's greetings.

Their orders called for the explorers to hand out medals, fancy coats, and presents to the chiefs and less expensive trade items for other tribal members. In an effort to impress their hosts they demonstrated the air gun that Lewis had brought along. Once the talks began the ceremonies went well, until Lewis and Clark decided to recognize a head chief. Although their interpreter stressed that each of the three villages had its own leaders and that any act that recognized one of them as the "head chief" would cause trouble, they ignored his warning. Instead the visiting Americans chose Kakawissassa, from the first village, as the "grand chief" and gave him the largest, most impressive medal. As predicted, this angered chiefs from the other two villages. To mollify the chiefs the

explorers gave each of them the same number of presents. Before leaving
the Arikara towns the explorers persuaded one of the chiefs to join leaders from other tribes along the Missouri and travel east to visit the
president.[22]

As the expedition moved north, one of the Arikara chiefs traveled with
it, because the explorers had promised to help make peace with the Mandans. Yet at the same time the leader of the third village warned that any
alliance with that tribe might cause the Sioux to turn against their Arikara trading partners. The most thorough analysis of the circumstances
suggests that Lewis and Clark had only a vague idea of the complexities
of this situation. No matter what the explorers thought, the trade ties
with the Sioux to the south remained more important for the Arikaras
than establishing peace and reopening commerce with the Mandans to
the north.[23] As they traveled upriver the American visitors created dis-
content by disregarding the tribal leadership structure and failing to
understand the existing trade patterns among the area tribes, so their
actions probably aggravated existing tensions between the traders and
the villagers.

At least in the short run, the explorers inadvertently created new issues by encouraging chiefs to travel east to Washington, D.C. In early
1805 the men who had agreed to visit the president began their downriver
journey to St. Louis. The record of this trip is somewhat unclear, but by
early the next year they had reached the capital city. In 1806, almost a
year after leaving home, the Arikara chief and several of the other tribal
visitors died. Officials in Washington had little information about their
guests. Secretary of war Henry Dearborn got the Arikara chief's name
wrong. When President Jefferson composed a letter to the village leaders
on the Missouri, he inserted and scratched out several names, finally set-
tling on "Arketarnawhar."[24] Early in 1807 Joseph Gravelines, the interpreter who had accompanied the headmen east to Washington, returned
to Dakota and reported that several of the chiefs had died. Assuming that
the whites had killed them, some of the Arikaras responded angrily and
treated the trader harshly.[25] In this instance plain bad luck caused American efforts to impress and establish good relations with the tribe to have
the opposite effect.

Later that same summer actions by the U.S. government and civilian
traders led to renewed Arikara violence. The causes for the incidents

appear interrelated. In early May 1807 Manuel Lisa led a party of forty-two men up the Missouri, expecting to trap and trade in the northern Rockies. The men moved their keelboat upstream without any trouble until they reached the Arikara villages. There several hundred armed men lined the riverbank and began shooting as soon as the traders came into range. They demanded that Lisa halt there, which he did. The Indians' actions remained threatening however, so the men on the boat leveled their weapons at the crowd on the shore. This persuaded the chiefs that talking might be better than fighting. They invited Lisa to meet in council, where they smoked, talked, and exchanged a few presents before allowing the white traders to continue farther up the river.[26]

Just a few weeks later army ensign Nathaniel Pryor set out from St. Louis with a squad of fourteen soldiers to escort Mandan chief Shahaka on his way back from the trip to Washington, D.C. Apparently wanting to make amends for the death of the Arikara chief Arketarnawhar, the government sent a medal, some clothing, and the presents that the Arikara leader had received for the ensign to deliver to the dead chief's son. To strengthen his small party, Pryor persuaded St. Louis trader Pierre Chouteau, Jr., to accompany him with another twenty-three men. They reached the lower Arikara village without incident, but the Indians there appeared to be anything but happy to see them. After Pryor spoke briefly and gave a medal to one of the chiefs, the party moved upstream to the other towns. As soon as they got there the villagers attacked, killing three of the civilians and wounding several others. At that point Pryor and Chouteau allowed their boats to drift downstream, and the soldiers brought the Mandan leader back downstream to St. Louis.[27]

At the time the Arikara attack on Pryor and Chouteau's men caught the group by surprise. In 1804 and again in 1806 Lewis and Clark had passed the towns without any particular difficulties. None of the white parties had any way to know whether the Indians might have been at war with the Mandans that summer. Still, at least Ensign Pryor had some ideas about why the violence had occurred. He blamed Manuel Lisa's actions toward the tribe just a short time before the soldiers reached the village and complained that the trader tried "to divert the storm which threatened *his own boat,* by diverting the attention of the Ricaras to ours."[28] Pryor went on to charge that the trader had supplied the Indians with guns and ammunition and had promised them that his party would bring large amounts of trade goods to the villages.

Pryor's charge made little sense, because the Indians attacked without asking about presents or trade. Certainly it was possible that the shooting came as revenge for their chief's death in Washington, because the Indians had learned of that just before the ensign's detachment arrived. Even this seems to make little sense: the chief had come from the lower village, while the attack occurred at the two upper towns. It appears likely that the ongoing war with the Mandans that summer played a decisive role. Not only had the Arikara chief died under suspicious circumstances, but Pryor's party was escorting the Mandan chief Shahaka, a leader of their enemies, on his way home. Had the men known about the war between the Mandans and the Arikaras, they might well not have tried to return Shahaka to his home that summer or at least might have anticipated a possible attack. At the same time Chouteau's men had trade goods that they wanted to bring upriver to the villagers' enemies and competitors. Even if no war had existed that summer, the Arikaras would have tried to stop Chouteau from delivering trade goods to the Mandans. So when his men continued their trip farther upriver the villagers focused their anger on the next group of whites to arrive.

The 1807 attack made American officials more careful two years later when they escorted the Mandan leader Shahaka up the river a second time. In early 1809 territorial governor Meriwether Lewis signed a contract with the Missouri Fur Company to bring the chief home. To ensure that Indian attacks would not prevent this, the traders hired forty American riflemen as a military escort. When added to the hunters, boatmen, and traders the group included nearly 350 men. Heavily armed and traveling up the river in a flotilla of thirteen keelboats and barges, some armed with swivel guns and many flying flags and banners, the expedition made an imposing sight. Just below the Arikara villages the forty riflemen went ashore, pulling their cannon with them as they followed the boats. This military display temporarily intimidated the villagers, who promised to remain peaceful. After demanding that they end their attacks on other river travelers, the traders left some goods behind and continued on to the Mandan villages to deliver their trade items and the long-absent Shahaka.[29]

For the next several years shifting groups of hunters and traders traveled up and down the Missouri. They had to push their way past Teton Sioux efforts to blockade the river and avoid sporadic raids by almost all of the Indian groups along that stream except the Mandans and Arikaras. Apparently Sioux depredations and disruption of earlier trade patterns frightened the village tribes so much that they decided to cooperate with the St. Louis merchants to survive. Whatever the case, the Arikaras temporarily stopped their depredations against the traders. For example, as they led separate groups up the Missouri in the summer of 1811, both Wilson P. Hunt and Manuel Lisa heard that all of the tribes along that river except the "Mandans, Arikaras, and one or two small tribes" were hostile.[30] Some days later the white traders met a war party of nearly three hundred Arikara, Mandan, and Hidatsa men headed south to fight the Sioux. Rather than attacking the traders, the Indians escorted them north to the Arikara towns. Apparently the villagers saw the Sioux as more dangerous to their trading economy than their visitors.

When the traders reached the villages, however, the Arikaras renewed their demands for a permanent trading post, because Lisa's men returned to St. Louis for much of the year. Hoping to force their visitors to agree, the Indians refused to trade; when that failed, they threatened to prevent the party from traveling farther up the river. For a time Manuel Lisa seemed to accept their terms and even persuaded his hosts to sell horses to Hunt's party. While the discussions went on, the visitors moved from one village to another, visiting, eating, and trading for a whole week. They claimed that the Indians had treated them well, and at one point Chief Left Hand even provided guards to limit thievery. While professing their regret about the 1807 attack on Ensign Pryor, the Arikaras blamed it on a "bad chief" who had rejected the decision by the other leaders to avoid violence.[31] One chief certainly could have led the attack, and the Indians may have told the truth here.

An incident the next year demonstrated how unpredictable the Missouri River Valley tribes appeared to the intruding whites. In the summer of 1812 Manuel Lisa returned to the area. A few days before his party reached the Arikaras, Chief Left Hand met them, so Lisa stopped to talk. The trader gave the chief a few presents and then continued up the river. When he got to the villages, instead of receiving the anticipated friendly greeting, two of the other chiefs refused to meet him at all. Fearing that they might attack, the trader took some armed men to the trading post and demanded that the villagers explain their behavior. They told him that by giving even small presents to Left Hand he had insulted and angered the others. So he hurried to give presents to them too. At that point the tension eased, and they brought out buffalo robes to trade. Lisa actually had hoped to close his unprofitable trading post there, but to keep peace with the villagers he just moved it a few miles.[32]

This example illustrated the volatility of Arikara relations. The Indians linked their own decline to the disruptions caused by the fur trade. As a result they had difficulty in deciding how to treat outsiders—either other Indians or white traders. Their critical need for a stable supply of trade goods led them to attack merchants whenever those men failed to meet that need. At the same time the Arikaras' competition with the Sioux, Mandans, and Hidatsas brought repeated raids and warfare against those groups. Their dependence on the traders for the manufactured goods that they wanted created a sort of love-hate relationship. Each of these tribes wanted access to the manufactured goods, while hoping to block their competitors from getting the same thing. They may not have realized that the white merchants continued the trade only as long as they profited from it and not to meet the needs of any one tribe.

By the time Lisa and most of his party returned to St. Louis, the War of 1812 had gotten underway. Most American merchants quit traveling up the Missouri. News that the Treaty of Ghent had ended the war with Britain in late 1814 brought renewed efforts to get furs and hides from the northern plains and Rockies, but the St. Louis entrepreneurs had some difficulty getting their Indian commercial activities restarted. Manuel Lisa and several other active merchants organized a newly reconstituted Missouri Fur Company, one of several groups trying to rekindle the upriver trade. By 1818 one of these operated small trading posts at Council Bluffs for the Omahas and another farther upstream for the Sioux. Few of the merchants tried to venture farther upstream, however, and those who did made no effort to open permanent trading posts there. That left the Arikara, Mandan, and Hidatsa villagers with little access to the manufactured goods that had become so crucial to them.

In 1820 Joshua Pilcher became head of the Missouri Fur Company and sent men to build Fort Recovery (later Cedar Fort) for the Sioux at the Big Bend of the Missouri River some 150 miles south of the Arikaras. From there the white traders supplied guns, ammunition, and other manufactured items to the Tetons. The next year Pierre Chouteau, Jr., headed the French Fur Company, which built several more small forts, one in direct competition with Pilcher and his associates for the Sioux business. As these outlets supplied the Sioux, they infuriated the upriver tribes, who lacked any reliable way to get similar goods. In 1820 a large war party attacked and robbed two of the trading posts.[33] At the time the repeated raids, petty theft, and random violence along the Missouri kept profits in the fur business both low and uncertain.

Two years later William H. Ashley and Andrew Henry revolutionized the entire western American fur trade. Rather than depending on small, scattered posts spread through the Indian country that were difficult to defend, they devised a new approach. In early 1822 they ran a series of advertisements in the St. Louis newspapers calling for "Enterprising Young Men . . . to ascend the river Missouri to its source, there to be employed for one, two or three years."[34] A few years earlier a few so-called free trappers had spent time in the mountains; but the effort proved dangerous and unprofitable, so the practice ended. The number and type of the new mountain men the partners recruited made their enterprise successful, and others followed their example for much of the next twenty years.

Ashley's and Henry's new strategy for the trade ignored existing Indian economic networks entirely. If white trappers succeeded in gathering large numbers of pelts, St. Louis business owners would have little need to risk their men and money sending goods to the Indians along the Missouri. Hiring the mountain men clearly threatened the villagers' economic survival and contributed directly to the 1823 confrontation. Henry led the first of the trappers up the Missouri in early 1822, but their hasty departure left them short of food and made the next year difficult. They had moved so quickly because they wanted to beat their competitors from other St. Louis fur companies in getting to the mountains. When the partners' boat the *Enterprize* sank, Ashley scrambled to gather another craft and new supplies. He met the party in western Missouri and managed to get the 125 men and their equipment to Henry's camp in about three months. Apparently the trapping party's size discouraged any attacks as it made its way up the Missouri. Ashley had been "somewhat apprehensive of danger" when halting at the Arikara villages, so he offered the chiefs a few presents and, according to Jedediah Smith, "said such things to them as he thought mostly likely to secure and continue their friendship."[35] After assuring the Arikaras that his men would not compete with them as traders, he persuaded them to sell him some much-needed horses.

No matter what Ashley told the Arikaras when he stopped to buy horses in 1822, his request for a license to trade in the Rocky Mountains brought immediate confusion in western Indian-white relations. The provisions of the 1802 Trade and Intercourse Act allowed the license-holder to deal with Indians that had a treaty relationship with the United States, but none of the tribes in the mountains had one. The right to trade also said nothing about bringing white men west to hunt and trap in direct competition with the Indians. Certainly Ashley knew that his actions violated or at least skirted the existing regulations, so he spoke with both General Henry Atkinson, then commanding U.S. troops in the area, and William Clark, superintendent of Indian affairs at St. Louis. Although Atkinson expressed some doubts about the expedition, Clark overlooked the obvious differences between trading and trapping. He not only ignored this effort to skirt the law but assured secretary of war John C. Calhoun that a trading license for Ashley's venture would not cause any difficulties with the Indians and urged approval of the application. Clark's action to help a fellow St. Louis leader set the stage for the 1823 violence that triggered the war.[36]

The next March Ashley traveled up the Missouri again, this time bringing more recruits and additional supplies. After two months of toil the boat crews had nearly reached the Arikara villages when Jedediah Smith, one of Henry's men, brought disturbing news. He reported that the mountain streams were not navigable, so the trappers needed many more horses than expected to carry the furs that they had gathered. At that point Ashley's party had few options. They could drop back downstream and try to get horses from the Sioux, but the Tetons demanded high prices for their animals. Otherwise they had to visit the unpredictable Arikaras and hope for a friendly reception. Even though Ashley had traded with them peacefully a year earlier, this time he worried. Describing his preparations, he reported using "all the precautions in my power for some days before I reached their towns," to prepare for trouble.[37] He had little choice. His partner's men had to have more horses or their enterprise would collapse.

Ashley's flotilla reached the Arikara towns shortly after several violent incidents between these tribesmen and other traders. In March 1823 a village war party had met some Missouri Fur Company men carrying furs and hides back to St. Louis. A few Sioux hunters accompanied them, and the Arikaras demanded that the traders surrender their hated enemies to them. When the fur men refused, the warriors robbed and beat them. Perhaps more anti-Sioux than antiwhite, this incident illustrated the villagers' frustration. They saw the Sioux and the traders working together, while the St. Louis fur people had repeatedly refused to operate a permanent trading post for the Arikaras. This had forced the villagers to become ever more dependent on the Tetons, their trading competitors and enemies.[38]

Soon after that confrontation a large party of Arikaras launched an unsuccessful raid against Cedar Fort, one of the Missouri Fur Company's trading posts for the Sioux. The attackers had taken several Teton women prisoner, and one of them ran toward the post trying to escape. When the warriors rushed after the woman, several of the traders opened fire as they tried to rescue her. They killed at least two of the Indians and wounded several others, including the son of the Arikara chief Grey Eyes. At least one account reported that the angry Arikaras swore vengeance against the whites. Given the villagers' custom to "cast their robes" or attack the next people they met if they failed at warfare or thievery, it is possible that they attacked Ashley's party because it arrived shortly after that clash. One account suggested that the traders then at Cedar Fort had purposely antagonized the Arikaras, hoping to focus their anger on Ashley to disrupt his venture. Whatever the combination of factors, by the time trapper's boats reached the two Arikara towns the villagers were in no mood for friendly talk or trade.[39]

On May 30, 1823, when their keelboats neared the lower town, the trappers reported seeing Indian women hurriedly carrying water, which may have meant that they feared trouble. Ashley and two men went ashore, meeting Little Soldier and Grey Eyes, chiefs from the lower village on the riverbank. The Arikaras demanded presents to "cover the blood" of their men killed at Cedar Fort. While he offered gifts, Ashley tried to explain that he had nothing to do with the traders who operated the trading post, who worked for his competitors. Surprisingly, this seemed to mollify Grey Eyes, even though his son was one of those who had died in the fight. Little Soldier, however, refused the presents, signifying that the traders might expect some act of retaliation. That same evening Grey Eyes told Ashley that tribal leaders had agreed to remain at peace and that they would sell the Americans the horses they needed the next day.[40]

On the morning of May 31, 1823, the trading began. During the day the Indians provided nineteen horses and several hundred buffalo robes. By late afternoon, however, they started to complain about the amount of trade goods they had received. At that point Ashley decided to take the horses he had and leave in the morning. Unfortunately a stiff wind the next day prevented them from moving the boats upstream, so they had to remain anchored in the middle of the river while forty of the trappers camped on the beach with the horses. That evening Chief Bear invited Ashley to the upper village. There Chief Little Soldier, from the lower village, warned them that some men from the lower town remained angry over the shootings at Cedar Fort and that they might attack in the morning. That is exactly what happened. At daybreak several hundred warriors opened fire on the men still on the riverbank, killing all of the horses and some of the men, while wounding many others. When the shooting ended, more than twenty of Ashley's men had been killed or wounded, and he had to lead the expedition back down the Missouri to Fort Atkinson.[41]

Later that summer the Leavenworth Expedition made its way north from the fort to punish the villagers. The campaign combined regular army troops, a contingent of fur men, and several hundred Sioux recruited to help fight their enemies. The expedition failed miserably. The soldiers could not aim their artillery pieces effectively and ran out of ammunition after most of their shots sailed harmlessly over the fortified villages. When Colonel Henry Leavenworth demanded that the Indians pay for the attack on Ashley's party, Chief Bear of the upper town refused. Later the colonel reported that "the people of the upper village would not give up their horses to pay for the mischief which the Chief Grey Eyes of the lower village had done."[42] After negotiations broke down and the artillery attack failed, the Indians slipped away during the night and the traders set the abandoned villages afire before returning to

St. Louis. So the actual campaign proved totally ineffective. The Arikaras escaped punishment or defeat.

In fact from their point of view the Arikaras must have seen these actions as a major victory over the Americans. Gradually they had come to realize that they could not compete economically or militarily with their Sioux rivals to the south, so they focused their anger on the whites who traded with them. Recognizing the danger to their economic survival that Ashley's use of the mountain men represented, they attacked and drove his expedition back down the river. When Colonel Henry Leavenworth led a force of U.S. Army regulars against them later that same summer, they refused to pay reparations for the property that Ashley had lost in the battle. Next they withstood the soldiers' futile assault, which inflicted almost no damage on their towns. Their crowning achievement was to make utter fools of the Americans, when nearly two thousand people along with their horses, dogs, and other property slipped away during the night without being discovered. Clearly the Arikaras won this first western Indian war.

Its causes illustrate the complexity and variety of challenges that proved so frustrating for Indians, American officials, and pioneers alike. The basic issues are evident. Long-term competition and conflict between the villagers and their Mandan and Hidatsa neighbors on the one hand and the ever more powerful Teton Sioux on the other shaped Arikara relations with the intruding fur traders. Local customs that called for retaliation when others failed to "cover the blood" brought violence. The avaricious activity and cutthroat competition among the fur trade companies tended to fuel existing antagonisms. A casual willingness by the St. Louis business community to overlook existing tribal customs and ignore the economic needs of the villagers in favor of short-term profits angered the Indians. Although the United States government had what appeared at the time to be only a modest part in these events, the actions of American civilian and military officials made a volatile situation worse.

Rarely did this conflict include elements that helped cause other Indian wars. From what little the historical record says, religious matters played no role in it. No Christian missionaries had tried to spread their faith within the villages, so Native prophets and shamans had no reason to denounce the intruders. Even though industrial technology had long since penetrated the villager economies, it came as the result of mutually beneficial trade and not as part of a government-supported acculturation program. The Arikaras and their neighbors lived so far removed from the rest of the United States that pioneer encroachment (except for the fur traders) had no impact either. The Indian groups signed no treaties. Their societies operated in clearly recognizable traditional patterns until well after the 1823 war. The villages exhibited the usual divided leadership of Indian communities, and the chiefs had little authority to prevent violence. As in many tribal societies, the actions of young men who followed the accepted paths to social and military prominence made conflict nearly unavoidable.

CHAPTER 4

The Black Hawk War, 1832

As the warm spring sunshine faded into early evening on May 14, 1832, Illinois mounted volunteers under Major Isaiah Stillman halted briefly. Before they could set up camp, scouts found the Indians' trail and the troopers rushed after their quarry. At the same time, a few miles away on Sycamore Creek, about twenty miles south of present Rockford, the large camp of Sauk, Mesquakie, and Kickapoo people finished a dog feast to honor some visiting Potawatomi chiefs. The aging warrior Black Hawk had invited them, hoping that the chiefs would encourage his followers to found a new village in Potawatomi territory east of the Mississippi River. The visitors' evasive responses persuaded him to discount earlier rumors of welcome by other tribes and of possible supplies from the British. Instead of the hoped-for opportunity to restart their lives in Illinois, his followers faced possible disaster. He urged the band council to lead the band back down the Rock River and to return to Iowa. Unforeseeably, that decision came weeks too late. As the visitors left his camp, the Illinois militiamen, now only a few miles away, rode pell-mell toward the Indians.

At that point one of the young Sauk men hurried up to the leaders and reported seeing several hundred mounted white soldiers approaching the camp. Black Hawk's version of what happened states that he sent three men with a white flag to parley with the militiamen and that another

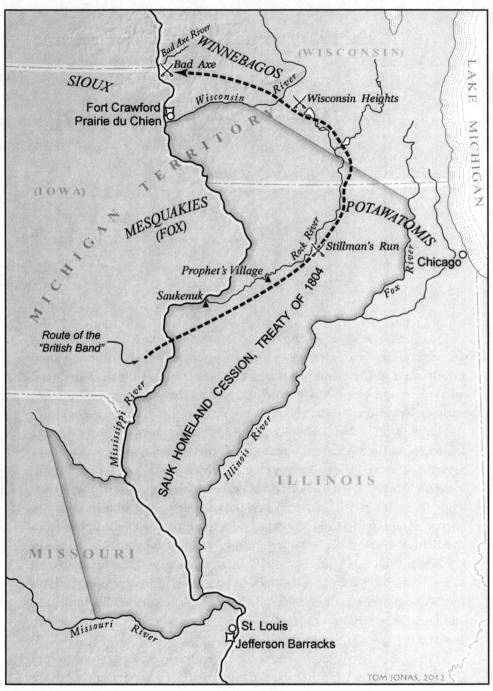

The Black Hawk War.

© 2013 University of Oklahoma Press, Norman.

five Sauks rode after them soon afterward to observe. White accounts
recorded no Indians with a white flag but instead mounted warriors acting suspiciously in the fading daylight. The untrained and poorly led Illinois volunteers had no interpreter with them. After taking the first three
Indians captive, they opened fire on the observers, who fled. The troops
galloped after them. As they neared the Indian camp, Black Hawk and
perhaps forty men charged, routing the terrified rangers, who fled in all
directions. The next day, Major Stillman counted twelve men dead and
another fifty-one missing. The Indians lost only three men, although the
attackers had outnumbered them by four or five to one.

Before this incident the Sauk leader had decided that his followers
would have to give up their dream of remaining in Illinois. Without back-
ing from the neighboring tribes they had no choice but to return to Iowa.
Now, as news of the fight at Stillman's Run spread across the frontier,
any chance for a peaceful solution disappeared. Illinois politicians and
pioneers alike called for war. A year earlier the Sauks and Mesquakies
seemed to have left the state for good. Now they had returned, but more
importantly they defeated Illinois troops and threatened its northern
frontier settlers. At the same time the Indians considered Stillman's attack on their peace envoys to be just one more act of white aggression.
Tribal custom demanded that the warriors retaliate for the militiamen's
attack, and a disastrous war followed.[1]

Unlike the other wars considered here, neither the United States nor the
Indians expected or wanted this conflict. It began by accident rather than
by design. Surely the Indians' determination to stay in their traditional
home area confused and angered American officials. By this time the bitterly debated Removal Policy, which the Indians refused to accept, had
become the law of the land. Despite having been pushed west across the
Mississippi River by military force just a year earlier, they "invaded" Illinois rather than staying on tribal lands in Iowa. Still, in the spring of
1832 their hope to find a new home posed only a modest threat. A
prompt military effort to push them out of the state might have encouraged them to leave without any violence. But General Henry Atkinson,
commander of the U.S. forces sent against the British Band, blundered
badly. Despite his distrust of civilian rangers, he allowed Major Isaac
Stillman's militiamen to move ahead of his slower-moving infantrymen.
By itself that might not have brought disaster, but he compounded his

first mistake with another. He did not foresee that the rangers might shoot first and ask questions later and made no effort to recruit any translators to send with them.[2] Without anyone who could understand what the Indians had to say, the pioneer soldiers started a conflict that the Sauks had not expected.

The Black Hawk War provides a classic example of the issues that led to frontier wars in the mid-nineteenth century. As in almost every case, land and its resources became a central issue framed by the federal Removal Policy on one side and the actions of U.S. officials, pioneers, and Indians on the other. In this instance, a Native prophet played a modest role for the band that stumbled into war, but probably not as directly as shamans affected the Creek Red Sticks earlier and the Nez Perces a generation later. Sauk and Mesquakie suspicions that federal officials favored their tribal enemies and the certainty that an 1804 treaty had stolen their land created long-standing anti-Americanism among them. At the same time continuing but unfounded American fears that agents and traders from Canada might influence these villagers led to branding the offending Indians as the British Band by the press and the government. Even before officials seeking removal focused on this group, repeated federal moves to persuade the Indians of the upper Mississippi Valley to abandon their traditional practices of clan retribution against neighboring tribes added tensions that further strained relationships with these people. Bitter divisions among village leaders over how to deal with the United States also rent the fabric of tribal life. When one adds the actions of Illinois state officials and the incursions and violence by pioneers to this mix, another Indian war comes as no surprise.

The Sauk and Mesquakie tribes had migrated west into the upper Mississippi Valley during the eighteenth century. By 1804 observers estimated that the Sauks numbered about 4,800 people and that another 1,600 lived in the Mesquakie villages, although often the population fell below those figures.[3] While not united, they lived near each other, shared a similar language and culture, intermarried, and occasionally carried out communal hunts and warfare. By the time Americans arrived in their homeland, the Sauks and Mesquakies lived in agricultural villages in southwestern Wisconsin, northwestern Illinois, and eastern Iowa. Each year they left to hunt in those states as well as Missouri and then trade with the British to the north and the Spanish at St. Louis. Members of both tribes dug lead from rich surface deposits in the region to use in their trade.[4] Still, some observers noted sharp distinctions in the political life of the two groups. The Mesquakies or Fox appeared far more individualistic, and by the 1820s Sauk agent Thomas Forsyth noted that among the Fox "the Chiefs are made fools of by the warriors."[5] In the Sauk villages, however, the chiefs commanded respect and directed communal activities most of the time, even though individuals could act in ways that might bring difficulties to the entire tribe.

Poor relations between the Sauks and Mesquakies and the United States began immediately in 1804 when American officials arrived in St. Louis to take charge of the vast Louisiana Purchase. From the start the Indians thought that the new government favored their long-time Osage enemies at their expense. First they watched as federal officers gave large amounts of presents to the Osages. Then the Americans turned back a 300-man Sauk-Mesquakie war party headed west to attack the Osages.[6] To make matters worse, no sooner had the United States taken control of Louisiana than American pioneers began squatting on long-claimed tribal hunting grounds not far north of St. Louis. Village leaders complained immediately about the settlers disrupting their hunting and the favored treatment of their enemies to Captain Amos Stoddard, who represented the federal government in St. Louis. At the same time they asked the United States to provide a resident trader. The captain, temporarily acting as territorial governor, viewed the two tribes as uncooperative and possibly dangerous, however, so he took no action.

This American unwillingness to restrain the invading pioneers quickly led to violence. Seeing that their chiefs' efforts had failed to protect their prime hunting grounds, young Sauks took matters into their own hands. In early September 1804 four or five of them raided a frontier Missouri settlement on the Quivre River, killing three pioneers and leaving their mutilated bodies "with their scalps taken off,"[7] then returned home. Clearly hoping to force their leaders to act more decisively, the warriors threw the scalps on the ground in front of their village council, taunting: "Now you make the land to smile, go cry with the whites."[8] Fearing retaliation, the chiefs acted quickly. They moved several of the villages away from the angry pioneers. When the women and children had been relocated, two of the Sauk leaders and one of their trusted French traders went to St. Louis to negotiate.

In the city American ethnocentrism and ignorance of tribal customs led to immediate friction: the chiefs' attempt to reach a settlement went badly from the start. They admitted that their young men had killed the whites and offered to "cover the blood" of the victims with payments to their families. This widely accepted practice among tribes of the region only further enraged the pioneers as they prepared to retaliate. In fact local officials claimed to have prevented such action only "with great difficulty, and upon promises of ample justice" toward the tribe.[9] A second cultural misunderstanding became evident when the Sauks protested that they could not hand the murderers over to the American authorities. They explained that as village leaders they lacked any coercive powers to do that, but Major James Bruff, the new commanding officer at St. Louis, rejected that argument immediately. He considered this little more than a stalling tactic to give the young men more time to escape and insisted that the chiefs surrender the attackers. He made no overt threat of retaliation but invited them to return later that autumn to meet Indiana Territory's governor William Henry Harrison, who was expected a few weeks later.[10]

After their brief meeting with Major Bruff, the two men hurried back to their village and reported the American demands. Fearing a disruption of their trade and possible warfare with the United States, the chiefs sent a small delegation representing both the Sauk and Mesquakie tribes back to St. Louis to settle the dispute. There the five minor chiefs surrendered one of the young men involved in the attack, but they hoped to secure his release and to persuade the Americans that they had no intention of going to war. But Governor Harrison had little real interest in their fears or in the fate of the imprisoned young Indian. His objectives stretched far beyond those minor local issues. Acting as the front man for President Thomas Jefferson's ambitious land-grabbing schemes for several years, he had negotiated a series of treaty cessions that acquired millions of acres of land for the expanding nation. In his St. Louis meetings with the small Sauk and Mesquakie delegation, the governor used their circumstances and his negotiating wiles to extract a land cession treaty from these chiefs too. Their only instructions from tribal leaders seem to have been to secure peace with the Americans and, if possible, obtain the release of their fellow tribesman. Certainly they lacked authority to sign away any of the tribe's land. No minutes of the negotiations survive; not surprisingly the Indian reports contradicted Harrison's account of what happened.[11]

Two rumors about the meetings circulated later. One was that the chiefs defended the attack as a proper response to the pioneers' unwanted sexual advances toward village women and blamed the whites for the incident and deaths. The other was that Harrison had kept the Indians drunk for some weeks. Whether this was true or not, all Sauk accounts of the negotiations agree that the men could not sell any territory because they did not belong to the clan responsible for safeguarding tribal land. When they returned home, Quashquame and his companions told village leaders that they understood the treaty as a peace agreement and not a land cession. Their visit did secure the eventual pardon of the imprisoned young Sauk, but before he could be freed the prison guards reported killing him as he tried to escape. Not a total failure from the Indians' point of view, the agreement achieved temporary peace with the United States. Without understanding the document's contents the chiefs gave away all tribal claims to much of western Illinois and southern Wisconsin.[12]

For this vast area the government paid them $2,234.50 immediately and promised annuities of $600 for the Sauks and $400 for the Mesquakies. When they returned north to their home villages, the treaty signers faced close questioning about what they had done. They assured the civil chiefs that they had gained peace with the Americans and insisted that they had not sold any tribal land. But from that day on disputes over the treaty brought repeated dissension and recrimination within the Indian villages. Their signing the treaty in 1804 proved a disastrous turning point in Sauk and Mesquakie history. From then on disagreements over its provisions and their meaning for the tribes and their relations with the United States became a fundamental cause for the war that broke out nearly three decades later.[13]

Nevertheless, the pact met some of the Indians' objectives. It convinced some of the Sauks that they had become U.S. allies and thus in their view had an equal footing with their Osage enemies. It recognized Sauk and Mesquakie land claims in Missouri, while ceding their land east of the Mississippi River to the United States. Yet one part of the treaty seemed to promise that it reserved their Illinois lands for them permanently under American oversight. This was a clear misunderstanding. It actually said that "[a]s long as the lands which are now ceded to the United States remain *their* [U.S.] *property* [emphasis added], the Indians belonging to the said tribes, shall enjoy the privilege of living and hunting upon them."[14] They clearly had no idea of this article's implications. Their heated denials of having ceded their eastern land to the United States, repeated for the next generation, demonstrate that they failed to grasp how the frontier land system functioned. The federal government had no intention of holding the ceded land but expected to sell it. When the sale took place, the Indians would lose their "privilege of living and hunting" on it. Whatever interpretations one offers to describe Harrison's wording and explanation of the treaty, his action created a situation in which ignorance, miscommunication, fraud, and later simple wishful thinking combined to exacerbate the growing tensions between the two societies.

Not all friction or violence in the Mississippi Valley stemmed from white-Indian disagreements. As in other regions many of the incidents and issues that disrupted peace resulted from the nature of the tribal societies themselves. For example, Sauk chiefs spoke the truth when they told American officials in 1804 that they lacked the authority to force the young men who had killed the pioneers to surrender. By U.S. standards at the time the tribal societies represented a sort of hyperdemocratic system that offered almost unimaginable personal freedom. For example, individual men could organize hunting expeditions or put together war parties to raid and fight almost whenever they chose. Their actions, like those of the Arikara men who chose to "cast their robes" and attack others without cause, repeatedly threatened the peace. True, the chiefs could try to dissuade the participants from what they saw as dangerous or unwise ventures, but they had only advice and moral suasion on their side.[15] U.S. policy makers never accepted that reality. Instead, as the instructions to Lewis and Clark showed, the government insisted on naming a "head chief" for each group. Even when that was not done, it wanted tribal leaders to control the actions of the entire band or tribe. The Indians rejected that expectation entirely.

In this context repeated minor intertribal incidents continued to keep the situation along the upper Mississippi in flux for much of the early nineteenth century. American officials there assumed that British traders and agents helped to cause this trouble while they worked ceaselessly to gain support from the tribes. When the United States declared war in 1812, villagers in the region had several options. Some of the Sauk villages chose neutrality, and a few even moved west of the river into Missouri to avoid the conflict. Many others, however, sided openly with the British. Their action seemed to support claims by U.S. frontier officials that most difficulties with the Indians resulted from continuing anti-American propaganda spread among the tribal people. For whatever reasons, many Sauk and Mesquakie men volunteered to fight alongside the British against the United States and participated in campaigns in Michigan, northern Indiana, and Ohio. Closer to home they raided south into Missouri, and along the Mississippi they attacked shipping, nearby army posts, and the soldiers sent against them.[16]

During the fighting the Indians helped to defeat American troops and militiamen; but the young men found that white tactics included long periods of inactivity, so they left. After having been away from their central village of Saukenuk on the Rock River in northwest Illinois for a year or more, many of them returned home during the winter of 1813–14. Their efforts had not contributed to any significant British victory, but the treatment that the Sauks received from their military allies strengthened their earlier ties. In the decade after the conflict, so many villagers traveled to Fort Malden across the river from Detroit that they created what the pioneers labeled the Great Sauk Road across Michigan.[17] Their annual visits to Canada kept alive American suspicions of foreign meddling with those tribes and earned some of the Sauks who made the annual journey to Canada the name of the British Band. Politicians and pioneers clearly found it easier to blame foreigners than to recognize the negative impacts that U.S. actions had on tribal peoples.

The war had another major impact within Saukenuk itself. In the autumn of 1813 militia units in both Missouri and Illinois raided Indian villages in western Illinois. In one incident the civil chiefs at the village feared an American attack. Because most of the fighting men from the community had joined the British and too few remained to protect the village effectively, they discussed temporarily falling west across the Mississippi. At that point young Keokuk, the Watchful Fox, volunteered to lead the defense of the village and became recognized as the war leader for the community through that act. When the warriors returned months later, the older and far more experienced warrior Black Hawk learned that Keokuk had supplanted him as the military leader at Saukenuk.[18] Apparently this caused no immediate public bickering, but personal competition and animosity between the two men grew for most of the next two decades.

As soon as he heard about this quarrel William Clark, the superintendent of Indian affairs and the American official most responsible for dealing with tribes in the area, moved to widen this split. He supported Keokuk publicly, showering him with presents to give his followers. He also arranged for Keokuk and some of the peace chiefs to visit Washington, D.C., expecting to impress them with the size and strength of the United States. This left the older and anti-American Black Hawk on the sidelines and furthered the growing rift between the two leaders. Of equal importance, without any chance to travel east, Black Hawk stayed isolated and ignorant of American numbers and power, so he remained less willing than his rival to cooperate with U.S. demands. The personal differences between the two war leaders gradually provided a focal point for dispute in the Sauk and Mesquakie villages and became a key element that led to the 1832 conflict.[19]

In the years after the War of 1812 increasing pioneer settlement in the Mississippi Valley and declining income from hunting and trade forced the Sauks and Mesquakies to venture farther west onto lands claimed by the Pawnees and the Sioux during their summer hunts. These same pressures also increased competition with Winnebago and Menominee hunters for game closer to home. As this competition sharpened, it brought increased intertribal raiding and with it American fears that an Indian war might spill over and involve the frontier population. Hoping to avoid that possibility elsewhere, federal officials continued to encourage tribal groups to abandon hunting as Benjamin Hawkins had tried among the Creeks two decades earlier. If successful this might have reduced intertribal violence and opened more land for the pioneers. By the 1820s, however, little effort had been made to implement this approach among tribes along the upper Mississippi River. Rather, during that decade the U.S. government shifted away from acculturation to a new approach, the Indian Removal Policy. Instead of persuading the villagers to clear land for farming, it first encouraged and then forced them to move west beyond the Mississippi River. In theory that would give the Indians more time to accept the acculturation program, but in fact it would open millions of acres of tribal land for white uses.[20]

Meanwhile, the government continued its effort to limit or end traditional practices. In particular it demanded an end to cultural practices such as "covering the blood" (paying for damage or injuries to others) as well as the related family, clan, and village retaliation that had brought peace or war to Native communities for generations. Because federal officials' attempts to prohibit clan retribution failed, officials led another Sauk delegation to Washington in 1824, hoping to encourage Indian cooperation. The chiefs who traveled to the capital saw the strength of the United States and realized that they could not openly resist its demands. Black Hawk had remained at Saukenuk, so he had no reason to change his strong anti-American views. This second visit to Washington and Clark's continued patronage gave Keokuk and his supporters a commanding position in Sauk society.[21] At the same time it gave dissidents someone nearby to blame when events angered them. Eventually it persuaded Black Hawk to oppose Keokuk and most of the peace chiefs when they seemed to accept the American demands.

During the 1820s continual intertribal raiding and small-scale violence kept the region in turmoil. As the Sauks and Mesquakies shifted their hunting farther west beyond the Mississippi, they intruded on lands claimed by the Iowa, Otoe, and Sioux tribes. That led to increasing violence. Traditional custom demanded clan retribution for injury, so theft or injuries gave the young men from each group repeated justifications for raiding. Small-scale violence continued. Fearing that the expanding frontier population might be targeted in these episodes, William Clark and Michigan territorial governor Lewis Cass called the tribes to a conference at Prairie du Chien in southwestern Wisconsin in 1825. There the two men hammered out multitribal peace treaties. Those agreements called for the chiefs to outline the land that each tribe claimed and to keep their hunters from encroaching on any of the others' territory. Even more importantly the new treaties required the chiefs to end the ongoing retaliatory raids. In place of clan actions they had to let the United States settle any new multitribal disputes.[22]

Surely Clark and Cass, as veteran negotiators who had dealt with Indians for a generation, realized the drastic changes that these provisions demanded. Yet they failed to anticipate the opposition that village leaders might face when they had to support these basic cultural changes. This suggests either an appalling ignorance of Indian customs or a blind determination to subjugate the tribes at all costs. In either case, Clark and Cass claimed that they had achieved peace. It seems likely that some headmen realized that the treaty provision threatened village stability because it struck directly at the long-standing custom of clan and family responsibility for personal defense. Certainly they knew that they had no authority to implement that treaty promise or else failed to understand the new requirement. Perhaps they thought that they had little choice but to try. As a result, rather than bringing peace, the 1825 agreement sharpened antagonisms within Sauk and Mesquakie society, gave malcontents an issue to use against the village chiefs, and had no positive benefits that the Indians could see.

In fact one part of the agreement had broken down by early 1827, just two years later. Sauk hunters reported finding a large Sioux encampment on land that the treaty guaranteed to the Sauks in Iowa. Hearing of this, Black Hawk and Morgan or Bear's Hip, a Mesquakie leader, both demanded action and began recruiting warriors to repel the intruders. Intervening quickly, the civil chiefs tried to dissuade both men. When that failed, they offered Black Hawk three horses and other presents, but he rejected their arguments and gifts. Instead he said that nothing but his own death would keep him from attacking the Sioux.[23] Realizing that they could not prevent the raid themselves, Keokuk and other chiefs warned their agent Thomas Forsyth about it. At first he threatened to have Black Hawk and his followers brought to St. Louis in chains. Then, realizing that was an empty threat, he warned the Sioux agent of the danger and made certain that the would-be raiders learned that their enemies knew of the plan. Apparently this convinced Black Hawk that an attack might be too dangerous. By mid-June the crisis passed, as Sioux chiefs sent messages calling for peace.[24]

Facing growing pressures from a weakened environment, neighboring tribes, and advancing pioneers, the Sauk and Mesquakie villagers had little chance to retain their tribal lands. This became clear in 1827 when Illinois governor Ninian Edwards demanded that the federal government force all Indians across the Mississippi. Their presence in the state, he wrote, "has been borne by the people for a few years past with great

impatience . . . and cannot be submitted to much longer."[25] Some months
later several minor incidents with the Potawatomis living near present
Chicago caused the governor to threaten that if federal officials delayed
action much longer "the Indians will be removed, and that very promptly,"
by the state.[26] Responding to Edwards's threats, the secretary of war
promised that the tribes would be out of Illinois by May 25, 1829.[27]

While they faced increasing tensions with the pioneers, the villagers
had growing ecological problems too. Each year the supply of wild game
shrank, so the hunters brought home less food and fewer hides and pelts
for trade. Soon the Indians could not pay their debts to the traders, and
agent Thomas Forsyth pressed the chiefs to move their villages to Iowa.
Some saw that they had little choice and did so. Others responded with
open defiance, using Quashquame's repeated claim that he had never
sold the tribal land north of the Rock River.[28] The federal land office decision to offer Sauk land for sale to pioneers in 1829 brought matters to a
head. Confused by the 1804 treaty article, which promised that the Indians could live on those lands as long as they belonged to the United
States, many Sauks and Mesquakies thought that the government had
cheated them. Some chiefs from both tribes opposed the sales. Bad
Thunder, Red Head, and Ioway all argued against cooperation with the
United States. These men represented the villagers with anti-American
ideas and opposed Keokuk and the tribal elements that he led. Their actions helped to form the hard core of what became the British Band that
stumbled into the 1832 disaster.

Several of the wars examined here included an aspect of religious revival or leadership exercised by shamans, and the Black Hawk War was
no exception. By the late 1820s Wabokieshiek or White Cloud, a half-
Sauk half-Winnebago prophet, lived in a multitribal village about sixty
miles up the Rock River from Saukenuk. His religious teachings remain
unclear, but he exercised some influence among the people of Saukenuk
and by 1827 had been invited to move there. Instead he chose to stay with
his immediate followers, but he continued to have some influence among
the Sauks and Mesquakies. In 1828 the local agent reported that the
prophet had promised to work for peace.[29] Nevertheless, by the end of
the 1820s he encouraged the traditionalists to remain in Saukenuk near
the graves of their ancestors. While he may have meant no harm, this
advice persuaded some members of the British Band to ignore white

demands that they move across the Mississippi. Later, on the eve of the war, his ideas and support offered false hope to a despairing people.[30]

Pioneer settlement in 1829, both illegal and lawful, increased white-Indian friction and violence at Saukenuk. Squatters arrived early that spring before the federal land sale and the Indians' return from their winter hunt. They fenced nearly all of the well-worked and carefully tended fields, tore down lodges, and began to plant their own crops. When the Indians objected to what they saw as the theft of their land, the pioneers threatened or beat them, took their horses and rifles, and generally made life miserable. Villagers appealed to agent Forsyth in May 1829, who told them that he had no power to remove the whites and advised them to leave Saukenuk. Quashquame repeated his earlier claims that he never sold the Sauk village land and Black Hawk denied that American officials had ever mentioned land to him in 1816 when they discussed a new treaty. In fact he claimed that the whites had added the land-related articles to the treaty *after* the Indians had signed it. While Forsyth gave the Indians no satisfaction, he misinformed his superiors, writing that only a few of the villagers would still be at Saukenuk by the end of that summer.[31]

By this time the long-standing divisions among Sauk and Mesquakie leaders had hardened so much that compromise became ever less likely. Keokuk and the peace chiefs had long recognized that moving from Illinois to Iowa offered their only hope for survival. Their opponents, perhaps 20 or 25 percent of the villagers, refused to accept that and would not budge. Despite the seizure of their best land, destruction of their lodges, occasional physical abuse from pioneers, and the threats of federal officials, they rejected the pleas of their tribal leaders. They had no intention of leaving Saukenuk and looked elsewhere for support. Some went to the Winnebago Prophet for advice. He assured them that they could remain in Illinois if they had not sold their village lands to the United States. Others visited British officials at Fort Malden in Canada. When they returned several of the men reported that those officers had told them the same thing.[32] Unfortunately the 1804 treaty had sold the land, despite all the Sauk and Mesquakie assertions, so the advice only encouraged the dissidents' false hopes.

Traditional gender roles in the tribal villages played another direct and unusual part in creating the confusion and bitterness that led directly to war. When the United States began selling the land along the Rock River, village and tribal leaders had to choose whether to abandon their major village and the graves of their ancestors or find some way to remain there. Black Hawk and Keokuk argued bitterly about this. The Watchful Fox promised that he would try to get the whites to exchange other lands for the villagers' traditional home. That effort failed, and soon he began recruiting people at Saukenuk to join most of the Sauks at their new villages in Iowa. This enraged Black Hawk. "I looked upon him as a coward, and no brave, to abandon his village to be occupied by strangers," he remembered.[33] Clearly the aging warrior felt that Keokuk's acceptance of white demands marked him as both unpatriotic and a coward, unwilling to defend tribal lands as any "real" Sauk male would do.

The Indian women had several reasons for supporting the men in their 1832 return to Saukenuk as well. Before any fighting began, pro-U.S. chiefs warned William Clark that rumors of government plans for dealing with the recalcitrant Sauks in Iowa had created near-hysteria among some of the villagers. One of the stories circulating that winter described how American officials expected to seize all of the Sauk males, "young and old, and deprive them of those parts which are said to be *essential* to courage."[34] The chiefs reporting this blamed that fear on the unusual amount of sexual mutilation of the whites killed during the war. The same rumor that threatened castration for the men promised that once that had been completed the government would bring "a horde of Negro men . . . to whom our wives, sisters, and daughters were to be given, for the purpose of raising a stock of *Slaves* to supply the demand of the country."[35]

Beyond those rumors, the women had other strong personal motivations for demanding a return to Illinois. By custom the land that they had tended for generations at Saukenuk belonged to them. During the 1831 negotiations with General Edmund P. Gaines, one old woman had testified that the chiefs could not have sold the cropland because the women would never have accepted such an action.[36] The fertile, well-watered fields near the village gave them large crops each year, and they did not want to abandon them. Moreover, they had constant trouble from the time they began work on new fields in Iowa. Their digging sticks broke in the hard ground. Thick grass with its deeply tangled roots made planting difficult and limited their crops. So this issue, when added to the feared emasculation of Sauk men and the rumored forced breeding with slaves, may help to explain "the enthusiastic madness with which our women urged their husbands to this desperate resort" of returning to Illinois.[37]

Repeated mistreatment of villagers at Saukenuk by pioneer settlers resembled similar experiences of both the Ohio Valley tribes and the Creeks earlier, as frontier toughs and criminals used violence and intimidation to drive the villagers from their homes. Every incident created new resentment among the Indians. When the Sauks complained, local officials warned that they needed to move west, so Indian anger and frustration grew. Black Hawk recounted incidents in which the whites' actions seemed totally inexplicable to him. In one case a Sauk man had found a bee tree and took part of the honeycomb back to his lodge. Several pioneers followed, shouting that he had stolen it from their tree. When he offered to return the remaining honey they rejected it. Instead they stole the packs of furs that he had gathered during the winter hunt and needed to pay his debts to the traders. Without them he had no way to get things for his family the next year. In other instances whites harassed the women when they tried to gather corn and beat a young man to death when he opened a fence to ride his horse down a road that the farmers had blocked. When Sauks complained to their agent, they learned that "the whites were *complaining* at the same time that *we* were *intruding upon their rights!*"[38] Responding to that charge, Black Hawk concluded: "[H]ow smooth must be the language of the whites, when they can make right look like wrong, and wrong like right."[39]

Black Hawk's bitter accusations illustrated the level of anger and frustration that developed among Native peoples across the country. In particular American actions that appeared to limit tribal independence frequently disrupted frontier peace. The 1825 Treaty of Prairie du Chien gives a clear example of this. It called on tribes in the region to allow federal authorities to settle disputes and struck at the heart of local custom and tradition. Only two years after signing the agreement, Sioux bands had knowingly moved into Sauk and Fox hunting territory. Although American officials prevented bloodshed, there is no evidence that the Sioux left their hunting spot. Some anti-American Sauks saw this as just another example of one-sided treatment by the United States. To them this fit into what appeared as a long series of actions that favored

Sauk competitors or enemies that dated back to the 1804 support of the Osage tribe.

The "Warner Incident" and subsequent U.S. actions in 1830–31 brought this issue to a head and illustrate the mistrust and poor relations among the Rock River villagers, competing tribes, and the government. This grew out of a situation in which intertribal raids and counterraids had continued despite the earlier 1825 promises made at Prairie du Chien. In 1829 a Sauk and Mesquakie war party had killed twelve Sioux, and the victims' families demanded that their warriors retaliate. At Fort St. Anthony near present St. Paul, Minnesota, Indian agent Lawrence Taliaferro warned William Clark that leaders of a war party of almost five hundred men had told him that they would attack the Fox villages. Desperate to avoid a war, Clark and his subordinates moved to "cover the blood" with payments of cash and goods. When it appeared that this might not be enough to head off a reprisal, Clark called for another round of negotiations at Prairie du Chien in 1830.[40]

Acting on orders from Clark, Wynkoop Warner, the new subagent at the Fever River settlements in northwestern Illinois, asked Mesquakie leaders from a village in northeastern Iowa to meet the Sioux, Winnebago, and Menominee chiefs and reconfirm their earlier peace. Having issued his invitation, Warner then told the Sioux and Menominees to expect the unarmed peace delegation. Instead of attending the anticipated negotiations, on the evening of May 5, 1830, nearly fifty Menominee, Sioux, and Winnebago warriors attacked the Mesquakie chiefs' camp. When the fighting ended, they had killed all but one of the chiefs who came seeking peace. They sent him home to carry news of the disaster. Ironically, all of those who died had favored peace.[41]

Other Sauk and Mesquakie leaders hurried to recruit a force of four hundred to five hundred men to avenge this attack. Again frontier officials scrambled to defuse the situation. Agent Thomas Forsyth urged calm and persuaded the outraged chiefs to take more than two hundred of the men south to meet with William Clark at St. Louis rather than traveling north to attack their enemies. There the angry chiefs denounced American policies as unfair and one-sided. To them the incident occurred because they had cooperated with federal officials. On their way to seek peace, in response to Warner's invitation, their unarmed party had been murdered, not killed in battle. Even Keokuk, who always spoke for peace, refused to meet for another parley. "I can't shake hands with the Sioux and Menominees, until we are paid for covering our dead," he announced angrily.[42] Modest payments to the enraged chiefs seemed to bring an uneasy peace, but only briefly.

Under tribal custom, relatives of the slain had the option of accepting the payments or calling for retribution. This time they spurned the blood money and insisted on revenge. So in August 1831 a Mesquakie and Sauk war party killed twenty-five Menominees near Prairie du Chien. When asked, the raiders explained their actions as necessary to keep harmony within their home community. Federal authorities viewed the incident somewhat differently. To them it demonstrated that they could not depend on the Sauks and Mesquakies to live up to their treaty agreements. Although they gave generous presents to the Menominees to "cover the blood" of this latest episode, frontier leaders feared that might not halt the continuing warfare. Next officials in Washington insisted that Mesquakie chiefs surrender the men who organized or led the attack. General Henry Atkinson received orders to meet the village leaders and seize the raiders. This action just reinforced Sauk and Mesquakie feelings that the United States would not deal evenhandedly with them. When the Sioux and Menominees had killed the Mesquakie peace delegation in the Warner Incident, the government had not insisted that the attackers be surrendered. Now, however, when the Sauks and Mesquakies retaliated, U.S. officials moved to arrest the attackers rather than giving presents to the victims' families. Certainly these events persuaded many Sauks and Mesquakies that the Americans refused to treat them fairly and appear to have encouraged some to join other dissidents already in the British Band.[43]

Even so that group might not have returned to Saukenuk in 1831 except for their continuing troubles in Iowa. The women harvested only a skimpy crop from their unfamiliar fields, while the men found little game for food or pelts. Coupled with the lost incomes from their profitable lead mining land east of the Mississippi, these hardships placed enormous strain on the villagers' lives. Their fond memories of happier times at Saukenuk exerted strong attractions, so in the spring of 1831 members of the British Band straggled back into Illinois. Their arrival terrified many of the pioneers, who fled from the village site. Black Hawk reported enjoying a few pleasant months there as the people planted, hunted, and carried out some traditional summer ceremonies.[44]

This could not last, however, because the pioneers who had fled quickly reported that the Indians had returned to their Rock River village. This news stirred Illinois governor John Reynolds into action. Insisting that the federal officials get the Sauks out of the state once and for all, he called up seven hundred mounted militiamen with orders to move the Indians "dead or alive" from Illinois. As soon as he heard about the governor's actions William Clark asked General Edmund P. Gaines to move soldiers north from Jefferson Barracks near St. Louis to prevent an Indian war.[45] When he learned that troops had been sent, Black Hawk traveled to the Prophet's village for advice. White Cloud said that his dreams told him that General Gaines only wanted to frighten the British Band into leaving the village. Later Black Hawk recalled that the Prophet had "assured us that this 'great war chief' dare not, and would not, hurt any of us."[46] Whatever his motivation, White Cloud told the aging warrior just what he wanted to hear, so he decided to remain in the village and to ignore or refuse to obey the general's orders.

When Gaines reached Saukenuk, he wasted little time on diplomatic niceties. Instead he called the chiefs together on June 2, 1831, and described the president's anger because of their return to Illinois. He reminded them that the United States had treated them well despite their anti-American actions for more than twenty years. Then he reviewed treaties that they had signed agreeing to leave the Rock River and migrate west. The time had come, he said, for them to live up to their promises. They had no choice but to cross the Mississippi and remain in Iowa. At this point their sense that they had been treated unjustly, their bitterness over the 1804 treaty of cession, and certainly their wishful thinking all came out in the discussion. As usual Chief Quashquame claimed that he had never sold their village, and this time one of the older women told the general that the village land belonged to the women, who had never agreed to its sale. Gaines remained adamant. The Indians had to go![47]

Black Hawk had recommended passive resistance, assuming that the general would not hurt the villagers if they did nothing. For a time that worked: Gaines spent several days getting his force ready for action while hoping to avoid any fighting. The situation changed abruptly on June 25 when Governor Reynolds and 1,400 mounted militiamen arrived. Seeing these rangers, Black Hawk reported that he feared "the multitude of palefaces, who were on horseback, as they were under no restraint of their chiefs."[48] The governor had guessed correctly. The mere presence of that many armed pioneers persuaded the Indians to leave immediately. The Sauks hurried across the Mississippi when darkness fell, and on June 30, 1831, a few of the leaders returned for a brief parley. There they agreed to stay in Iowa permanently. At this meeting the general arranged for them to receive enough corn to feed themselves during the next winter.[49] That done, he reported that the Indians would remain west of the Mississippi and that even Black Hawk appeared reconciled to having a new home. Gaines thought that he had succeeded, as the last of the Sauks and Mesquakies moved west into Iowa without any fighting.

Yet the new 1831 agreement failed to resolve any of the issues that had caused the standoff in the first place. In the spring of 1832, despite all expectations to the contrary, the British Band returned. Now, for the first time, it had a formal organization that included an identifiable council of chiefs and recognized war leaders. It appears that some of the leaders took advice from the Winnebago Prophet Wabokieshiek and that he served as their spiritual mentor. Former residents of Saukenuk made up the largest element of the group. Estimates and scholarly accounts of how many people the band included have varied from 1832 to the present. Keokuk reported the number of men at 500 to General Atkinson. Former agent Thomas Forsyth's account gave the figure of 368 men, by far the lowest count at the time.[50] Whatever the exact count of potential warriors, the British Band included all members of their families, old people, women, and children. Even with only three or four people in each family, this would have raised band membership to a minimum of 1,200–1,500 people.[51]

To that number should be added a motley variety of other adherents. A village of Kickapoos, who had left their tribe in 1819 when the chiefs had ceded the tribe's land in Illinois to the United States, composed one part. This group included about a hundred fighting men and their families, perhaps another three hundred to four hundred people. They had asked the Saukenuk chiefs to let them build a village near the Rock River and had moved there in the early 1820s. By 1832 they could not rejoin their Kickapoo relatives and at the same time had no claim to Sauk or

Mesquakie land in Iowa. So they faced an uncertain future at best.[52] Two
other small parties joined the larger British Band adherents that spring.
When General Atkinson continued to demand the surrender of the Mesquakies who had retaliated against the Menominees for the 1831 Warner
Incident, their friends and relatives followed the fugitives into the larger
group. After the party crossed the Mississippi into Illinois, some Winnebagos, Sauks, and métis from the Prophet's village threw their lot in
with the dissident Sauks as well.

With this many elements in the British Band, the motivations for each
subgroup that spring varied substantially. Some had rejected the need to
cooperate with the United States as essential for their survival. Others
like Black Hawk had no desire for war but expressed a stubborn refusal
to abandon northeastern Illinois. They shared that fierce attachment to
their home territory with many tribes. Later it motivated both the Apache
leader Cochise and Nez Perce Chief Joseph. When the aging Sauk leader
recognized that he could not return to his former village, he accepted the
Prophet's invitation to settle near his village farther up the Rock River in
northern Illinois.[53] Wishful thinking played an important role too. The
village women complained that the ground was difficult to work and that
they could not raise enough food for their families. Men looking for ex-
cuses to move back to the Saukenuk area needed little convincing. Together they ignored General Gaines's warnings of June 1831 when he
had told the stragglers at Saukenuk that they had to abandon the village
and never return or face sure destruction.

Seeing themselves as beset on all sides by other tribes, white settlers,
and government officers while their own tribal leaders appeared unable
or unwilling to stand firm, the Indians chose to ignore the reality of their
circumstances. One expert suggested that their actions grew out of a
"combination of panicky fear about losing personal integrity by giving in
to a powerful and contemptuous adversary, stubborn legalistic argument,
and wild fantasy."[54] For him Black Hawk became the personification of
those frustrations and fears. To make matters worse, that spring the Winnebago Prophet invited the British Band to settle at his village and
assured them that the whites would allow them to stay as long as they
remained peaceful. Diplomatic good news followed this religious assurance. Neapope, one of the band chiefs, returned from Canada and,
clearly lying, reported that the British had promised to bring men and

supplies to Milwaukee if the Americans attacked the peaceful Indians. Claims that nearby tribes welcomed the refugees and would help them circulated too.

Because of this variety of factors, it took until May 14, just prior to Major Stillman's attack on the Sauk camp, for Black Hawk and some of the other leaders to realize that the nearby tribes wanted nothing to do with his people and that the British Band had to return to Iowa as quickly as possible.[55] By then time had run out: the war began. Clearly the British Band members did not expect conflict that summer. If they had, the elderly, women, and children would have remained in Iowa. Even with their fantasies of cooperation with the Winnebago or Potawatomi tribes and the more unrealistic hope for military aid from the British, they would not have led their families into such danger. The conflict, then, resulted from an intricate assortment of causes that have led scholars to depict it as a war of complex issues. Set within the framework of a fraudulent treaty and forced removal, this unexpected, unwanted, and accidental war stemmed from a tangled pattern of intratribal and intertribal relationships as much or more than most.

During the actual campaign against the British Band that summer, American forces rarely found more than small raiding parties. Using their accustomed tactics of scattered attacks and rapid withdrawal, the Indians avoided large fights with their pursuers most of the time. Atkinson's slow-moving infantrymen rarely saw their foes, but the Illinois mounted rangers had better luck. After the Indians moved north up the Rock River into southern Wisconsin they turned west toward the Mississippi. At that point the militiamen discovered their trail. As they often did, the military leaders recruited Winnebago, Dakota Sioux, and Menominee auxiliaries to help. It is likely that these tribal allies captured or killed as many of the fugitives as the whites had, except for the near-slaughter during the August 2 Battle of Bad Axe when the troops overtook the fleeing Indians on the bank of the Mississippi. By early August 1832 the fighting had ended and many of the survivors had been brought to Prairie du Chien in southwestern Wisconsin. From there the army sent Black Hawk, the Prophet, and some of the other British Band leaders south to Jefferson Barracks to be imprisoned there.[56] The next spring the government moved the captives east to Fort Monroe in Virginia then, after giving them a quick tour of eastern cities, escorted them back to Iowa.

The war cost the Sauks and Mesquakies dearly. The villagers who lived in Iowa faced the same treatment received by a majority of the Creeks who remained neutral or even served as allies to Andrew Jackson in 1814 during the Red Stick War. Just a few weeks after the fighting ended, in September 1832 General Winfield Scott and Illinois governor John Reynolds extracted a treaty that seized nearly one-third of eastern Iowa for the United States. It took a strip of land fifty miles wide along the west bank of the Mississippi that included some 6 million acres of the tribes' best land. That started a period of rapid population loss and cultural decline among both tribes. By the 1840s they had been pushed south and west into Kansas. Just over twenty years later they had to move again, this time to Indian Territory in present Oklahoma.[57]

Most of the tribes whose men served as allies and helped defeat the British Band fared little better. During the winter of 1835–36 the Potawatomis and their allies living along the shore of Lake Michigan faced removal to Missouri and beyond. The next year (1837) the Dakota Sioux ceded their claims to land in western Wisconsin. Then in 1840 the government pushed the Winnebagos west too. Just a few years after the Battle at Bad Axe, the tribes of northern Illinois, southern Wisconsin, and eastern Iowa no longer occupied their traditional areas. The Dakota auxiliaries from Minnesota avoided removal for another generation, but during the early 1860s they too would fight and lose a war against the United States and be driven from their homes. Within just a few years the Native people in the region disappeared. Thousands of white pioneers poured into the area, often erasing most signs that Indians had ever lived there.

CHAPTER 5

The Minnesota Sioux War, 1862

As they headed home after a failed hunt in the Big Woods on August 17, 1862, four tired, thirsty young Wahpeton Dakota Sioux men rode toward the combined home and store of Robinson Jones at Action, Minnesota. Near the house they saw a nest with chicken eggs along the fence, and one of the riders stopped to take them. When a companion cautioned that they might get into trouble if they stole the eggs, the would-be thief called him a coward. Responding hotly, the hunter promised to show his bravery and dared the others to help him kill the nearby white settlers. Members of an active soldiers' society, the others agreed. The hunters entered the little store and asked Jones for some whiskey. When he declined and walked across the road to visit a neighbor's farm, the Indians followed. There the Dakota hunters and pioneers had a friendly target-shooting competition. Suddenly, without any warning, the young Dakotas shot three of the men and one woman. While fleeing past the Jones house, they shot a teenaged girl as she looked out the door.

The hunters stole a couple of horses and raced back to their village at the Yellow Medicine Agency, described the killings, and demanded that their chiefs lead them to war. As news of the incident spread, men from some of the lower villages hurried to the camp, where bitter debate raged during the night. Little Crow and several of the more experienced chiefs opposed any attack on the white settlers, reminding the others that the

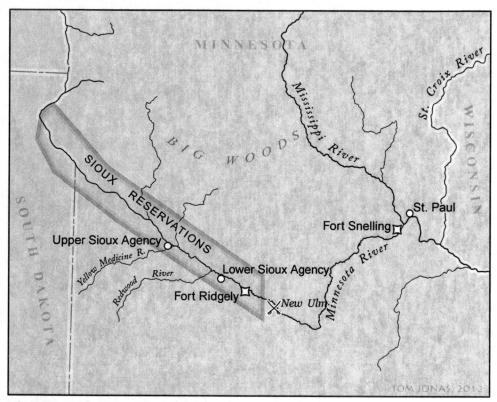

The Minnesota Sioux War.
© 2013 University of Oklahoma Press, Norman.

overwhelming numbers of Americans made fighting against them sui-
cidal. He predicted that "you will die like the rabbits when the hungry
wolves hunt them." His arguments failed to keep peace; responding to
the taunting by some of the soldier society warriors, he declared: "Ta-
o-ya-te-du-ta [Little Crow] is not a coward: he will die with you."[1] The
next day, August 18, the villagers attacked the Lower Sioux or Redwood
Agency. What had begun as a minor argument among a handful of tired,
hungry young men shifted rapidly into a bloody incident that touched off
what came to be called the Minnesota Sioux Uprising or sometimes Little
Crow's War.[2]

Although the local Sioux agent and the commanding officer at Fort
Ridgely should not have been surprised, this conflict caught the pioneers
almost completely unaware. Before the 1850s the Dakota Sioux had rarely

even threatened the incoming settlers. Instead their wars focused on traditional Indian enemies. This time the fierce assaults provided a dramatic reminder of frontier dangers, far exceeding any earlier interracial violence in the region. Striking without warning, the tribesmen inflicted heavy casualties among the settlers and the local militia. When the war ended, authorities never presented an official count of the dead and wounded, but existing accounts suggest that between four hundred and eight hundred settlers, fewer than one hundred soldiers, and about one hundred Indians died in the fighting. News of the war spread quickly from Minnesota to eastern Wisconsin and west as far as Denver, igniting fears of a broader Indian war.[3] But the immediate causes for this violence grew directly out of the local situation that summer.

Having first encountered Europeans when French traders entered the Upper Mississippi Valley in the seventeenth century, the Dakotas had enjoyed mostly peaceful relations with the white traders and settlers for almost two centuries. Unlike the Lakota Sioux, who had moved farther west and adopted horses and a nomadic lifestyle, they had remained in present Minnesota and western Wisconsin. By the 1830s they numbered about six thousand and lived in four distinct bands. The Mdewakanton and Wahpekute people, known as the lower bands, lived along the Mississippi and lower Minnesota Rivers. After 1851 their villages stood near the Lower Sioux or Redwood Agency. The other two bands, the Sissetons and Wahpetons, lived farther up the Minnesota River and dealt with officials from the Upper Sioux or Yellow Medicine Agency.[4]

These villagers had inhabited the region for generations. Each fall the men crisscrossed the prairie and forest land, hunting the abundant deer found there and east into Wisconsin. The women gathered wild rice along the streams and lakes as well. In March they began their yearly maple-sugar making while the hunters set out to gather smaller animals for meat and pelts to trade. In summer the people fished and gathered fruit, nuts, and roots to round out their diet. Although not serious farmers, the women planted small plots of corn and certainly exchanged it with nearby tribes for other foodstuffs. After their early meetings with the French, the Dakotas opened trade for manufactured goods with them and with other Europeans. This mix of traditional and trading economies sustained them for generations. But by the middle of the nineteenth century two developments had changed their lives dramatically. First, the preceding hundred years of increased trade-based hunting had reduced the supply of animals sharply. That threatened their very survival unless they moved or changed their way of life. Second, as Dakota self-sufficiency weakened, the influx of American settlers further undercut the traditional life that the Indians had enjoyed for generations.[5]

As in many Indian societies, their world had two kinds of people: the members of their own band or village and everyone else. Customarily they regarded all others as strangers, even potential enemies. For generations the Dakotas competed with and fought against neighboring tribes such as the Ojibwas (Anishinaabes) in the St. Croix River Valley to the east as well as the Winnebagos (Ho Chunks) in central and western Wisconsin and the Sauks and Mesquakies in Illinois and Iowa. Despite these traditional rivalries, all the area tribes had customs that helped them to accommodate outsiders and make them part of the village, band, or tribal kinship networks. Gradually they accepted the traders. Many of them married Indian women and became part of the village societies, along with their mixed-race children. For decades these newly incorporated people seem to have had few negative results in the villages, but that began to change soon after the 1819 arrival of Americans. From then on whites came to have increasingly divisive roles in the Indian villages and in tribal dealings with the newcomers.[6]

This process took several decades, but the Americans' entry into the Dakota homeland had more immediate and long-term impacts on Native life. In the summer of 1819 Colonel Henry Leavenworth led troops of the U.S. Fifth Infantry to occupy land at the confluence of the Minnesota and Mississippi Rivers. There they built what later became known as Fort Snelling. That garrison of several hundred soldiers remained small for decades but gradually attracted an increasing number of merchants who encouraged the Dakota hunters to kill ever more animals for the trade in pelts and hides. This increased hunting reduced some species to near extinction, and soon the hunters could no longer get the necessary trade goods or enough fresh meat to feed their families. That made them increasingly dependent on credit from the traders, as economic stability in their communities disintegrated.[7]

Struggling to get the pelts they needed for survival, many of the young hunters slipped farther east into Wisconsin, encroaching on the territory of their long-time Ojibwa enemies. Soon that became too dangerous, so they traveled south into areas claimed by the Sauks and Mesquakies in northern Iowa. Each of those tribes faced similarly weakened environments, so each repeatedly trespassed on the others' hunting territory. By the end of the 1820s the need to overcome the increasing scarcity of food and their ever-growing dependence on credit from the resident traders led directly to expanding intertribal violence.

The American soldiers and federal Indian agents who came into Minnesota added new elements to this increasingly volatile situation. In a few decades their actions, combined with those of the traders, changed the Dakota world forever. In 1819, just a year after U.S. troops began work on the garrison at Fort Snelling, Lawrence Taliaferro arrived to serve as agent at the nearby St. Peter's Agency. An honest and hard-working man, he appears to have had the Indians' well-being at heart. As agent he strove to implement the federal government's ongoing efforts to acculturate tribal people, as Benjamin Hawkins had done a generation earlier among the Creeks. Taliaferro urged the villager leaders to shift from their traditional dependence on hunting, gathering, and borrowing from the traders to farming. To encourage that, in 1834 he had a plow shipped to Chief Big Thunder's village. There the chief and war leader Big Iron both tried plowing, but the novelty soon wore off. Physically demanding work, farming ran head on into traditional Dakota cultural practices. Women raised food crops, men did not.

A few years later Taliaferro hired whites to do the work, but this backfired. When the villagers saw that others would plow for them, they refused to do it themselves. When Big Thunder learned that Taliaferro had paid the white men to do this work, he demanded that one of his mixed-race relatives get the job and salary. The agent balked. The Indians saw his refusal to share what he had as a failure to follow Dakota social customs, so they destroyed farm equipment and killed the draft animals to sabotage the program. There is little evidence that Taliaferro understood the Indians' actions. When he resigned twenty years later, he had failed to change the Dakotas' social and economic practices. At that point nearby white farmers planted and harvested almost the only crops grown in the area.[8]

Some years later when a few Indians did begin to shift from hunting to farming, their actions had an immediate impact. To succeed in a market economy, each person needed to withdraw from the group-oriented village community. That meant ignoring some of the traditional rituals and clan obligations, such as sharing their food and other wealth with neighbors or taking part in ceremonies that called for personal exchanges and present giving within their own village or clan. When people ignored those tribal customs, they weakened the unity of Dakota society, undermined the Indians' ability to live without having to accept the government acculturation program, and created growing intratribal divisions. These changes came gradually and for a time lacked the almost immediate and destructive force of Benjamin Hawkins's efforts among the Creeks in Alabama a generation earlier. Still, after a decade or two the changes began to disrupt the Minnesota villages as directly as they had done in the South.[9]

The situation for the Sioux people during the early and middle decades of the nineteenth century shifted dramatically as agent Taliaferro, army officers, and other federal officers all intervened actively in their lives. The multitribal treaties that William Clark and Lewis Cass concluded in 1825 at Prairie du Chien, Wisconsin, are an early example. There American negotiators tried to get tribes in the region to end their culturally driven raids in revenge for insults or injuries from other Indian groups. The treaties required that retaliation cease and pledged that the United States would pay intertribal damage claims instead. Next the U.S. officials asked each tribal delegation to outline the borders of its territory. Then Clark and Cass tried to persuade the chiefs to stop their people from traveling through or hunting on land beyond their own borders. Writing this into the treaties, they promised that Indian compliance would end the violence and threatened to punish anyone who refused to remain at peace.[10]

Even though the chiefs signed the agreement, they gave little evidence of having any intention to enforce that demand. In fact the provision that called for an end to raiding brought protests from the young men in the soldier societies of each tribe. Their hopes for prestige and chances for future leadership roles required that they demonstrate personal bravery in the raids that stemmed from meeting clan obligations or in success as hunters. Not only had U.S. officials asked the men to stop hunting and become farmers, but now the treaty also prohibited their time-honored military actions against tribal enemies. Together these changes that white officials tried to impose posed a major challenge to Dakota culture and autonomy.

Still, although the American representatives had written those ideas into the agreement and the chiefs had initialed it, little changed. Certainly both William Clark and Lewis Cass recognized the centrality of clan retribution in the tribal societies. Only blind wishful thinking could have persuaded them that getting a few headmen to sign the treaties would erase that long-held traditional imperative. Despite reporting that they had pacified the region, they must have known that any lasting peace remained unlikely. To complicate matters, governmental inaction ensured the new treaty's failure, because local officials never completed the boundary surveys that would clearly have identified the home territory for each tribe. At Prairie du Chien the U.S. officers had insisted that the Dakotas and others stop raiding their enemies, but the Americans could not enforce this part of the treaty effectively. Sporadic violence continued.[11]

By the late 1820s, as more settlers and miners moved into the Upper Mississippi Valley, federal officials worried that Indian warfare might cause attacks on the incoming pioneers. To avoid that William Clark summoned the tribes to Prairie du Chien again in 1830. There he repeated earlier demands that the intertribal raiding cease. Again the veteran negotiator continued to ignore the centrality of warfare in the village cultures. Whatever conclusions were reached in the discussions with the chiefs about the intermittent raiding, this issue did not appear in the new round of treaties. This time the federal negotiators decided not to rely on the Indian leaders' assurances. Instead they convinced the chiefs to accept small land cessions between tribes meant to keep peace by locating the warring groups farther apart from each other. In return for the proposed land surrenders, Clark offered each tribe a modest ten-year annuity.[12]

For the next generation these agreements brought few direct changes to the intertribal situation in the region because the government lacked any way to enforce them. At the same time the fluid nature of the Indian societies limited the village chiefs' authority. They could only advise the men to remain at peace, not stop them if they chose to raid. Because neither the government nor the village councils could do anything effective to end intertribal violence, it continued. Just two years later the unchecked intertribal raiding became a major factor leading to the Black Hawk War that erupted in 1832. Rather than urging the nearby tribes to remain neutral, hard-pressed army leaders called on the Sioux, Menominees, and Ho Chunks to join them against the Sauks and Mesquakies. Several groups of each tribe responded, and the Dakotas slaughtered several hundred of the defeated fugitives as the war ended.[13] Not surprisingly, these contradictory American efforts to control how the tribes related to each other confused and angered many Indians. The government repeatedly urged them to remain at peace but then asked for their military help when necessary, as in 1823 against the Arikaras, in 1827 against the Ho Chunks, and in the 1832 Black Hawk War.

Agent Taliaferro's continuing effort to implement the government's acculturation program caused repeated arguments and divisions in Dakota villages. His frequent demands that tribal leaders end raids against other tribes surely weakened his influence on other issues and created widespread opposition. Some of the chiefs recognized that the Dakotas benefited more from peace than from war, but this failed to satisfy the young men's desire to prove their bravery. They often ignored their leaders' urgings and slipped away to attack their enemies or hunt in their territory. Even chiefs who spoke for peace ignored the raids. In fact they feared that Sauk and Mesquakie or Ojibwa neighbors might overrun Sioux hunting areas without the threat of continued Dakota retaliation.[14] Their concern about losing even a few of the remaining game animals remained central to the discussions. By the end of the 1820s so few deer and beavers remained that the Dakota men had turned to killing muskrats for pelts and food. Although the traders paid almost nothing for the skins, the animals became central in the Indians' diet and a decade later constituted nearly the entire catch.[15]

Part of the government's effort to turn the Indians into farmers included inviting Christian groups to send missionaries to the region. By 1835 men representing the Protestant American Board of Commissioners for Foreign Missions (ABCFM) had established their first two frontier outposts among the Dakotas. With several decades of experience working in other Indian communities, they quickly developed an extensive nongovernmental acculturation program in Minnesota. At first they avoided calling for economic changes in village life. Instead the newcomers

established schools to teach basic literacy. Although they were not the
only religious group among the Sioux, they had the most workers and
remained when several other organizations ceased operations.

At least seven ABCFM-supported men moved into the Dakota territory, and the organization operated seven missions among the tribe by
the early 1840s. In theory the missionaries expected to use literacy as a
means of converting the Indians to Christianity. Like the agents' efforts
to change the economy from hunting and gathering to agriculture, the
missionaries' plan to undermine tribal religious practices had only a modest impact for the first few decades. They seem to have misunderstood
the basic connections between Dakota religious ideas and day-to-day practices. Disappointed at their failure to gain converts, they turned to mixed-
race individuals and their families to begin the first Christian groups. By
1842 the missionaries claimed to have converted thirty-nine women and
three men among the Dakotas, but soon after that some of their adherents moved away.[16]

While federal officials and the missionaries tried to reshape Dakota
society, they had little success. But by the end of the 1830s the U.S. Indian Removal Policy brought other problems for the villagers. This new
government plan sought to push competitors and traditional enemies
such as the Sauks and Mesquakies and Winnebagos west of the Mississippi
into southern Minnesota and northern Iowa, territory that the Sioux had
claimed for generations. This brought additional hunting in an area
where decades of excessive hunting and trapping had almost eliminated
the animals. By relocating tribal groups the federal action opened new
regions for pioneers, and more land seekers moved into the upper Mississippi area. In 1836 Wisconsin became a territory, adding new demands
that the government end Indian title in the region.[17]

By then agent Taliaferro had reported that his Dakota charges faced
starvation as their hunting and gathering economy neared collapse and
urged the government to accelerate its acculturation program. To him
that policy offered the Indians a better chance for survival than any other
options. At the same time it might avoid tribal collapse and prevent frontier violence. Local white leaders concurred, reasoning that a shift from
hunting to farming would open new areas for pioneer farmers. If the
Dakotas sold much of their land to the government, it could give them
the seeds, equipment, and training that they needed to become farmers.

The agent and some other observers concluded that a flood of pioneer settlers would overwhelm the Sioux if they failed to change their society. Yet this view ignored village leaders' repeated opposition to any major cultural restructuring of their lives.

The Dakota leaders' continuing rejection of the federal acculturation program apparently persuaded them that new treaty talks might achieve their goals. The 1830 Prairie du Chien treaty had provided modest annuities that enabled the Sioux to continue their traditional hunting and gathering economy. Now, just a few years later, many of the villagers depended entirely on that modest income, and the chiefs hoped to get increased government payments. In September 1837 agent Taliaferro led a twenty-one-man Dakota delegation to Washington, D.C., where they met secretary of war Joel Poinsett and the commissioner of Indian affairs Carey Harris. During the talks these men offered tribal leaders $1 million for their claims to land east of the Mississippi River in present Wisconsin. Some of the chiefs hesitated to make such a large cession, particularly one that surrendered much of their best hunting territory. Others asked for a larger payment, claiming that the land in Wisconsin had far more game than land on the Minnesota side of the river. However, bad timing disrupted the talks. Facing budget shortages following the Panic of 1837, Secretary Poinsett refused to negotiate further.[18]

Instead of the $1 million payment offered originally, the government agreed to only modest annuities spread over a long period. With little hope of getting more money for their land and needing to bring something back for their impoverished people, the chiefs accepted the new terms. These included a twenty-year annuity of $25,000 for food, clothing, and farm tools. In addition they provided a smaller perpetual annuity of $15,000.[19] Even with this new income these Indians faced an uncertain future. The U.S. Senate took until June 1838 to ratify the agreement, and pioneers began moving into the area during the months before the ratification took place. Once the treaty went into operation, delivery of the promised goods proved erratic. Often the materials arrived weeks or even months late and included fewer and lower-quality items than promised.[20] While the Dakota leaders complained at times, these issues appear not to have undermined their trust in American promises to treat them fairly and honestly.

The 1837 treaty did little more than buy the Indians a few more years to avoid the government's acculturation program. They continued to hunt and gather as usual, but with little success. Ever more hard pressed to find game, the young Dakota men ignored the new agreement and continued to intrude on the newly ceded Wisconsin land. Repeated contacts with Ojibwa hunters there kept alive the raiding cycle between the two tribes. At the same time increasing numbers of pioneers filtered into the area. In the late 1840s both Iowa and Wisconsin became states, and in 1849 Minnesota Territory opened. That attracted new groups of pioneer farmers and business owners looking for new opportunities. As always, the growing numbers of whites made life harder for the Dakota hunters and their trading partners. The Indians' needs for goods continued; but they had already killed most of the game animals, so they had trouble feeding their families. The Dakotas' inability to gather enough pelts to pay their debts made the traders ever less willing to extend credit. In fact several times these merchants tried to force the Sioux to return essential items like axes, traps, or weapons.

To escape these difficulties, some of the Indians turned to the missionaries and Christianity. The American Board of Commissioners for Foreign Missions had sent men to the Sioux in the late 1830s, who gradually attracted converts from among the mixed-race families and some Indian women. They operated several schools teaching in both English and Dakota, but these seem to have had only a modest impact. Once Little Crow (Taoyateduta) became recognized as a chief, he briefly led efforts to reduce alcohol consumption and even invited the missionaries to restart their activities. A few of the tribal leaders learned to write in Dakota, while an even smaller number acquired some English. But even the usually cooperative Little Crow seems to have taken little personal interest. A few other headmen considered learning English helpful and attended classes or sent their children to the local schools. As half-hearted as these acts appear now, they divided the Sioux: some traditional opponents of acculturation threatened children who went to school.[21]

While the chiefs quarreled about the impact of the federal program, settlement in Minnesota grew steadily. Land seekers, traders, and the newly appointed political leaders all wanted access to the Dakota land, but for different reasons. Those trying to boost settlement sought to open more land for incoming farmers. The traders knew that the Indians could no longer survive by hunting. These merchants assumed that the United States would soon buy the tribal land. They expected that federal negotiators would accept their claims to a large part of the annuity funds as repayment for Indian debts as they had done in the past. Even the resident missionaries supported the new effort to reduce the tribal land base. Overlooking their own repeated failures, the clerics hoped that the Sioux would realize how few resources remained and would become farmers. To bring that about they urged the United States to negotiate new land cession treaties with the Minnesota Sioux.[22]

Some chiefs in the four bands saw a new land cession as another way to raise cash. They could pay their trade debts and use the surplus to help retain their traditional economic patterns. The headmen thought that the United States had treated them fairly in the past, so they expected calm and honest negotiations. By this time, however, the situation in the upper Mississippi Valley had changed dramatically. The federal Removal Policy had pushed most eastern tribes out of their traditional homes and into the West. When the Dakotas began negotiations, they seem to have worried more about their Ojibwa enemies and being able to continue hunting than about retaining their traditional land. In fact they saw a cession as a way to deflect continuing white encroachments. This aligned their ideas with those of the American negotiators, who talked of establishing two reservations next to each other along the Minnesota River. This land lay farther upstream and west of the Mississippi than some of the chiefs expected, but at least for a while it would keep them separated from the intruding pioneers and their tribal enemies.[23]

The new talks came as the traditional Dakota economy neared almost total collapse. In this circumstance both the traders and local officials sought to profit from the land surrender, but by now tribal leaders had gained more experience as negotiators. They asked why the government had not paid what it had promised during the 1837 treaty discussions and why they had never received most of the annual payments for tribal schools. Despite their complaints they got neither answers nor dollars. In 1849 Alexander Ramsey (newly appointed territorial governor) and John Chambers tried to negotiate a purchase of Dakota land, but the talks failed. A year later the political leaders and traders tried to create good feelings by extending credit and giving presents to the villagers. During the spring of 1851 Ramsey traveled up the Minnesota River to Traverse des Sioux to negotiate with the Sisseton and Wahpeton villagers. When the two sides came to an agreement, the bands surrendered most of their land in Minnesota and all of their land in Iowa. The new treaty promised to pay them $1,665,000, most of which supposedly went into an interest-bearing trust fund. From that the two tribes would theoretically receive $68,000 each year, some in cash payments and the rest for food and to pay for the continuing acculturation program. The commissioners also set aside $305,000 in so-called hand money to pay tribal debts to the traders and the costs of removal to a new reservation along the Minnesota River.[24]

On the same day the chiefs signed the document several of the traders, helped by missionaries and mixed-race men, persuaded them to sign a "traders' paper." This private agreement gave the merchants $210,000 of the hand money and paid another $40,000 to the mixed-raced people who had helped get the needed signatures. From the start this second paper brought bitter controversy. Dakota leaders claimed that they thought it was only a second copy of the treaty, not a promise to give the traders most of their promised cash. Agent Nathaniel McLean objected that it included no way to verify the merchants' claims. But long-time missionary Stephen Riggs considered the amounts claimed and the signing of the traders' paper reasonable actions that had been explained clearly to the Indians. When several of the chiefs produced a list of their mixed-race relatives and of the traders to be paid, some others objected. The continuing disputes over the "traders' paper" within the tribes certainly undermined the villagers' trust that American officials had dealt fairly with them.[25]

When Ramsey and Lea turned their attention to the Mdewakantons and Wahpekutes in late July 1851, they found these people far less eager to negotiate than the other Dakotas. Negotiator Luke Lea offered his listeners $800,000 for their land, assuming a quick agreement because the other two tribes had already signed a treaty. To his dismay Chief Wabasha asked why the money promised to the Sioux for education in the earlier 1837 treaty had not been paid. First Lea tried to avoid this issue. When that failed, he promised that the chiefs would get the money as soon as they accepted the new treaty. When they said no, the talks broke off. The visiting negotiators tried to force the Dakota leaders to accept the government's terms by halting the Indians' food rations. After several tension-filled days the chiefs signed the treaty when they saw almost no other options. It promised a twenty-mile-wide reservation along the Minnesota River abutting the land assigned to the Sissetons and Wahpetons just days earlier.[26]

The new agreement did little to calm Indian-white tensions in southern Minnesota. These negotiations actually spread confusion within the tribes. The traders' paper led to complaints and divisions within the villages as well as active political infighting among the territorial politicians and the traders. Before the ink on these two agreements could dry, white squatters rushed onto the Sioux land long before the U.S. Senate got around to ratifying the treaties. During the ratification process the senators removed the articles establishing the two new reservations along the Minnesota River without telling the Indians about their action. That act ended all Dakota claims to land in Minnesota. Now all the Sioux had left was a small cash payment and some annuities, but no homeland. After bitter objections from the tribal leaders, sharp infighting among the traders and their political allies, the coercion and bribery of some of the chiefs, and a congressional investigation, the situation calmed. The Sioux tribes settled on the two promised reservations, apparently not fully realizing that they had no formal title to the land and could be pushed west whenever the government decided to do so.[27] Many of the villagers saw the actions of government officials and groups of traders as a betrayal because of the Americans' unwillingness to live up to Indian expectations about traditional kinship duties. For more than three decades the Sioux had accepted white actions as being supportive, but the new treaties and their results clearly suggested otherwise.

Just a year after the dispute ended, Willis A. Gorman replaced Alexander Ramsey as Minnesota territorial governor and superintendent of Indian affairs there in 1853. He faced immediate demands from pioneers to move the Indians onto their reservations but had spent most of the money set aside for removal costs to feed the Indians, so little remained. With the Sioux facing starvation, the new agent, Robert G. Murphy, moved ahead with plans for farming, but these stalled because of federal reluctance to invest enough money. After all the Dakotas had no title to their reservations, only the president's promise that they might remain there for up to five years. Then irregularities in awarding supply contracts and rumors of misconduct against the agent and governor persuaded commissioner of Indian affairs George W. Manypenny to reduce funding. This may have made some sense politically, but to the Indians cutting off already appropriated funds seemed just another example of a dishonest move by the whites.[28]

In spite of these difficulties the two new reservations began to take shape by 1854. The Upper Sioux Agency for the Sissetons and Wahpetons stood at the mouth of the Yellow Medicine River, while what became the Lower Sioux or Redwood Agency for the Mdewakantons and Wahpekutes lay directly to the southeast and downstream. As the Indians settled into these two new locations, the agents and missionaries continued to insist that they had to stop hunting and become farmers. Many of the Dakotas still faced starvation, however, so some of the men left to get food for their families. The new governor Willis Gorman only made the situation worse when he responded angrily by withholding the annuities that would have eased worries about getting enough food. For the next half-dozen years local officials repeatedly used that short-sighted tactic. To the Sioux this looked as if the government now refused to live up to the promises that it had made in the 1837 and 1851 treaties.[29]

American officials at all levels used the withholding of annuities as a club to force the Sioux to cooperate with government demands. Whenever the young men left to hunt or the families went on their traditional gathering rounds to obtain desperately needed food, they risked punishment. Above all the whites continued to demand an end to the continuing raiding cycle that pitted young Dakota and Ojibwa men against each other. Federal officials had done this often since the 1825 treaties but failed to disrupt the pattern of clan or village retribution, which lay at the center of tribal culture and identity for both people. Related efforts to encourage farming led to suggestions that the government consider breaking up the reservations and allotting them for individual family farms. In theory this would speed acculturation, while at the same time it promised to open more tribal land for the white settlers.

By the mid-1850s the reservation communities began to change. A small but growing number of men quit hunting and turned to farming. Some families accepted Christianity, began wearing white clothing, and withdrew from traditional ceremonies. That disrupted the clan obligations for sharing food and work that lay at the center of village life. Meanwhile, some of the chiefs leveled charges of corruption against the agents, so Indians who might have cooperated with those officials chose not to do so. In the summer of 1856 Francis Huebschmann, the new superintendent, decided that he would end the intertribal raiding between the Sioux and Ojibwa young men once and for all. He ordered that a raiding party of twenty-one young Mdewakanton men be arrested and put in irons and threatened to withhold the villagers' annuities until they surrendered. Despite Chief Little Crow's spirited defense of the warriors' actions, the superintendent refused to back down. He posted armed guards to keep the rest of the Indians from breaking into the warehouse to get much-need food.[30]

Even jailing the young men failed to bring peace. While the prisoners waited for the government to try them, their Ojibwa enemies killed nine Sioux men in a raid near the Upper Agency. Shortly after that incident Huebschmann asked that the Sioux be released. Apparently he realized that it made little sense to punish the Sioux when the army could not prevent their tribal enemies from committing similar depredations. This incident highlighted the near-total ineffectiveness of the entire system for supervising Indian affairs. The agent had little recourse but to free the young men, because he had no money to pay for conducting trials of warring tribesmen. Huebschmann's act had at least one other negative result. After the chiefs succeeded in persuading the raiders to surrender, the young men endured two months in army custody. That angered many of them, who came to view their chiefs as having abandoned tribal customs. From this time on the soldiers' lodge became a vehicle used to protest the actions of the village council. In particular those determined to continue traditional Dakota practices used the growing power of the soldiers' lodges to oppose or even threaten the chiefs if they openly supported the government's actions.[31]

Continuing incidents, particularly the Spirit Lake or Inkpaduta Massacre, illustrated the growing unrest among the Sioux. Inkpaduta's band had been expelled from the Wahpekute Tribe. In March 1857 he and a few others attacked an Iowa frontier village. They killed thirty-five people in two days and took a few women captive. Agency and military officials recruited other Indians to rescue the captives. In July Little Crow led some one hundred Sioux to find and punish the raiders, but Inkpaduta fled west and escaped. Even though the raid happened in Iowa, it increased white settlers' apprehensions about their Dakota neighbors and likely fueled the growing anti-Indian sentiment in Minnesota. For the Indians it demonstrated clearly that the white officials lacked any effective way to punish those responsible for the attack.[32]

In this context dissension among the Dakotas intensified. Some of the villagers recognized that they could not depend on hunting, and each year a few more of the Indians turned to farming. That infuriated the militant traditionalists, who rejected any effort to change their lives. Growing disputes among the villagers weakened the bonds that had held their society together and increased the stresses that they faced. At the same time federal officials charged with implementing the acculturation program chafed at its lack of progress. In 1857 special agent Kintzing Prichette called the effort to make the Indians into farmers only a dream. Nevertheless, by the late 1850s policy makers had decided to push acculturation forcibly and called for new treaty talks to achieve that goal. Local white leaders and traders supported the move too. For the politicians any reduction in the Sioux land base meant more opportunities for settlers. At the same time the traders expected that they would be able to establish large claims for the Indians' debts.[33]

By late fall 1857 Superintendent William Cullen persuaded the Dakota leaders to visit Washington and "readjust the treaty" drawn up just a few years earlier. That winter a twenty-four-man delegation from the Mdewakanton and Wahpekute villages started east. The Sissetons and Wahpetons sent their own nine-man party along. In March 1858 the talks began just as Minnesota became a state. At first they made little progress. Mdewakanton leaders reminded Indian commissioner Charles Mix of past government inaction and failures to fulfill earlier treaty provisions. Little Crow pointed out that while funds had been appropriated, even reputedly sent west, they never reached the Dakota people. The commissioners could do little but promise that the government was keeping the Sioux funds safe. Mix could hardly tell his visitors that the government was loath to spend the monies on improvements that would soon be lost because they held no title to their land.[34]

Having failed to get any commitment to make long overdue payments repeatedly promised by the agents and listed in earlier treaties, the Sioux delegation turned to the issue of white encroachment on their land. Little Crow pointed out the influx of German pioneers and complained that they had moved far beyond the boundary set earlier. "You gave me that

line," he noted, but now "your Dutchmen [Germans] have settled inside
of it."[35] Unfortunately, whatever Indian leaders thought American negotiators had told them, the commissioner's maps failed to support the chief's
claims. For a time the negotiations halted. Perhaps the government chose
to drag out the talks because the Indians had to pay their own costs for
this trip. In June 1858 Mix finally told the Sioux leaders that they had no
formal title to their land. He made it clear that they had to surrender
their claims to land that they occupied north of the Minnesota River or
they would lose everything. Responding for the astonished Indians,
Little Crow complained that in 1854 officials had promised that the Dakotas would always have this land but now the whites wanted half of it. As
Black Hawk had done thirty years earlier, the frustrated chief questioned
their honesty. He remarked bitterly that "it appears you are getting papers all around me, so that, after a while I will have nothing left."[36]

When the discussions ended on June 19, 1858, the discouraged Indians accepted a treaty that gave them title to land on the south side of the
Minnesota River. Now they had a clear title, but the agreement also included a new provision. They had to accept federally assigned eighty-acre
allotments within the new reservations. Having just surrendered half of
their land, the returning chiefs struggled to persuade fellow Dakotas of
the future benefits that the treaty provided. They promised large payments that never came, and many Dakotas thought that their leaders had
accepted bribes. Some members of the soldiers' lodge threatened to kill
the chiefs for giving away half of their land. Others looked for new leaders and gradually accepted Red Owl as their spokesman.[37]

At the same time, Joseph R. Brown, one of the traders, became the
new agent. He had years of experience among the Sioux and realized
that they had no options but to become farmers or move west. So he began a program to build individual homes. Then he hired white settlers to
plow five-acre plots so that each family could have a garden and become
able to feed itself. Married to a Sisseton woman and speaking Dakota,
Brown understood the villagers' customs. He began paying Indian men
to do many of the farm tasks. By accepting government money, the men
obligated themselves to try to do what the agent wanted, living as farmers
rather than hunters. Brown's program made a noticeable impact in some
villages, as workers completed the new houses and the gardens began to
provide at least some food. Next the agent and Superintendent Cullen

encouraged a few of the more acculturated men to form what the officers called the "pantaloon band" or at other times the "Improvement Sioux." These individuals agreed to cut their hair, something the traditional Indians refused to do. Once they did that, the white officials gave each man several complete sets of white clothing, a pair of oxen, and a cow. Within a year nearly two hundred of the village men accepted the presents and began trying to change their way of life.[38]

While this may have been the only chance that the Indians had to retain their Minnesota land, it only exacerbated the bitter divisions among the villagers. Often the farmers sold their surplus crops to the traders or the agent rather than sharing what they had raised. Because of their short hair and white clothing, they were less than welcome at the traditional ceremonies, dances, and feasts that the Dakotas had observed for generations. In the meantime, the young hunters continued their treks off the reservation but had to travel farther each year to avoid the growing number of white farmers just across the river. Many of the pioneers had claimed former Indian land well before the Senate ratified the treaty; but local officials supported their actions, so they remained. The squatters' presence angered many Dakotas, who resorted to their traditional practice of destroying property and livestock to show their outrage. These acts in turn increased antagonism between the reservation dwellers and their neighbors, so tensions within the reservation communities and between Indians and white settlers remained.[39]

By this time the Sioux no longer believed that the government had treated them fairly or honestly. They watched as agents and superintendents arrived, tried to impose their wills, and then left, only to be replaced by others who had little or no understanding of Dakota traditions or beliefs. In 1858 Minnesota became a state, and by then its population and leaders had little sympathy for the original inhabitants. White squatters moved north onto tribal lands. Rather than removing them Congress recommended that they be allowed to stay and to file 160-acre claims on the reservation. Abraham Lincoln's victory in the 1860 election brought yet another set of new appointees as superintendent and agent to the scene. Their inept dealings with the Sissetons and Wahpetons at the Yellow Medicine Agency led to violence as the traditionalists launched bitter attacks on the Sioux farmers there.[40]

Almost from the start of their service in 1861 superintendent Clark Thompson and agent Thomas Galbraith faced growing divisions in the Sioux villages. The encroaching settlers gave liquor to the hunters, who in turn destroyed the equipment and killed the animals belonging to the tribal farmers. At the Yellow Medicine Agency most of the Sissetons and Wahpetons ignored the officials' efforts to force them to become farmers. Instead they attacked the families that had moved onto individual farms. That intimidation persuaded some of the farmers to rejoin their villages for a time. A large number of the Mdewakantons at the Lower Sioux Agency had begun farming. When an infestation of cutworms destroyed much of their expected corn crop just before the harvest, they faced starvation. That forced many of the families to leave the reservation and return to hunting and gathering in what they called the Big Woods.[41]

After a difficult winter, conditions for people on the reservations in early 1862 remained desperate. Many of the men continued hunting. Agent Galbraith made the situation worse and used their absence as the excuse to refuse to give those who remained any food. At the same time he gave some food to the farmers who needed it the least. Rumors that Civil War defeats would prevent the government from sending the annuities later that summer circulated widely. The traders continued pressing individual families to pay off their debt. This infuriated the Indians, who thought they had cleared their accounts in the negotiations just completed months earlier. They rejected any further claims made by the merchants. The traders quickly learned of this. When they heard rumors that the government lacked money to pay the annuities, they refused to give any new credit.[42]

By June 1862 the angry soldiers' lodge members and the farmers all faced starvation. Some men sold their weapons to get food. Others stole tools, equipment, and even livestock from the agency to sell. They could not expect any money from the government until later that summer, and the merchants refused to advance them any supplies. The farmers' crops needed weeks or even months to mature, and they had no more cash than did the hunters. A month later the soldiers' lodge at Yellow Medicine insisted that the agent give them the annuities rather than handing them to the traders, because "they take all our money out of our hands."[43] Meanwhile, Galbraith did little to alleviate the misery around him even when nearly a thousand desperate men demanded that he give them food. On August 4 the Indians broke into the warehouse and took hundreds of bags of flour, but that calmed things only for a few days.

Leaders from all four Dakota tribes met Agent Galbraith as well as some of the missionaries and traders at the Upper Sioux Agency the next day. They stressed their desperate need for help, but the agent had few supplies left to give them. Little Crow suggested that he borrow food from the traders and repay them when the annuities got there in a few weeks. As spokesman for that group, Andrew Myrick was reputed to have said that as far as he was concerned "if they [the Indians] are hungry, let them eat grass."[44] When translated, that remark set off an angry demonstration; but troop reinforcements from Fort Ridgely that arrived later that day helped prevent another major incident. Captain John Marsh, the troop commander, oversaw talks between the agent and tribal leaders for the next few days. He persuaded Galbraith to give out whatever food he still had in the government warehouse, which satisfied the Sioux temporarily. On August 9 the situation quieted as most of the people at the Yellow Medicine Agency left for a buffalo hunt. When fighting erupted less than two weeks later, the warriors killed Myrick, stuffing his mouth with grass.[45]

This conflict had many causes. Some it shared with the other wars, including land loss, forced acculturation, corrupt treaty negotiations, and the Indians' gradual loss of the ability to feed themselves. As in the Red Stick conflict, bitter divisions between the traditionalists who clung to an annual hunting and gathering cycle and those who accepted parts of the acculturation program created disagreements and violence. The determination of the soldiers' lodge members to continue retaliatory raids against their Ojibwa enemies resembled earlier similar actions by the most of the tribes in the Upper Mississippi Valley that had led to the agreements at the 1825 Treaty of Prairie du Chien. The pioneers' encroachments certainly had a role in this story. The Minnesota Sioux and the tribes of the central plains shared the unstable situation caused by the government's need to focus its attention on the Civil War, while pioneer farmers pushed onto tribal land from several directions.

But the war also had some distinct origins. Sioux beliefs and kinship customs regarding reciprocal obligations shaped many of their relationships with government officials, trading partners, and other Indians more clearly than in some of the other examples studied here. In this case the U.S. troops rarely clashed with the Dakotas. The federal Removal Policy had an impact as other tribes moved west into areas on the fringes of Sioux territory, but this seems to have brought only modest changes to their lives. While all of the indigenous groups experienced some collapse of their traditional economic activities, the specter of actual starvation set this conflict apart from the others. Continuing disputes with their trading partners added another unusual element in the drift toward war. This combination of causes gradually shifted the situation from uneasy peace to violent warfare.

This war differed from many earlier ones because the encroaching pioneers had not committed a long series of thefts, beatings, or other atrocities against the Dakotas, as had happened elsewhere. Government officials certainly had dealt harshly with them and local traders frequently cheated them. But when fighting erupted on August 18 members of the soldiers' societies, not frontier rangers trying to drive Indians off their land, fired the first shots. Yet at the same time sharp internal divisions split the Dakota tribes. Many of the established civil chiefs openly opposed going to war, and their opposition limited the warriors' success. Although the militants had persuaded Little Crow to lead, they often ignored his effort to plan coordinated attacks. As a result they raided frontier settlements in a series of scattered attacks and thus failed to overrun the small garrison at Fort Ridgely or the defenders of New Ulm in the fiercest fighting. Persistent disputes over what to do with the several hundred captives they held also distracted and weakened the efforts of the soldiers' societies to keep the fighting going.

While the Indians fought and argued, news of the outbreak spread fear in many frontier communities. For example, in Colorado authorities used the scare to call for more troops. In Minnesota authorities quickly raised 1,200 men, and Colonel Henry Sibley immediately moved them to the reservation. Calling on the Indians to surrender, he promised to punish only the men who had committed atrocities. Yet, in another case of white lies to the Dakotas, when nearly two thousand Indians laid down their weapons and freed the white captives they held, he set up a military commission that convicted and sentenced 393 Sioux men to death with virtually no evidence. Eventually President Lincoln pardoned all but thirty-eight, who were hanged in December that same year. When the troops halted their pursuit, Little Crow and his small band traveled north into Canada but eventually returned. The chief died when a couple of pioneers shot him while he and his son were picking berries some time later. By then the government had moved many of the Dakota survivors west into Dakota, as the Minnesota Indians experienced the same fate as many indigenous groups in nineteenth-century America.

CHAPTER 6

The Cheyenne and Arapaho War, 1864–1865

On April 11, 1864, a small party of Dog Soldiers, members of one of the Southern Cheyenne warrior societies, rode north to join their northern relatives in an attack on the Crow people. As they neared the South Platte River, they found four mules wandering loose on the plains and took the animals to their camp. That evening W. D. Ripley, a local rancher, rode up to claim the mules as his. When the young men requested presents for having gathered up the animals, he refused and rode to nearby Camp Sanborn, complaining that the Indians had stolen his livestock. The next morning Ripley guided a forty-man detachment of the First Colorado Volunteers, then in federal service, to the Cheyenne camp to recover the mules. By then the Dog Soldiers had crossed the Platte River heading north, but they stopped when the cavalrymen rode up. Contradictory first-person accounts of what happened next suggest that the Indians and soldiers met, but without an interpreter, neither understood the other. Although the Cheyennes returned three of the four mules, the soldiers' commander, Lieutenant Clark Dunn, ordered his men to disarm the Indians. When the tribesmen refused to turn over their weapons, shooting broke out.[1]

Just three days later, in a second incident, Lieutenant George S. Eayre led another patrol of the Volunteers looking for Indian thieves to the village of Crow Chief's band. The soldiers had no evidence that these Indians had any connection to the earlier incident but attacked anyway. This time the Indians escaped. With the villagers gone, the troopers halted to loot and then burned almost everything that they could not steal. A few hours later they came to a second Indian camp, but this time the people had fled before the soldiers arrived, taking most of their belongings. Finding little to take, the command rounded up nineteen cattle grazing nearby, apparently part of a herd reported stolen. The presence of these animals convinced the officers that the Cheyennes had stolen the cattle. They forwarded this information to Colorado territorial governor John Evans and Colonel John Chivington, the commander of Colorado militia units. Those men in turn used the report to justify harsh reprisals against the Indians, including unprovoked attacks on other peaceful villages. This infuriated the most warlike elements among the Cheyennes. They thought that the victims of the attacks were innocent and increased their raids along the immigrant trails in retaliation.[2] According to Chief Black Kettle, these incidents provided the spark that set off the fighting on the central plains that year.

This conflict appears to have been less "avoidable" than some of the others examined here. The experiences of the Plains tribes differed markedly from those of the Creeks, Sauks, and Mesquakies or Dakota Sioux. Those groups all had decades, even generations, to adjust to incoming white Americans. By contrast, it took only fifteen or twenty years for national developments and local actions to disrupt the lives of the Cheyenne people. Those events challenged the hunting peoples to surrender their cultures immediately and gave them almost no time to recognize that they had no choice. The process began in 1846 when the United States settled its dispute with the British over the Oregon Country and extended the nation's western border to the Pacific. That in turn encouraged more pioneers to head west over the Oregon Trail. Just two years later America's 1848 victory in the war with Mexico and the discovery of gold in California at virtually the same time brought tens of thousands of would-be miners and farmers west. The newcomers traveled through and into regions where the indigenous people had little prior experience with Americans. The travelers' animals used the water and ate the grass, while their creaking wagon trains frightened the native animals that Indians depended on for food.

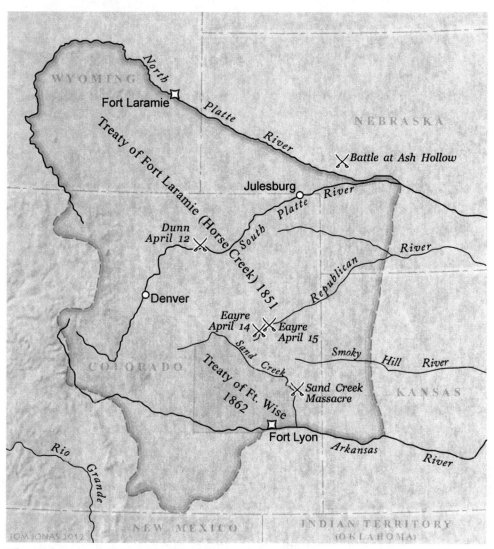

The Cheyenne and Arapaho War.
© 2013 University of Oklahoma Press, Norman.

As citizens moved into the West, federal authorities took steps to gain control of the region. First they moved troops west. Then they established governments there. In 1850 California gained statehood, while Utah and New Mexico became territories. Just four years later Kansas and Nebraska became territories as well. These political developments, coupled with the lure of mineral wealth and good land, attracted ever-increasing numbers of Anglo-Americans to what had been Indian country just a few years earlier. Most contacts between the newcomers and the Native Americans remained peaceful, but minor disputes and incidents occurred repeatedly. Because neither the U.S. government nor tribal leaders could prevent the continued friction or control their own people, it was only a matter of time before warfare erupted.

The flood of Anglo-Americans into their homeland affected Cheyenne and Arapaho societies immediately. Primarily nomadic buffalo hunters, they moved across the central plains every year. During the fall and winter they lived in sheltered valleys along the Front Range of the Rockies. In the spring, as soon as the new grass had grown enough to feed their horses, they moved east onto the plains. Depending on the season, the availability of animals, and the locations of their tribal enemies, they hunted and raided from eastern Wyoming south to western Kansas. The Overland, Santa Fe, and Smoky Hill Trails all passed directly through their hunting territory during the 1850s and later. The hundreds of wagon trains that carried thousands of white settlers west decreased the buffalo herds noticeably. By mid-century the tribes' mounted hunting tactics had been so successful that they had reduced the numbers of bison so sharply that scholars now depict their lifestyle as unsustainable.[3] In 1853 agent Thomas Fitzpatrick reported that some of the Cheyenne and Arapaho bands "are actually in a starving state. They are in abject want half of the year."[4]

It seems likely that the Cheyenne bands had begun to separate by the 1820s and 1830s, though it is unclear exactly when. Gradually one group became allied with the Lakota Sioux and usually remained north of the Platte River. The other lived and hunted along the Arkansas River farther south. Eventually they became two distinct people, the Northern and Southern Cheyenne tribes. Before the division a council of forty-four peace chiefs made the important decisions; but as the villages and bands moved apart geographically it became increasingly difficult for the chiefs to meet. At the same time five distinct warrior societies had developed, and their actions complicated tribal political and social practices. Led by respected war leaders rather than by the recognized village chiefs, these groups policed summer migrations, planned the hunts, and led raids against tribal enemies. By offering young men chances to prove their skills and bravery, the war society leaders gained their support and strengthened their position when they disputed the traditional chiefs' decisions. As had happened among the Dakotas in 1862, the soldier groups often ignored the tribal council's wishes and opposed its decisions whenever they appeared to restrict the warriors' hunting or raiding.[5]

As late as the 1850s tribal life followed its traditional patterns. Each spring and summer the people scattered, living in separate villages or temporary hunting camps until cold weather approached. Then they found sheltered valleys where they camped for their winter. What frontier whites saw as a single society controlled by the chiefs bore little resemblance to reality. Rather than having any clear tribal identity, the Cheyennes' long dependence on summer hunting had produced a society of people who thought in local, familial terms. They gave primary allegiance to their particular village or hunting band, which rarely joined others. While the Cheyennes had a recognized tribal council, the chiefs met as a group only sporadically. In these circumstances a fundamental struggle for effective leadership ensued. The civil leaders came to represent Cheyenne unity and peaceful activities, while those who spoke for the warrior societies vied for personal influence among the young hunters and fighting men. The Dog Soldiers or Dog Men became the most well-known of the soldier societies. By the early 1860s they had organized a separate new band, almost independent from the rest of the tribe. This made it difficult to avoid incidents or misunderstandings that might lead to war.[6]

The advancing American frontier society also lacked effective unity. Responsibility for dealing with the Indians was shared by the distant federal government and local territorial officials, who saw the situation on the central plains differently. Colorado leaders wanted access to the land, water, and other available resources. To get those things territorial officials needed to push the Indians aside, so they took forceful steps to do that whenever possible. They called repeatedly for the army to establish new garrisons as the nearby white population spread. Once the forts appeared they acted as if the soldiers had to help them achieve territorial goals by moving or destroying the local Indians. National political leaders saw the situation differently. Facing bitter sectional debates over extending slavery into the West, they hoped to avoid costly and destructive wars with the powerful tribes of the plains and took only a few cautious steps to extend federal presence into that area.

Not only did national and territorial officials have different objectives that shaped their approaches toward the Indians, but from the start federal officials lacked any effective means for dealing with the tribes. After 1849 the Office of Indian Affairs (OIA) operated as part of the newly established Department of the Interior and held the responsibility to supervise programs for the indigenous groups. These civilian officers negotiated treaty agreements, supervised the payments of annuities, established new agencies, and listened to the concerns of Indians and whites alike. But frequent violence between Indians and settlers forced them to share authority for dealing with the tribes with the U.S. Army. The military had to protect the pioneers and keep peace. Unfortunately the civilians and soldiers on the scene rarely trusted or cooperated with each other. They frequently disagreed on what actions to take, which made keeping peace with the plains dwellers difficult.

In September 1851 the first major effort to begin formal relations between the federal government and the tribes on the northern and central plains began. At Fort Laramie in present Wyoming federal negotiators came to talk peace in order to protect the crowds of pioneers pushing west. The Cheyennes and their Arapaho allies joined thousands of other Indians near Fort Laramie to meet the Americans. In the middle of that month they signed the Treaty of Horse Creek, which the whites called the Treaty of Fort Laramie. As the earlier 1825 Treaty of Prairie du Chien in Wisconsin had done, this agreement asked each tribe to identify its home territory. The Cheyennes claimed land that stretched from Wyoming south across the central plains to the Arkansas River and from the Rocky Mountains east to western Nebraska and Kansas. The chiefs agreed to stay in this region and also promised to avoid hunting near the crowded immigrant trails.[7] In return the treaty promised the tribes annuities of $50,000 a year for fifty years to compensate them for the expected reduction of the buffalo herds. Months later, while discussing ratification of the agreement, the Senate Committee on Indian Affairs changed its terms. It reduced the fifty years of payments to ten without bothering to tell the Indians, hardly a good start toward future cooperation and goodwill.[8]

Implementation of the Fort Laramie Treaty proved difficult from the beginning. At first its provisions had little direct impact on the Cheyennes, but not all the Plains tribes had the same experience. For the first several years finance and transportation problems delayed the arrival of annuity goods for weeks or even months. That angered the thousands of Indians who had signed the treaty. They gathered near Fort Laramie each summer, expecting to get the promised food from the government. While the Indians waited for weeks their animals ate the nearby grass and the women ran short of wood for their cooking fires. This forced them to shift camps often and delayed their start on their important summer buffalo hunt. Bored, hungry, and probably disgusted at having to waste time near the fort, some of the young men looked for excitement. High Forehead, a visitor to the Brulé Sioux near the fort, killed an old, broken-down cow that wandered away from a passing wagon train.

The migrants reported the incident and asked Lieutenant Hugh Fleming, the commander at the fort, for help. The band chief Brave Bear offered to pay for the cow, but the commander ordered that the Indians surrender High Forehead to the soldiers. When the chief said that he had no authority to do that, Fleming sent Lieutenant John Grattan and a small detachment to the Indian camp to arrest the young man the next morning. There Brave Bear repeated his offer, but Grattan insisted that High Forehead surrender. When he refused, the young officer ordered an attack. This was a terrible mistake. More than one thousand Sioux warriors obliterated the twenty-nine-man detachment, attacked nearby traders' warehouses, and left for their summer hunt. The army only made matters worse when it ordered General William S. Harney to punish the Sioux the following summer. When the Brulés withdrew, raids on the northern plains increased dramatically.[9] Responding forcefully, General Harney attacked and destroyed a peaceful Sioux village under Chief Little Thunder at Ash Hollow.

This destructive assault terrified many plains dwellers accustomed to only a few fatalities and injuries resulting from traditional intertribal raiding. It also set the pattern for continuing violence between the army and tribal fighting men for the next generation. Not only had General Harney's force smashed an entire village, but the victims had taken no part in the incident that brought the general's retribution. He clearly had little understanding of the situation or the peoples that he faced. After browbeating Sioux leaders, he demanded that they and other tribes cease attacking each other, which they had been doing for generations and had no intention of stopping. Once again Americans tried to force basic changes on an Indian society about which they knew almost nothing.

True, the 1851 treaty had called for the warriors to quit raiding their tribal enemies, but few Indians knew or cared about that.[10]

For the next several years minor incidents between Plains hunters and the intruding whites occurred repeatedly as suspicion on both sides remained high. As the highest-ranking officer in the area, General Harney may well have increased the tensions through his crushing 1855 victory against the Brulé Sioux at Ash Hollow. Certainly that defeat achieved the government's immediate objective of pushing the Lakota bands farther from the main immigrant trail to hunting grounds farther west. To the Plains Indians, however, the army's action signaled a new level of violence by the white soldiers that went far beyond the Native custom of intertribal raiding. News of the defeat spread terror, confusion, and anger among many Plains groups. So Harney's victory failed to bring any real peace to the region or to end the warriors' harassment of pioneers moving west.

Until the mid-1850s most white pioneers had traveled along the fringes of the Cheyenne homeland, but by 1856 that began to change. The government sent survey teams to locate a wagon route along the Kansas, Solomon, and Smoky Hill Rivers. This new track cut directly through the center of Cheyenne territory, as the 1814 federal road had done in Creek country. It encouraged hundreds of pioneers to enter a prime buffalo-hunting area. The Indians objected immediately. Ignoring their complaints, a year later another survey party moved across tribal land north farther along the South Platte River. With these two new roads marked, migrants and settlers began to drift into both regions. Their increasing presence raised the Indians' fears that the newcomers would drive away the buffalo and increased the likelihood of interracial violence along the newly opened immigrant routes.[11]

Even before the survey crews finished their work, violence flared in eastern Wyoming. While visiting the small army detachment stationed at the North Platte Bridge near present Casper, a party of Northern Cheyennes captured some wandering horses. Soon a messenger came with news that the owner promised a reward and asked them to bring the animals to the soldiers' camp. The hunters returned three of the horses and when asked about the fourth said that they had not brought it because it did not fit the owner's description. Instead of thanking the young men for returning most of the animals, the commanding officer ordered his troops to arrest them and put them in leg-irons until the others returned the last horse. The Cheyennes customarily killed male prisoners; fearing that was what the soldiers planned to do, they tried to escape. In the melee that followed the soldiers killed one man, shot another, and locked the last two in chains. The wounded man escaped and raced back to the village with news of the incident. Fearing that the troopers might attack them as General Harney had attacked the Sioux camp at Ash Hollow a year earlier, the villagers fled, leaving much of their property behind for the advancing troops to steal or destroy.[12]

None of the white officers had charged the men with having stolen the horses, so the Indians saw the soldiers' actions as an unwarranted attack in response to their peaceful cooperation. The local commander's excessive reaction to the disputed ownership of a single horse reinforced a pattern repeated frequently for almost a decade. With almost no evidence that Indians had done anything wrong, the officers refused to accept or investigate any explanation. Instead they often directed murderous attacks on civilian populations. One of the small Cheyenne party returning the lost horses to the army post, Bull Shield, had been killed. Another, Two Tails, escaped although wounded; and a third, Wolf Fire, died in prison while still in chains. Then the post commander infuriated the Indians when he refused to let the dead man's family have his body for burial. In addition, the attacking soldiers killed civilians and destroyed all of the personal property of the entire village. Cooperating with the soldiers was clearly dangerous at best and often brought misery and destruction. Similar disputes about livestock ownership continued to shape life on the plains for years.

To be sure, not all of the aggression came from the invading civilians or the army. Careless and dangerous acts by young Indian men played significant roles too. For example, in late summer 1856 a group of Cheyenne and Arapaho warriors, seeking their Pawnee enemies, camped near the road to Fort Kearney in Nebraska. When the mail wagon for the fort passed, several of the young men rode after it, hoping that the driver might give them some tobacco. The Indians' approach frightened the driver, who tried to ignore them. When one of the two kept insisting, he panicked, pulled out his pistol, and fired at them. The young Cheyennes responded with arrows and wounded the teamster slightly before he got back to the fort. Angry about this unexpected attack on a white man that would surely cause trouble, the chiefs whipped the two young men soundly. At the fort the driver's story and fresh wound brought Captain George Steward and forty-one cavalrymen in pursuit. The Cheyennes had left, hoping to avoid trouble, but the soldiers overtook them the next morning. When the troopers rode up, the Indians dropped their bows and arrows and indicated that they would not fight. But the soldiers attacked without any warning. They killed at least six men and seized all of the party's horses and camp supplies, leaving them on foot and destitute.[13] In this instance something as simple as a young Indian's determined begging for tobacco led to unexpected fighting and the loss of Cheyenne life and property.

This unexpected assault infuriated the Cheyennes. They saw the incident as another unprovoked attack by the Americans and shifted their attention from their Pawnee enemies to the white settlers. In retaliation they struck at pioneers traveling along the Platte River, killing men, women, and children and taking several captives. At that point the chiefs hurried to stop the violence and sent men to Fort Laramie to explain what had happened. First they pointed out that their young man could have killed the mail wagon driver but chose not to do that. Then they asked why the soldiers had started shooting once the warriors had put down their weapons. When agent Thomas Twiss had no good answer, the chiefs told him that they could not prevent the young warriors' efforts to get revenge for the murder of their unarmed friends.[14] Despite their lingering anger, the band leaders agreed to free the white captives and repeated their desire for peace. In return the agent tried unsuccessfully to persuade the army to halt its attacks.

These efforts failed completely. Instead General Persifor Smith, commander of troops in the West, did just the opposite. He ordered that the Cheyennes should be punished for the raids. In June 1857 Colonel Edwin V. Sumner led a command of nearly four hundred soldiers west from Fort Leavenworth against them. By late July his men had located their quarry, and on July 29 a line of soldiers and warriors faced each other. Before the colonel gave his troops any orders, Fall Leaf, leader of his Delaware scouts, shot at the Cheyennes. When they returned his fire Colonel Sumner shouted that "an Indian fired the first shot" and ordered his men into battle.[15] Earlier two respected shamans had persuaded the Indians that their religious ceremonies would make the troopers' carbines ineffective, so the young warriors had little to fear. They faced the charging soldiers bravely until the cavalrymen unexpectedly drew their sabers. Apparently believing that the shamans' powers did not protect them from these weapons, the Indians broke ranks and fled. Neither force suffered large casualties, but the army column found and destroyed the tents and property belonging to an entire 170-lodge village, a major blow to the tribe that only weakened efforts to keep peace.[16]

After that debacle the tribe avoided contact with the columns of soldiers still on the plains for the rest of the summer. In October 1857 a delegation of chiefs visited William Bent, one of their longtime traders, at his new fort on the Arkansas River in southeastern Colorado. Having married into the tribe years earlier, he understood its society well and reported that tribal leaders wished to be left alone. Unexpected events the next year changed the situation dramatically. Prospectors discovered modest amounts of gold in the area promised to the Cheyennes by the 1851 Treaty of Fort Laramie. Within a single year several thousand gold seekers arrived. From that point on life changed for all of the indigenous peoples of the southern and central plains. Now they could no longer avoid contact with the incoming whites. The intruders' presence and actions threatened the annual summer buffalo hunt farther east on the plains, endangered the tribe's food supply, and disrupted winter camping sites near the mountains.

From the start at least some tribal leaders recognized that their situation had changed. For example, Chief Black Kettle told their new agent Robert Miller at an 1858 multitribal meeting that the Cheyennes had no desire to fight the soldiers. As Miller reported, the chief went on to say that the Indians hoped that the government would "give them a home where they might be provided for and protected against the encroachments of their white brothers until . . . they had been taught to cultivate the soil and other arts of civilized life."[17] This idea had been proposed more than a decade earlier, but no one had paid much attention to it at the time. Now the agent happily reported the news. Unfortunately, as so often happened, the men he talked to represented only a small minority of the tribe. No headmen from the northern bands or leaders of the five soldiers' societies among the southern bands had taken part in the meeting.[18]

When the handful of civil chiefs expressed their willingness to lead the Cheyennes in a new direction, heated arguments broke out and they got little support. The warriors' societies objected heatedly. Buffalo hunting, horse thievery, and raiding enemy peoples lay at the center of their traditional social and economic life. As in many other Indian societies, the women had always farmed a little. Most men saw farming in gender terms, as women's work that they should avoid. During the discussions they seemed to agree to halt new attacks on the white newcomers, but even that decision lacked full support. While the Indians shivered in their lodges during the 1858–59 winter, gold seekers moved to build permanent settlements on tribal land. In early 1859 the rumors of gold discoveries in Colorado spread east, and hundreds more would-be miners rushed to take part on trails that cut directly through tribal hunting grounds. By August that year William Bent reported that the groups on his agency were "pressed upon all around by the Texans, by the settlers of the gold region, by the advancing people of Kansas, and from the Platte, are already compressed into a small circle of territory." If the government failed to act quickly, he wrote, "a desperate war of starvation and extinction is therefore, imminent and inevitable."[19]

By then the earlier separation of the related bands and their development as two distinct entities had become clear. The Northern Cheyennes spent most of their time between the North and South Platte Rivers and gradually became allied with the Lakota Sioux. Their southern counterparts lived between the South Platte and the Arkansas Rivers, often hundreds of miles away. The heavily traveled trail to the Colorado goldfields followed the Platte River and passed directly between the two groups. The Indians living to the north had access to a better hunting territory and encountered fewer white gold seekers than their southern relatives. Because their location placed them nearer their traditional Pawnee and Ute enemies, they saw less reason to accept white demands to stop raiding or to cede any more of their tribal land. Suggestions that they abandon the hunt and shift to settled agriculture generated little support among them; in fact, some unhappy members of the southern bands drifted north to join their ranks. Often U.S. officials had no clear understanding of this division when they wanted to conclude treaties with the Cheyennes.

In September 1859 commissioner of Indian affairs Alfred Greenwood met with Arapaho and Southern Cheyenne leaders. At the time most of the Cheyennes had not finished their summer buffalo hunt several hundred miles away. When White Antelope, Black Kettle, Little Raven, and a few other chiefs arrived for the talks, what they heard must have been discouraging. Commissioner Greenwood proposed that they accept a much-reduced homeland in an area that had little water for agriculture and no sizable buffalo herds. Despite those limits at the end of the talks the headmen accepted what became the Treaty of Fort Wise (1861). The commissioner ignored or failed to realize that most of the chiefs and no leaders of the warrior societies took part in the negotiations. They never saw the agreement, much less signed it. When the treaty was signed in February 1861, it included the names of only six men from the tribal council of forty-four. Still, for a time at least the southern bands seem to have accepted the new land despite its severe limits on both their mobility and their ability to feed themselves. In return the U.S. government promised to pay $450,000 for the cession and up to $5,000 annually to build sawmills and gristmills as well as a mechanic's shop.[20]

Why the handful of peace chiefs accepted a greatly reduced home land remains unclear, as was white officials' mistaken assertion that the chiefs exercised effective control over their fellow villagers. Virtually all of the evidence and experiences to the contrary for the preceding seventy-five years suggested that officials could not hold band and village chiefs responsible for actions of anyone in their group. This idea caused unending trouble and frustration for the chiefs, who never exercised such authority, and continuing white dissatisfaction. Apparently it resulted from a willful wrongheadedness that allowed or encouraged Americans to blame Indian leaders for actions over which they had little if any control. When incidents took place, federal officials could use Indian noncompliance with American demands as an excuse to act in ways that would achieve their short-term goals without having to consider the long-range implications of their decisions or actions. Frequently these actions lay at the heart of the disputes between the two societies and encouraged the continuing violence.

By the end of the 1850s almost all of the Plains tribes saw their living conditions worsen and white actions becoming a direct threat to their traditional way of life. More miners streamed west, and settlements in Kansas and Nebraska expanded rapidly. In this situation the confusing and frequently changing boundaries of the Office of Indian Affairs administrative units dealing with the tribes on the central plains added to regional instability. For example, in 1846 the Upper Platte [River] Agency began its oversight of groups living near the trail that followed that stream overland to the west. Nine years later the OIA established the Upper Arkansas Agency (1955) to supervise Indians who lived farther south. Just a year after that the Colorado Superintendency came into being, charged with responsibility for overseeing tribes on the central plains. These three offices dealt with many indigenous groups, including the Cheyenne, Arapaho, Sioux, Pawnee, Ute, Comanche, and Kiowa peoples.

Because the individual tribes moved across an area that stretched from Wyoming south to Texas and from Colorado east into Kansas and Nebraska, it often remained unclear which set of bureaucrats held the ultimate responsibility for each band. Local agents came and went quickly, further confusing the situation. Between 1856 and 1864, the years leading directly to the war, Thomas Twiss, Robert Miller, William Bent, Albert Boone, Samuel Colley, and John Loree all served as agents to the Cheyennes and sometimes others as well. In addition, special agents, superintendents, and commissioners arrived to investigate conditions or negotiate agreements. It is no wonder that the officials knew little about their charges or that the village chiefs lacked confidence in the local government officers.

In 1861, while the indigenous groups struggled to deal with their rapidly changing situations, pioneers, territorial leaders, and Indian Office officials faced new pressures as the Civil War tore the nation apart. In a life and death struggle with the Confederacy, the United States removed most of the regular army units from the West. This left the defense of the swelling Colorado, Kansas, and Nebraska populations up to state and territorial Volunteer units temporarily under federal supervision or less well regulated territorial militia. Composed of mostly untrained men and commanded by local political leaders, these forces reflected the pervasive anti-Indian feelings of many new westerners. At times that led to unreasonably harsh actions, such as those described earlier. They occurred often during the early 1860s because of the almost complete lack of federal oversight to limit anti-Indian excesses.

Early in the Civil War settlers heard about Confederate agent Albert Pike's effort to sign alliances with the southern Plains tribes and to raise troops for a military invasion of Arkansas and New Mexico. Both of those actions frightened the local Colorado leaders and increased settlers' fears about the danger of Indian raids.[21] Yet when territorial governor William Gilpin established militia units for local defense, he did so more out of fear of Confederates than of Indians. During the drought-ridden summer of 1861 he postponed the delivery of the Indians' annuity supplies for several months to ensure that the tribes would have enough food to survive the winter. He seems to have given little thought to where the Indians might get food before then. Despite withholding tribal supplies Gilpin's excessive spending brought his dismissal in 1862, and President Lincoln appointed John Evans as his replacement. In a few months the new governor joined other business leaders to promote land speculation, ranching, and mining in Colorado. Hoping to boost those ventures, he called for a transcontinental railroad that would pass through Denver.[22] Because those economic developments would need Indian land, resources, and peace, the territorial promoters viewed the tribal people as obstacles to local economic development as well as being a physical danger.

To get at the land the leaders used rumors of dangerous incidents and factual reports of Indian raids to focus white fear and racial hatred on the indigenous people. While this situation was certainly not unique to Colorado, its territorial political, business, and military officials repeatedly stirred the settlers' fears of Indian hostilities so that they could shape public actions later. For example, the August 1862 Dakota Sioux attacks on pioneer settlements in Minnesota sent a wave of panic across the frontier from Colorado east to Wisconsin. Yet this Sioux war took place hundreds of miles east of Denver. Not only did Indians pose little danger to pioneers on the central plains, but that year the Cheyennes and Arapahos spent a peaceful summer hunting, not raiding white travelers or taking their property.[23]

Even though the Indians remained peaceful, agent Samuel Colley and Governor Evans started efforts to limit or end their annual buffalo hunts. This followed well-established policies to transform tribal social and economic practices. The negotiators of the 1861 Fort Wise treaty had promised to take some of the band leaders east to visit the president. As usual they assumed that the chiefs would avoid going to war once they saw the large cities and the size of the American population. In March 1863 agent Samuel Colley took Cheyenne, Arapaho, Comanche, Kiowa, and Caddo delegations to Washington. Cheyenne chief Lean Bear told the president that his people wanted peace with the whites and asked Lincoln to force the pioneers to stop their attacks. The president urged his visitors to stop hunting and warned them that he could see no way for them "to become as prosperous as the white race except by . . . cultivation of the earth."[24]

Meanwhile, in September 1863 Governor Evans and Colonel John Chivington, territorial militia commander, moved to implement the Fort Wise Treaty provisions. That agreement called for the Cheyenne and Arapaho bands to stop hunting and remain on their new reservation. Evans sent emissaries to the scattered camps to persuade the Indians to end their buffalo hunt and return west to meet him. A few of the band leaders reluctantly agreed, but none of them appeared when the governor traveled to the rendezvous. After Evans returned to Denver, he sent Elbridge Gerry as his messenger to find out why the chiefs had boycotted the meeting. They informed Gerry that only a handful of the forty-four-member tribal council had signed the document in the first place. Hence the rest of the tribe saw no reason to obey any stipulations of the treaty. Their arguments echoed those used by the Sauks and Mesquakies in regard to their 1804 treaty with William Henry Harrison. Like the Sauks, they had not seen the agreement provisions, had not agreed to cede their prime hunting lands along the Republican and Smoky Hill Rivers, and refused to surrender them to the whites. Of more direct importance, no buffalo grazed on the new reservation, so they had to leave it each summer just to survive.

The chiefs told Gerry that they resented even being asked to meet the governor. They complained that an army sentry had shot one of the Cheyennes earlier that summer. True, the agent had given gifts to his family to "cover the blood" according to Indian practice; but his relatives had rejected the gifts, so the raiding would continue. Seizing the initiative, the Indians boldly denounced the United States, telling Gerry that "the white man's hands are dripping with our people's blood, and now he [Evans] calls for us to make a treaty!"[25] Negotiations did not resume. These disputes reflected the situation in the Cheyenne camps. The chiefs who had not signed the treaty as well as leaders of the warrior societies demanded to be heard. Almost to a man they refused to curtail their hunting. Surely their presence at this council inhibited some of the treaty supporters, who remained silent. Whatever else the Indians' complaints did, they persuaded Gerry that the Cheyennes remained hostile and would not live up to their 1861 agreement, as he reported to Governor Evans. Yet for a time Evans took no action. After he heard rumors in November 1863 that the Plains tribes had agreed to unite and attack the white settlers, he hurried to investigate what he called "this foul conspiracy among those poor degraded wretches."[26]

When Evans found no evidence that supported his conspiracy charge, he adopted a less belligerent stance. For a while he depended on the local newspaper to depict the Indians as dangerous physical and military threats. It is not clear what impact local newspaper ranting about Indian savagery and depredations had on the governor's thinking, but it supported his views on dealing with the Native groups. During much of 1863 William Byers, editor of the *Rocky Mountain News,* filled its pages with bitterly anti-Indian material. Whether he feared that the tribes would see the absence of federal troops as an excuse to attack pioneers or simply wanted to sell more newspapers remains unclear. In either case, his columns called for extermination of Indians, whom he described as "a dissolute, vagabondish, brutal and ungrateful race" that "ought to be wiped from the face of the earth."[27] Whatever impact the editor's efforts had, they provided plenty of viciously anti-Indian stories that built support for Evans's effort to force the Cheyennes onto their diminished reservation.

By this time the governor faced a real dilemma. He wanted to gain clear title to much of central Colorado's land and resources. Many Cheyenne leaders refused to sign the Treaty of Fort Wise, however, while others who had acquiesced earlier now rejected the location of their new reservation. So Evans felt that he had little choice. He needed to find a way to force the tribes away from the territorial settlements. Yet if he succeeded, his actions might well provoke a war with the Plains groups. To gain support, he played on existing fears and rumors that Sioux and Northern Cheyenne bands had sent recruiters to the Southern Cheyenne and Arapaho camps to gather men for a united attack on white settlers. This move brought little public response because no such attacks happened during the fall and winter of 1863–64 even though some of the Cheyenne bands along the Arkansas River faced starvation. Still the governor did not trust them, and he ordered agent Colley to withhold any weapons or ammunition from the hunters. Like similar actions against the Dakota Sioux in Minnesota, this move to limit their ability to hunt only further antagonized the hungry villagers. Certain that he faced a major Indian war the next spring, Evans hurried east to Washington, D.C., to get more federal military support and authorization to reopen treaty talks with the Cheyennes and Arapahos the next spring.[28]

War-weary federal officials in the capital offered the worried governor little assurance. In fact soon after he returned west, in March 1864, a Confederate probe into Kansas persuaded General Samuel R. Curtis to shift all U.S. troops from Colorado east to defend against this move. Fearing the worst, Evans acted quickly, asking agent Colley to recruit spies among the Arkansas River Cheyenne bands. Yet by the spring of 1864 Colley worried more about intertribal warfare than about raids against white settlers. He reported small incidents involving Utes, Cheyennes, Arapahos, and Kiowas, who repeatedly stole horses and mules from each other. At one point he remarked that "if the Indians go to war among themselves, I fear that it will extend much further."[29] Nevertheless, the agent's reports of the frequent small-scale raids said nothing about possible violence by the Arkansas River bands. If the governor wanted an excuse to begin an Indian war against them, he had to look beyond Colley's reports.

During the next few months frequent poorly understood actions by tribesmen set the stage for the conflict that followed. In early April 1864 government contractors along the Smoky Hill River reported that young Indians had stolen a herd of their cattle. Responding to that and other minor incidents farther north along the Platte River, Colorado militia commander John Chivington issued orders to retaliate. His subordinates repeatedly attacked Cheyenne camps. The troopers often struck villages of people who had not committed the acts that sent the soldiers into the field. Operating with limited knowledge and often without interpreters, the Volunteers' operations made the situation worse. They had orders to kill the thieves and to disarm men in the peaceful bands whenever they could. Yet the troopers had no idea which Indians had stolen any livestock, and hunters depended on their weapons to kill game in order to keep their families from starving. That spring the military's actions on the plains started many of the fights.[30]

The Cheyennes then camped near Fort Lyon along the Arkansas River apparently worried that they might be blamed for the raids farther north and told the agent several times that they feared an attack by the white soldiers, but none came. Major Edward Wynkoop, commanding Fort Lyon in 1864, judged that the Cheyennes living near his post posed no danger to the white settlers that summer. While they remained peaceful, other bands and warrior societies did not and skirmished repeatedly with the militiamen in Kansas, Nebraska, and northern Colorado. On April 19 it was reported that drunken Indians had frightened white settlers from their homes and ranches along the Platte and then had robbed the unoccupied dwellings. After raiders stole a herd of horses from an Overland Stage Company station near Julesburg, Major Jacob Downing led a force of forty men after the thieves. When they found a small Cheyenne village, he ordered a charge. In the ensuing battle the troops killed and wounded a number of the Indians.[31]

As often was the case, the major had no evidence suggesting that the people he attacked had taken part in the earlier incident. Yet he reported quickly that "we have punished them pretty severely in this affair" and went on to predict a coming "war with this tribe, which must result in [our] exterminating them."[32] Downing's actions failed to bring peace. Instead they infuriated the Dog Soldiers and other militants who considered the Americans guilty of repeated unprovoked attacks on peaceful villagers. A handful of peace chiefs scrambled to persuade the Arkansas River bands not to retaliate, while the militants complained bitterly about the continued white aggression. As soon as they learned of this latest fight, the peace chiefs led a 250-lodge party toward the Smoky Hill River in May 1864, trying to avoid retaliation by the militia.[33]

But troops led by Lieutenant George Eayre intercepted the party. One of the chiefs, Lean Bear, decided to meet the troop commander and rode toward the soldiers, showing them the peace medal that President Lincoln had given him earlier. Rather than parley, however, the lieutenant ordered his men to open fire, killing the chief, one of only six Cheyenne leaders who had signed the 1861 Fort Wise treaty. Almost before the troopers could reload, hundreds of Indians responded, threatening to overrun Eayre's outnumbered men. At that point peaceful Indian leaders halted the charge and withdrew. This gave the cavalrymen a chance to retreat to safety. If the warriors had not broken off the fight they probably could have destroyed the entire command or at least inflicted heavy casualties on it.[34]

The motivations leading to the attacks on the Cheyenne and Arapaho bands beginning in April 1864 remain unclear. Some scholars suggest that they resulted from the response of territorial officials to General Samuel Curtis's March 26, 1864, order directing them to send all available troops east to help him repel a Confederate threat to eastern Kansas. They based this on comments made by George Bent (son of the trader William Bent and his Cheyenne wife, Owl Woman), who lived through the events. He recalled hearing from political enemies of Colonel Chivington that in his effort to avoid sending his troops east he thought that "the easiest way out of his difficulty was to attack the Indians and stir them up."[35] Then Chivington could tell General Curtis that frontier violence forced him to keep his units in Colorado. Other analyses suggest that the repeated rumor mongering of *Rocky Mountain News* editor William Byers also kept the local anti-Indian feelings at a fever pitch. Governor Evans apparently expected to link Chivington's call for military action with Byers's anti-Indian ravings to build his political stature and to strengthen the movement for Colorado statehood.[36] Actions by both Evans and Chivington appear to support these assertions.

Other events provided reasons for the continued suspicion and fear of the Indians. Even those Cheyenne and Arapaho bands hoping to remain at peace with the whites continued their raids on traditional enemy tribes despite their treaty agreements to halt those actions. They attacked the Utes to the north, Pawnees to the east, and Kiowas to the south. The chiefs lacked authority over individual young men or members of tribal warrior societies who carried out those raids. At the same time the Dog Soldiers and other militants continued attacking the white settlers despite the peace chiefs' warnings that their raids would bring disaster. The warrior societies followed traditional imperatives that they seek revenge or restitution for injury, death, or loss of property to band members. Their raids, thefts, or kidnappings just kept white fears alive.

For territorial citizens this situation came to a head on June 11, 1864, when a few raiders killed Ward Hungate, his wife, and two daughters at their ranch only about thirty miles southeast of Denver. After the attack searchers found Hungate's arrow-riddled body, with his face smashed in by an axe or war club and his head scalped. His wife, after having been raped, had been stabbed several times and scalped. Both the four-year-old and the infant girl had their throats cut and had been scalped. The baby also had been disemboweled. When the searchers put the mutilated bodies on display in Denver, the barbarity of these killings raised hatred of the Indians to a fever pitch and lent graphic support to Governor Evans's warnings about Indian hostilities. News of the incident spread quickly, and dozens of people hurried into Denver seeking protection. At the time authorities blamed the outrage on the Cheyennes, but evidence gathered later showed conclusively that the Northern Arapaho Roman Nose and three companions had committed these atrocities.[37]

When the governor requested help from Washington, Colonel Chivington repeated his calls for punishing the Indians while continuing preparations for war. Claiming that he wanted "to protect friendly Indians from being killed through mistake," on June 27, 1864, Evans issued a proclamation that directed friendly Indian groups to report to their agents in Kansas, Nebraska, and Colorado. He ended it saying that "the war on hostile Indians will be continued until they are all effectively subdued."[38] This proclamation failed to bring any calm. Most of the Indians were still hunting on the plains and had no way to hear the governor's offer. More importantly, authorities had no certain way to distinguish the peaceful and hostile bands. The militants still seeking further retribution for the earlier white attacks clearly had no reason to stop raiding or to expect peace if they camped near the forts.

The scattered violence continued. The difficulty of distinguishing peaceful from hostile groups remained and led to the infamous massacre at Sand Creek later that year. To spread news of his proclamation, Governor Evans sent emissaries to track down tribal groups still out on the plains. In late August the trader William Bent carried the governor's message to a camp with nearly two thousand Cheyennes and Arapahos, accompanied by a large party of Sioux. At an extended council meeting the peace chiefs convinced some of the others to stop fighting. They accepted Evans's invitation, requested an exchange of prisoners, and urged the governor to conclude peace with the other Plains tribes at the same time.[39] Black Kettle eventually led some five hundred villagers to a camp near Fort Lyon, where Major Edward Wynkoop promised them safety. On September 28, 1864, the Indian leaders met Governor Evans at Camp Weld near Denver hoping for peace, but he refused. Instead he told them that there could be no peace as long as some of the tribe continued their raids. Thinking that they would be safe at Fort Lyon, the peaceful Cheyenne leaders set up their village on nearby Sand Creek.

That decision proved disastrous. Early on the morning of November 29, 1864, the men of the First and Third Colorado Cavalry units thundered into the Indian camp in an unprovoked attack. When the fighting ended, they had destroyed the village. The Sand Creek Massacre probably included more atrocities than any other American military engagement. The militiamen scalped and mutilated all of the men, women, and children that they killed in the assault. News of the carnage spread rapidly, eventually leading to three investigations by both houses of Congress as well as the War Department. Wisconsin senator James Doolittle, who chaired the Joint Special Commission to investigate the incident, reported that when he asked the Denver residents which policy toward the Indians the United States should follow they shouted: "Exterminate them!" A few years later he wrote: "[W]hile it may be hard to make an Indian into a civilized white man, it is not so difficult to make white men into Indian savages."[40]

On the plains the Dog Soldiers, Northern Arapahos, and some Sioux bands declared war, attacking Americans wherever they found them. During the winter of 1864–65 war parties raided the immigrant trails and nearby towns as well. In January 1865 they destroyed ranches, bridges, and stage stations and also looted the town of Julesburg on the South Platte. The next month they stormed back into Julesburg and burned it to the ground.[41] By August 1865 many of the Indians felt that they had achieved their revenge and agreed to stop fighting. In October of that year federal officials met the assembled tribes and signed another peace agreement. The Treaty of the Little Arkansas included an apology for the attack at Sand Creek and even offered reparations to Indians who had lost family members in the massacre. The chiefs agreed to move to a new reservation in Indian Territory, but the agreement failed to bring peace because the Dog Soldiers had not participated in the talks. After the negotiations the army built two forts along the Smoky Hill route as Indian raids repeatedly brought military pursuit for the next few years.[42]

By 1867 relations with tribes on the southern plains followed two diverging paths. The army ordered General Winfield Scott Hancock to pacify the Arkansas River Valley with 1,400 men. Later that same year

the Indian Peace Commission opened negotiations with tribal delegations at Medicine Lodge Creek, hoping to gain peace and persuade the
tribes to accept reservations that would keep them away from the ever-
encroaching pioneers. Among other groups the Cheyennes and Arapahos signed new agreements that moved them to western Indian Territory. They got the right to hunt beyond the reservation boundaries but
little else. Again the militant warrior societies moved back to their favorite hunting grounds and attacked travelers and settlers, while the other
bands tried to stay out of harm's way. Seeing that the latest round of treaties had not brought peace, the army renewed its campaign. In late November 1868 Lieutenant Colonel George Custer destroyed Black Kettle's
village on the Washita River. The next July Major Eugene Carr routed
Tall Bull's Dog Soldier village, ending the fighting. The Indians had few
choices. Having suffered crushing defeats and facing rapidly shrinking
buffalo herds, they faced starvation unless they agreed to stay on the
reservation.

As in the Ohio Valley War nearly eighty years earlier, fighting between
the Cheyennes-Arapahos and the United States continued for more than
a decade. Both cases included bitter interracial violence marked by armed
white incursions, Indian raids, and army campaigns. Although some
tribal chiefs tried to avoid military actions, those leading the young warriors rejected negotiations. Facing American demands that they change
their way of life entirely, they refused. Spurning the treaties that some of
the civil chiefs had accepted, they fought for both their independence
and their cultural survival. The Cheyennes–Arapahos also shared some
experiences with the Dakotas in Minnesota. The Civil War occupied federal authorities in both instances. Because national leaders focused their
attention elsewhere, local leaders pushed their efforts to seize and develop tribal land whenever they could. When the tribes resisted, U.S.
forces defeated them. By the end of the 1860s the government had moved
them farther from the advancing pioneers.

CHAPTER 7

The Chiricahua Apache
War, 1861–1872

The two bands of Apaches struck quickly. According to rancher John Ward, the January 27, 1861, raid netted them twenty head of his cattle and his twelve-year-old stepson, Felix. The ranch stood twelve miles south of Fort Buchanan, east of present-day Tubac in southern Arizona, an area then dominated by several Apache bands. After the attack the Americans hurried to the fort asking for help, and the next morning Lieutenant Colonel Pitcairn Morrison ordered Lieutenant George Bascom to investigate. His party found only a few tracks that seemed to point toward the home country of the Chokonen Band of the Chiricahua Apaches, led by Cochise. Without any physical evidence, the nearby settlers blamed the chief's people for the raid. The Chiricahuas had no history of taking captives, however, while other bands of the Western Apaches had done so repeatedly. Whether aware of the divergent practices of the many Apache groups or not, the next morning Colonel Morrison sent troops to Apache Pass, in the heart of Cochise's home territory. This move led directly to the so-called Bascom Affair and the bitter raiding and warfare that followed.[1]

Leaving Fort Buchanan on January 29, Lieutenant Bascom mounted his fifty-four infantrymen on mules and rode northeast for several days, taking rancher John Ward along as his interpreter. On February 3, 1861, they halted near the Butterfield Stage Station just beyond the pass and about two miles from the Apache camp. There Bascom invited Cochise to

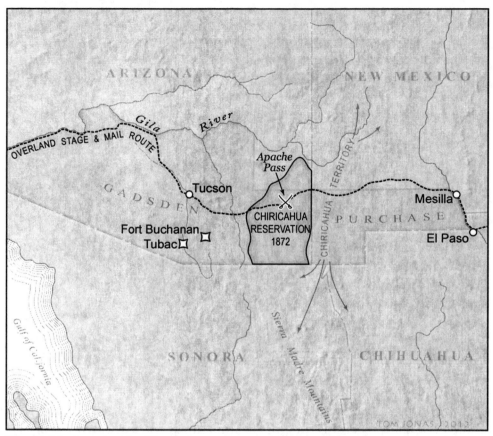

The Chiricahua Apache War.
© 2013 University of Oklahoma Press, Norman.

meet the soldiers for a parley. When no Indians appeared the next day, he tried again. He sent James Wallace, one of the stage company employees, to the Apache camp, once more asking the leaders to visit. Some hours later Cochise arrived. Military units had moved through the area frequently, so meeting them was nothing new for these Indians. The chief had no reason to think that the visit might be dangerous and brought his brother and several other Apache men as well as his wife and two of his children along.[2]

At the soldiers' camp, the chief and two of the others joined Lieutenant Bascom for a meal in his tent. When their meeting began, the young officer spoke pleasantly but soon accused Cochise's people of having raided

Ward's ranch and kidnapping the boy. The chief denied any knowledge of that raid but offered to send runners to several Coyotero Apache bands that he thought might have Felix. Cochise promised to do whatever he could to return the missing child to his family once his messengers found him. He told Bascom that this might take as long as ten days and asked the lieutenant for patience. What followed remains confused and disputed. But all accounts agree on the parley's outcome. Bascom claimed to have accepted the chief's offer and told him that he could leave but then demanded that his companions remain in camp as hostages until the Indians returned with young Felix. The chief's actions suggest that the lieutenant said nothing of the kind. Instead, thinking that Bascom intended to imprison him, the Indian leader jumped up, slashed a hole in the tent side, and escaped. The startled soldiers started firing and apparently wounded him in one leg as he ran from the camp.[3]

This incident quickly escalated. Cochise had plenty of experience with parleys and flags of truce. He denounced the lieutenant angrily for being dishonest, while the troops retreated to the stagecoach station, the only place that offered any protection from an attack. The next morning, February 5, the soldiers reported seeing large numbers of Chokonen men gathered only a few hundred yards away. The Indians left quickly but sent a single man with a white flag to request another parley. A short time later Cochise and three companions met Bascom with two sergeants and the interpreter Ward. During the next half-hour the chief tried to persuade the officer that his people had not taken the boy and asked that the hostages be released, but Bascom refused.[4]

When it seemed that the talks had reached a standoff, three of the stage company workers tried to intervene. They walked toward the Indians, who captured James Wallace and shot one of the others. Nervous soldiers shot and killed the third man, Robert Walsh, as he tried to scramble back into the fortified stage station. That ended the negotiations, and the Apaches and soldiers exchanged gunfire until late that afternoon. Each side had tried to settle the dispute in its own way but had failed. The gunfire that followed brought injury and death to both sides. When the shooting ended, each group held prisoners. It seemed possible that an exchange might yet end the incident without more fighting.

In the middle of the next day, February 6, Cochise led a bound James Wallace to the top of a nearby hill in full view of the troops. From there the chief offered to exchange his prisoner and some stolen army mules for the soldiers' Apache hostages. The lieutenant refused. Instead he insisted that the Indians return the captive boy, ending the talks. Later that same evening the Chokonen men captured a small wagon train moving into the area. The Apaches seized three Americans and several Mexicans, killing the latter almost immediately. They moved their new American prisoners back to camp, apparently hoping that four captives might make a hostage exchange more likely than their first effort when they had just a single man. The chief had his original prisoner James Wallace write a note reported to have said: "Treat my people well and I will do the same to yours,"[5] promising to return for more talks the next day. It took the frightened soldiers two days to find the message, so they failed to respond as the chief had expected.

While waiting for an answer, the Indian men ambushed the eastbound stagecoach early on February 7, but that attack failed. During the next several days sniping and minor skirmishes continued. Because the Apaches' accurate shooting forced the soldiers to stay near the fortified stage station the Indians managed to capture many of their mules. After two days of intermittent gunfire, on February 9 Cochise decided that Lieutenant Bascom would not exchange the prisoners, so the Apaches killed their four American hostages and left, retreating south into Mexico. Once the siege ended and the troops began their trek back to Fort Buchanan, they found the corpses that the Indians had left and hanged the six male Apache hostages in retaliation, including the chief's two nephews, but they did release the women and children.[6] Whatever the state of earlier Apache-American relations had been, these events led directly to the reported death of as many as 150 whites in the bitter raids that followed.

Both sides shared blame for the disastrous results. Certainly Cochise bore some responsibility for what happened. He gave up trying to settle the dispute, ordered or allowed the killing of the four prisoners, and led the Chokonen people south into Mexico. At the same time Lieutenant Bascom's refusal to accept the Apache leader's denial of having kidnapped the boy from the Ward ranch illustrates the Americans' repeated unwillingness to believe Indian leaders. It put the chief in a difficult position at best. The Apaches held honesty to be essential for a leader's character, so having the Americans question his veracity infuriated Cochise. The tribesmen assumed that the officer's invitation to share dinner had guaranteed their safety. To them his effort to seize his guests marked Bascom as entirely untrustworthy. The lieutenant's insistence that the Chokonen people with Cochise had kidnapped Felix and his refusal to exchange hostages made it impossible to end the incident without bloodshed. Of crucial importance for Apache-American relations in the Southwest, this breakdown of what began as a peaceful meeting made the Apache leader so suspicious of the soldiers that for the rest of his life he never fully trusted them.

In fact, the violence that erupted in Arizona may have been more impossible to avoid than any other of the wars examined here except for the 1790s conflict in the Ohio Valley. In both instances the wars followed extended struggles. Even if Lieutenant Bascom had acted differently, the later events fit into decades-old established patterns that pitted these Indians against every other group in the region. From the start, when Anglo-Americans met Apachean peoples during the nineteenth century, they became enmeshed in fluid and often dangerous events that they did not understand but could not ignore. The Apaches had migrated into the American Southwest centuries earlier, drifting south for generations after leaving their Northern Athapaskan relatives in northwestern Canada. Scholars differ on the starting point for their migration, on when they arrived at the locations where the European invaders first met them, and even on when these events happened.[7]

Whenever the Apaches migrated into the southwestern mountains, they occupied an area stretching from the west Texas plains across New Mexico and into much of southern Arizona by the time the first Europeans reached that area. Never a single tribe, they included groups now called the Jicarillas, Lipans, Kiowa-Apaches, Navajos, Mescaleros, Western Apaches, and Chiricahuas. The Chiricahuas included four distinct bands: the Chihennes, Nednhis, Bedonkohes, and Chokonens. Each of these bands included even smaller groups of just a few families that lived and hunted together and occasionally united for marriages, dances, and other social or religious ceremonies. People in each of the larger bands recognized and generally followed a single chief. As usual in Indian societies, that person retained his position only as long as the others respected and chose to cooperate with him. Despite their differences from other tribal groups, the Athapaskans' lifeways shared elements with many other indigenous peoples.[8]

The Apaches made their camps or *rancherías* in secluded valleys, near often scarce food and water sources. Some of the family groups occupied seasonal camps with small gardens, but Indian tradition and the challenging environment limited their size. Instead the villagers hunted, gathered, and traded for most of what they needed whenever they could. As relative latecomers to the area, they found most of the fertile and well-watered areas occupied and either continued long-established raiding practices or developed new ones. By the time Europeans arrived, Apache forays had brought repeated fighting with Pueblos and other indigenous farmers. When the Spanish began edging into the region, they provided just one more target for the Athapaskans' attacks.[9]

For at least the first hundred years, the Spanish limited most of their settlements to areas south of the present U.S.-Mexico border, except for a few missions and presidios in southwest Texas and northern New Mexico. In Arizona the Mission San Xavier just south of Tucson and the presidio at Tubac farther south represented the northern limit of the intruders' penetration. Still, the distance separating the Apaches and Spaniards did little to limit repeated violence between the two. By the 1670s, if not earlier, intermittent warfare plagued the region as Indian attacks often provoked retaliation by the local settlers. Spanish policies varied from a reliance on sedentary forts or missions to frequent military campaigns against the Indians. Rarely did these prove effective. By the last third of the seventeenth century Apache raiding and warfare had led to chaos: abandoned ranches, widespread loss of property, and dangerous travel conditions became common. Responding to that situation, authorities in Sonora created "flying companies" of what later became frontier rangers to hunt and destroy Indian raiders, but they only spread violence to wider areas and so failed to bring any lasting peace.[10]

As scattered settlements of ranchers or miners grew in northern Mexico during the eighteenth century, they offered ever more inviting targets to Indians looking for livestock, food, captives, or weapons. Spanish frontier officials occasionally led successful anti-Indian campaigns such as those in the 1770s by Hugo O'Conor and a decade later by Juan Bautista de Anza. These inflicted heavy casualties on some Apache groups but failed to secure lasting peace. In fact the continuing barbarity practiced by men on both sides practically ensured a continuing cycle of reprisals. One officer remarked that the Spanish "accuse the Indians of cruelty. I do not know what opinion they [the Indians] would have of us: perhaps it would be no better."[11] A colleague remembered killing an Apache leader, cutting off his head, and charging into battle with the head on his lance. During the same era the government paid cash for pairs of Apache ears, their own early version of scalp bounties.[12]

In 1786 Spanish leaders began a new policy that they hoped might bring peace or at least significantly reduce the fighting. They promised to give food and weapons to Indian leaders who established permanent camps near presidios or towns. This early proposal shared similar goals with those of later U.S. officials dealing with indigenous people. Both governments wanted to undermine the tribal culture and economy by urging the Indians to become farmers while increasing their dependence on European goods. Once a village or band settled near a presidio, the officers tried to appoint head chiefs, but the Indians rejected that. The Spanish approach differed from that of later official American efforts because they gave alcohol to the Indians, while the Americans tried to prevent its use. Seeking to limit raiding and fighting, presidio leaders tried to control when and where the Apaches could travel. In public the indigenous people who settled at the Spanish outposts seemed to accept these limits, but local shamans, war leaders, and chiefs apparently continued to meet their cultural obligations. It seems clear that some local officers realized that they received only partial cooperation. Yet while feeding the Indians may have reduced the local depredations at times, it failed to change basic economic practices. Indian raiding and thefts of livestock continued. Some Indian groups ignored or resisted this peace initiative. Others just added the Spanish handouts to their other food sources for the rest of the Spanish era.[13]

When Mexico gained its independence from Spain in 1821, the new government brought immediate changes for the Apaches and their neighbors. At first the connections between Mexico City and the far northern settlements weakened, so local authorities had less money than earlier to buy supplies for the Indians. That meant smaller food rations, so the Indians stepped up their attacks on nearby ranches and farms to replace the lost goods. Reports of chaos in northern frontier areas persuaded the new government to modify its approach. It decided to continue giving rations, but only to the individual Apaches actually present in the Indian camps on the days chosen to issue the goods. That meant that men who left the villages to supplement their modest rations by hunting or gathering risked their chance to get anything from local officers on ration day. This decision persuaded some Indians that the Mexicans wanted them to starve, and they increased their rustling of cattle and horses for food. That in turn fueled growing Mexican suspicions that they could not trust the Apaches.[14]

After Mexican independence, frontier officials supplied the Indians camped near existing presidios in the state of Chihuahua for a time, but soon the system began to disintegrate. Robbery, kidnapping, and warfare replaced it as the central features of Indian-Mexican relations. Authorities heard continuing reports of Apache uprisings, while the Indians feared that the Mexicans would turn the Comanches against them. During the 1820s local commanders became aware of small-scale Apache thievery and raiding but did little more than complain. Cattle rustling continued, but frontier officials felt that they had little choice but to avoid angering the Indians. Apparently they feared that any response would drive the scattered bands into a unified uprising. They also recognized that often local gangs of Mexican thieves stole Apache animals too.[15]

During the 1820s officials on the northern frontier tried to continue the earlier Spanish effort to "civilize" their Apache neighbors. They encouraged village leaders to settle in one place permanently and to work to support themselves. One scholar claims that these programs included as many as two-thirds of the Chiricahuas during that decade.[16] Still, these efforts to "buy" peace had little impact: minor livestock raiding and other thievery continued. In 1831 the tentative and uneasy relations between Indians and Mexicans broke down when the commandants general of both Sonora and Chihuahua ended their peacekeeping efforts completely. Within just a few months the indigenous people who had lived at the so-called peace establishments for years drifted away and returned to full-time raiding on the isolated settlements. Facing increasing violence and disorder by mid-October that year Mexican officers declared war on the Apaches and began a major campaign to regain control of the frontier. Whenever the Indians attacked, the troops pursued them, so for a few years the situation remained dangerous and peace illusive. As Mexican forces ranged widely against the raiders, the Indians adopted a long-standing custom. They sought peace when it appeared necessary. In August 1832 a new truce ended the hostilities briefly, but it disintegrated before the year ended.[17]

A cycle of intermittent peace and war followed for the next decade, and in 1842 the two sides concluded another cease-fire. This time it lasted for only three years. When the frontier officials' efforts to supply their indigenous neighbors as promised in the peace agreement, the Indian men stepped up their horse thievery and other raiding to feed their families. Continuing issuance of alcohol did little to prevent local incidents, and genuine hatred on both sides also kept tensions high. Presidio commanders and their superiors realized that they lacked enough troops, arms, or equipment to ensure peace, so their actions remained tentative. The governments of both Sonora and Chihuahua briefly turned to paying scalp bounties, which further outraged the Indians. Instead of cooperating by sharing their limited resources, or even information, the two states followed independent policies. For example, at times Sonoran troops crossed the border into neighboring Chihuahua and attacked Apaches there, causing further violence. As a result the northern frontier region endured continuing fighting with the Apaches as well as the Comanches, who raided south from west Texas. By the time the United States and Mexico signed the Treaty of Guadalupe Hidalgo in 1848 and the Americans prepared to take control of the present Southwest, the Apaches had developed a bitter hatred of Mexicans. Their perpetual raids gave little reason to think peace might come to the region anytime soon.[18]

Article 11 in the 1848 Treaty of Guadalupe Hidalgo pledged that the United States would enforce peace along the new border. Accepting assertions that Indian "incursions within the territory of Mexico would be prejudicial in the extreme," it committed the victors to act so that "all such incursions shall be forcibly restrained . . . and that when they cannot be prevented, they shall be punished" by the United States.[19] Fresh from their victory over Mexico, American officials apparently had little or no knowledge of the situation in the new international border region. Had they realized that Apache and Comanche raids as well as Spanish and Mexican military retaliatory campaigns had prevented any sort of real peace for generations, they might not have taken sole responsibility to pacify the area. In earlier decades the Indians had used distance or difficult terrain as protection from Mexican retaliation. After 1848 tribal leaders came to realize that the border offered a refuge, so they raided in one country and fled across the line into the other to escape pursuit. Their continuing forays into Sonora and Chihuahua brought outraged demands from Mexican officials that the United States live up to its promise to restrain the Indians. This proved nearly impossible, although during the next five years the U.S. Army shifted nearly two-thirds of its troops to the southwestern border. The newly deployed American forces had little more success than their Spanish and Mexican predecessors as Apache and Comanche raids south of the new border continued.[20]

The soldiers' presence along the Gila River boundary did almost nothing to stop the raids, kidnappings, and other violence. In fact many of the most successful Indian leaders lived south of that river, so stationing soldiers near it had little impact. Led by Mangas Coloradas, Cochise, and several other chiefs, large Apache forces frequently penetrated deep into Sonora and Chihuahua, killing civilians, taking prisoners, and seizing hundreds of horses and cattle. In response, during the 1850s officials in both Sonora and neighboring Chihuahua alternated between signing treaties with many Apache bands and retaliating when the peace that they sought collapsed. In 1850 Sonoran leaders reported that Apaches had killed at least 111 people and pleaded with the government in Mexico City for help.[21] Later that year Chiricahua war parties of several hundred men swept across the state, inflicting serious damage before heading north with at least 1,300 stolen cattle and horses. On January 19, 1851, a 100-man Mexican force overtook the Apaches and attacked. The fighting raged all day, and by evening the Indians had badly defeated their outnumbered pursuers. The Mexican force had twenty-six men killed and another forty-six wounded (including all of their officers) in one of their worst losses to the raiders.[22]

Raiding continued during the years when this treaty article remained in force, while the United States spent more than $12 million in futile efforts to keep peace. Army leaders on the scene complained that they needed many more troops, while officials in northern Mexico denounced the Americans' promise to keep them safe from Indian attacks as a lie. Hoping to recoup some funds, they submitted large depredation claims to the U.S. federal government, asking it to pay extensive reparations for their losses to the Indians. But Washington officials rejected their claims. After nearly five years the issue became part of the negotiations leading to the Gadsden Purchase. That agreement shifted the border south from the Gila River to its modern location in order to get land in southern Arizona and southwestern New Mexico as a route for a southern transcontinental

railroad. Article 2 of the new treaty repealed the earlier American commitment to keep peace along the border and included some funds for
reparations.[23]

While American and Mexican officials squabbled over boundary issues, the California gold rush brought thousands of newcomers through
the Southwest. At first most of the pioneers passed through on their way
to the west coast. When many failed to strike it rich, some returned to
Arizona hoping to change their luck. Others wanted land for ranching
or farming. Whatever their reasons for coming into the Southwest, most
of the newcomers had little idea of the danger that the indigenous
groups posed. Some early pioneers opened modest trade with the Native
peoples prior to the 1853 treaty and occasionally later. In some cases this
led Mexicans to accuse the Americans of exchanging the stolen livestock
brought north by the Apaches for arms and ammunition that the Indians then used in their next round of attacks south of the border. Given
the lingering hatred between the citizens of the two countries after the
war, the evidence tends to support those charges. If the early Anglo-
Americans did supply weapons to the Apaches, they paid dearly in just a
few years.

The newcomers missed two central issues that kept the region in turmoil. First, it appears likely that the incoming Americans failed to recognize the long-standing enmity between the Apache and the Mexicans.
Second, they had no idea of how essential and deeply embedded raiding
had become in the Indian economy and social practices. As in other instances where Indians met the intruders, almost none of the newcomers
knew or respected the indigenous values or practices. Certainly they had
no idea of the place that clan obligations for blood retribution held in
tribal culture or, more importantly, of the need to continue raiding for
group survival. The few individuals who may have understood chose to
ignore those factors. This failure made it difficult for pioneers or their
officials to credit Apache actions with any rational basis.

Rather, to the white newcomers, these violent people appeared to be
dangerous, even subhuman, savage creatures. Many pioneer newspaper
editors gave their readers a steady diet of anti-Indian views. Writing from
Tubac, one newsman rejected the idea that indigenous people had enough
intelligence to understand the ideas being used by missionaries trying to
convert them. To him the idea that the tribesmen could accept the new

beliefs was preposterous. In fact he wrote: "[E]veryone who has any knowledge knows that there would be just as much reason in sprinkling a little water upon the head of an ox; or just as much in preaching to a herd of cattle" as in doing either of those to the Indians.[24] Within just a few years that thinking shifted into cries for extermination or total removal of the Indians from Arizona.

The records offer no clear picture of when the Chiricahuas first became aware that American troops had replaced those of Mexico or that the 1853 Gadsden Purchase had established a new international border. During the 1850s the situation in Sonora and Chihuahua had spiraled downward into an unending cycle of violence. At the same time the new treaty no longer required U.S. troops to police the border. That encouraged Apache leaders to use it as a refuge from Mexican reprisals. While that simplified their relations with authorities in Sonora, now they faced the newcomers moving into their own home territory. By this time Mangas Coloradas, chief of the Chihennes or Warm Springs Band, began stepping back from actively leading war parties. Cochise became prominent as a Chokonen leader. This brought him to the center of the evolving relationships with the American pioneers and the army.[25]

The United States hesitated to exert its authority in the territory acquired through the 1853 Gadsden Purchase for several reasons. First, it took until 1854 for both nations to ratify the agreement. Then it took two more years before they agreed on the new international boundary. Not until 1856 did American troops replace the Mexican soldiers remaining north of the border. Their local commander rejected Tucson as a reasonable site for stationing his men, and in early 1857 the army established Fort Buchanan southeast of present Tubac. Never much more than a collection of wretched hovels, it housed the soldiers for several years, although the location of that post offered little protection for local settlers. Despite that, more than one scholar has suggested that the local citizens saw the nearby troops as a major economic benefit and hoped to profit from the army's presence.[26]

Early reports suggested that the Apaches in southeastern Arizona seemed friendly, but troop commanders assumed the worst and acted as if they needed to protect Overland Mail Company wagons passing through the region. Local difficulties began in June 1857 when Captain Richard S. Ewell led a small force of mounted dragoons into the

Chiricahua Mountains. There they attacked an Indian camp without any provocation and confiscated a small herd of presumably stolen horses. The Apaches retaliated the next day, recapturing most of their animals. It is not clear that the abortive raid really changed relations between the newcomers and the Indians, but the following events suggest that the Chokonens and their relatives might expand their raids to include the newly arriving Americans. Later that year Chiricahua raiders attacked an immigrant train moving through the mountains and then slipped away before any pursuing troops got there. Except for these scattered incidents no major fighting took place.[27]

In 1858 the Office of Indian Affairs sent Dr. Michael Steck to begin his duties as the new agent for the Indians in southern New Mexico and Arizona. In particular, his superiors wanted him to persuade the Chiricahuas to let the U.S. mail wagons travel through Apache Pass in their territory. Although that area had remained peaceful for more than a year, Steck called for troops to be stationed there to protect the mail service. His motivations remain unclear. At the time most of the Chokonens lived in Mexico at too great a distance from Apache Pass to pose any serious threat, and the mail coaches carried almost nothing of value to the Indians. While the incoming Americans worried about Apache attacks in Arizona, the Indians feared Mexican treachery. Late that year Cochise returned north into the United States.[28] In January 1859 the agent and the chief met. Steck agreed to give the Indians some food and supplies at Apache Pass each year, and the Apache leaders raised no objections to the stage and mail stations being built in the center of their home territory.

Still, sporadic thefts of horses and mules along the border never ended. These depredations often happened just as the Indians returned from their frequent raids south of the border. The Apaches considered their attacks in Sonora and Chihuahua separate from their dealings with the Americans. One chief reportedly promised that they would "not molest the whites" if the Americans ignored the Indians' forays into Mexico.[29] Because none of the military commanders or civilian officials could do anything to stop the Apache raids, they continued. Yet scattered violence took place in the United States too, because neither the Americans nor the Indians trusted each other fully. In March 1859, after a brief absence, Steck returned to southern Arizona. He met with Western Apache groups just north of Tucson trying to arrange a peace with them. In those talks the Indian leaders agreed not to attack the pioneers or steal their property, and in return the agent promised to give them rations.[30] Basically the early U.S. effort to buy peace with food followed the earlier Spanish and Mexican policies and likewise failed.

Some Arizona settlers objected to the agent's even talking with the Apaches. They wanted the army to destroy the Indian groups rather than having the agent work for peace. One local newspaper suggested that "when troops go into an Indian country, they should go to fight."[31] Despite the aggressive measures that the pioneers demanded, efforts to keep peace continued. On April 1 agent Steck returned to Apache Pass and gave out the food and supplies that he had promised to deliver. Yet the agent's gifts seem to have had no impact on long-standing band customs. As soon as he left, the Chokonen leaders led another campaign into Mexico, where they swept across the countryside, murdering, robbing, and burning as they went. In early summer 1859 they returned north, driving large herds of stolen animals into the mountains. Once at home they avoided the Americans much of the time.[32]

Gradually the Apaches' frequent cross-border incursions into Sonora led to incidents north of the border too. The Apaches stayed away from the overland stage route but continued their raids elsewhere in Arizona. Repeated complaints about the Chokonens brought new pressures on the authorities to act against them. Even agent Steck, who usually defended them, changed his view. He called the Chokonens "the most warlike band [of Indians] west of the Rio Grande, and the least reliable," and complained that their actions did little to reduce tensions.[33] In the winter of 1859–60 American civilians and Apaches with Cochise clashed several times, as white settlers killed several of the warriors while pursuing small parties of Indians with stolen cattle. In retaliation the Chiricahuas attacked one of the stage stations and soon after that stole part of the Santa Rita Mining Company horse herd near Tubac. During much of 1860 the Indians took their loot back and forth across the border into Mexico as they eluded pursuers in both countries and kept nearby residents on both sides of the line frightened and angry. Their January 1861 raid at John Ward's ranch and the Bascom Affair at Apache Pass a few days later changed the situation dramatically. Because both sides killed their hostages, what had been low-level scattered violence escalated into bitter interracial warfare that lasted for the next twenty-five years. At that point the conflict became what one scholar labeled "a war of blood vengeance."[34]

On April 12, 1861, the Confederate attack on Fort Sumter in Charleston harbor opened the American Civil War. Far removed from southern Arizona and the festering Indian-white violence there, that conflict had both immediate and long-term impacts on U.S.-Apache relations in the Southwest, as it had in both Minnesota and Colorado. Just a few months later, in June, practically all of the U.S. troops left Arizona to reinforce units in New Mexico as Confederate forces threatened there. Indians, Mexicans, and whites alike watched the army close posts from Fort Defiance in Navajo country to Forts Buchanan and Breckenridge in Apache country. As they saw the soldiers march away, some of the Apaches may have concluded that they had defeated yet another group of enemies. They had little to celebrate, however, because in less than a year units of Volunteers belonging to the California Column moved in to reestablish the abandoned forts and try to enforce peace in frontier Arizona.[35]

During the few months before these Volunteers arrived, miners continued to drift into the same area. Their frenzy to dig gold confused and angered the Indians. They saw the metal as practically useless, being too soft for tools or even musket balls. More importantly, they considered gold to be a symbol of the sun and sacred to the spirit Ussen and feared that mining would provoke "the Mountain Gods."[36] Later Indian informants reported that in 1861 the Chihennes chief Mangas Coloradas had tried to persuade the miners at Ojo Caliente to stop work there. In response they tied him to a tree and beat him severely. To the Apaches there was "no humiliation worse than that of a whip."[37] That unprovoked insult to their most respected leader enraged his people. It increased Indian suspicion and hatred of the whites just before the new troops reached Arizona.

The California Volunteers' arrival made U.S.-Apache relations more difficult and certainly more violent than earlier. Their commander, General James H. Carleton, had no love for Indians and almost from the start ordered his troops to "attack all Apaches" unless they came in to parley with a white flag.[38] When that policy failed to end the raiding, he became more belligerent and ordered his men to kill all of the male Indians they met. In June 1862 he placed Arizona under martial law and then sent some of his command east toward Texas. As the troops moved into

Apache Pass, Indians under Mangas Coloradas and Cochise attacked but withdrew after two days of heavy fighting in mid-July.[39] Late in the battle one of the soldiers wounded Mangas Coloradas. Having failed to defeat the Americans, the Apaches traveled south into Chihuahua, where their chief got medical attention.

Scattered raiding continued, but no major change came for another six months. In the meantime, Mangas Coloradas wanted to end the fighting and get a permanent home for his people. Having recovered from his wound, in September 1862 he asked if he could "come in to treat for peace."[40] General Carleton rejected this plea. By early October he wrote a subordinate that "Mangas Coloradas sends me word that he wants peace, but I have no faith in him."[41] Despite the lack of a positive American response and ignoring warnings from other Apache leaders, Mangas Coloradas had returned to Pinos Altos in southwestern New Mexico. When the chief and several of his men met a group of American miners there in January 1863, the miners took him prisoner and turned him over to troops under General Joseph West. In their meeting West told the Apache leader that "you have murdered your last white victim." Mangas Coloradas replied that his people had only defended themselves when "we were attacked by the white men who came digging up my hills for the yellow iron."[42]

That night the soldiers kept Mangas Coloradas under guard in the rubble of former Fort McLane. Reputedly the general told his men that he wanted the chief dead before morning. Although the accounts of what happened relate the events differently, they all agree that sometime after midnight on January 19, 1863, the men guarding Mangas Coloradas began to burn his feet and legs with their heated bayonets or threw hot coals from the fire on him. When he objected, they claimed that they shot him when he jumped up and tried to escape. The next morning some of the Volunteers buried his body. Later that same day the unit surgeon had the corpse dug up so that he could cut off its head. After boiling it clean he sent the skull to an eastern phrenologist.[43] Mangas Coloradas had tried to open peace talks and failed, and soon the Apaches learned that the soldiers had murdered and dismembered their leader. Rage swept through the Indian camps. His death, like the earlier Bascom Affair, increased the Indians' distrust of the soldiers. It also led directly to increased violence as other Apache leaders such as Victorio, Nana, and

Loco joined Cochise against the Americans, ending any serious chances to bring peace.

This incident resembles the unjustified army attacks on Cheyenne villagers on the central plains during the same period. While it involved killing only one chief as compared to destroying an entire village, it brought similar results: a renewed cycle of Indian raids and American retaliation that drew ever more Apache attacks. These events terrorized the civilian population, frustrated military commanders, and infuriated Indian communities for the next eight years after the soldiers had murdered the chief. Yet despite what had happened to Mangas Coloradas when he tried to open peace talks and the violence in 1865, Cochise wanted to end the fighting. He traveled to Fort Bowie, but the officers there sent him home, telling him to wait for twelve days. Rather than bringing negotiators to the Apache camp, Major James Gorman led a surprise attack against the Apaches. It failed entirely. Instead of coercing the Indians to make peace, the attack gave Cochise another example of American treachery. He responded by leading raids on both sides of the border. Now fully persuaded that the white leaders were liars who could never be trusted, he rejected new invitations to meet for talks during the next few years. Still, Cochise could not escape the troops entirely, and in late 1869 he sent a message to Chihenne leader Loco that he might be willing to end the fighting. Nothing resulted from this effort, but in August 1870 the chief visited Camp Mogollon to discuss peace again.[44]

By this time the Chokonen leader realized that his people could not survive continuous war with both the Mexicans and the Americans. Later that same year, while special Indian agent William F. M. Arny held talks with two other Chiricahua bands at Cañada Alamosa in New Mexico, Cochise came in unexpectedly. Insisting that he be given truthful answers, he told Arny that "if the government talks straight I want a good peace." At the same time he objected to moving his followers to a reservation, using arguments like those of the Cheyennes in Colorado. "The Apaches want to run around like a coyote," he asserted, adding that "they don't want to be put in a corral."[45] The agent responded that the government wanted to supply the Indians with food and blankets so that they could learn to live in peace with the white settlers. When the talks ended, the chief promised to discuss the plans with his people.

While the Indians considered how to respond, the government, with its usual bad timing, replaced the local agent with a new man, Orlando Piper, whom Cochise had never met. From the start a shortage of funds and supplies undercut the new agent's efforts and delayed any move toward peace. U.S. officials had promised the Apaches food and clothing but could not provide enough of either, so Cochise led his people back to their favorite homesite in southern Arizona. These events occurred during the early stages of President Ulysses Grant's Peace Policy, which incorporated civilian reformers to investigate and oversee the actions of agents on the reservations. Under this plan federal officials sent Vincent Colyer, derided by many southwesterners as "Vincent the Good," to oversee Indian affairs in Arizona and New Mexico. He wanted to meet Cochise, but his repeated efforts failed to overcome the chief's suspicions. While Cochise rejected American peace feelers, Lieutenant Colonel George Crook took command of troops in Arizona. In an ill-timed move in July 1871 the new leader set out with 204 men to defeat or capture the illusive Chokonen chief. This act only reinforced Cochise's fears about American double-dealing.[46]

During the winter of 1871–72 Cochise and his band lived at Cañada Alamosa, but they traveled south into Mexico when the government closed the reservation that spring. After a few months there they returned north to their mountain homeland. In March 1872 the chief met American officials again. When they urged him to lead his band to the new reservation at Tularosa, he declined. At that meeting Colonel Gordon Granger invited Cochise to visit Washington; but Cochise had little reason to trust the army, so he refused. Instead he disappeared into the mountains. From there the Chokonens renewed their attacks, joining other Apache bands raiding and killing people across southern Arizona.[47]

Just a year earlier the continuing violence had provoked Tucson leaders to organize and arm a civilian force that killed more than a hundred Aravaipa and Pinal Apaches, mostly women and children. Reports of this massacre sparked national outrage and persuaded President Grant to send General Oliver O. Howard west as a peace envoy.[48] His orders had two central objectives. First they called for him to negotiate peace with the Indians. That proved no easy task. Then the secretary of the interior told Howard "to induce them [the Apaches] to abandon their present habits of life and go upon permanent reservations."[49] Thus the established federal plan to force acculturation on all of the indigenous peoples came to Arizona, bringing with it many of the same difficulties that it had caused elsewhere. At first Cochise declined to meet the general, so Howard turned his attention to several groups of Western Apaches. In June 1872, using a long-standing tactic, he took a small delegation of those Indian leaders east to meet the president. He assumed that when they saw America's large cities they would realize that military resistance was futile.[50]

No sooner had the general completed this assignment than he received new orders: return to Arizona and negotiate a lasting peace with Cochise. In early September 1872 Howard reached Tularosa, New Mexico, and sent messengers who sought the elusive Apache leader. The residents persuaded him to get Thomas Jeffords, a local trader, as a guide because he was the only white man Cochise appeared to trust. Then Howard's small party visited Cañada Alamosa, which the general decided was a good location for the Apache reservation. With only four other men he reached the Apache camp, and Cochise arrived on October 1, 1872. In their first talks Howard said that he had come to make peace, and the Apache leader responded that "nobody wants peace more than I do."[51] Despite that positive beginning, it took several weeks to get the other Chokonen leaders to the camp. On October 12 the two sides agreed to a treaty. Howard promised a new reservation at Cañada Alamosa where the Apaches wanted it and appointed Thomas Jeffords as their agent. In return Cochise promised to keep the peace.[52]

After this pact Apache raids diminished noticeably. although the government lacked enough cash to buy the supplies that it had promised the Indians. Rather than establish a firm peace with the Apaches in southern Arizona, Howard's effort merely deflected the violence southward, as the Chokonen and Chihenne men continued their generations-long raiding in northern Mexico. The agreement with Cochise never became a formal treaty, and Indian leaders appear not to have understood or accepted the need to remain in the United States. Continuing Chiricahua forays into Sonora brought angry protests from officials there, but the Americans lacked a way to prevent the raids or to police the border effectively. While that situation continued for the next two years,

Cochise became increasingly enfeebled and died in June 1874. His death ended the uneasy peace, and renewed fighting between Apache bands and Americans moving into Arizona continued for the next twelve years. The agreement that Cochise made with General Howard in 1872 had ended the first and most bloody phase of the Apache wars, however, if only for a brief time.

Efforts to pacify the Apache bands continued for the next fourteen years. General Crook hired scouts from one Apache band to help track and fight Indians from the other groups. Once the raiders learned that they could no longer just fade into the mountains to escape the pursuing soldiers, Crook's scouts helped bring shaky peace. Within just a few years the government forced most of the Indians onto what became the San Carlos Reservation. There authorities dumped people from several Apache bands together, mostly to make it easy for the army to control them. By 1874 the government had moved the Chiricahuas from the mountainous homeland that General Howard had accepted to San Carlos as well. They hated this new home. Almost from the start individual leaders, whole villages, and even parts of entire bands fled the wretched conditions on the reservation. Their breakouts led the army to bring ever more troops into the Southwest for the last stages of the Apache wars.

These campaigns, which were less wars than the pursuit of small groups of Indians trying to escape the miserable life at San Carlos by troops using Apache scouts to force them back to the reservation, lasted until Geronimo's 1886 surrender and exile from Arizona to Florida and later Oklahoma. During the 1870s and 1880s reports of Indians leaving the reservation kept white settlers in southern Arizona terrorized and generated repeated calls for all Indians to be removed from the territory. Unlike each of the earlier conflicts examined here except the 1823 Arikara War, the violence between Apaches and whites in the Southwest resulted less from the invaders' hunger for good land than from terror of Apache attacks and white determination to exterminate Indians whenever they could. That motivation most resembled attitudes expressed during the Ohio Valley conflict of the 1790s and the 1860s views expressed by Colorado pioneers.

CHAPTER 8

The Nez Perce War, 1877

Responding to General Oliver O. Howard's ultimatum that they move onto the reservation, nearly six hundred members of the five nontreaty bands of Nez Perces gathered near Tolo Lake in western Idaho to consider what to do. Angry at being ordered to leave their traditional home territory but divided about how to respond, they could not reach agreement; their talks stalled. Some thought that they had little choice but to go to the reservation as the one-armed soldier insisted. Others argued against moving. On June 13, 1877, the leaders called for a *tel-lik-leen* ceremony, in which the men circled the camp slowly while telling stories of past deeds. As a young warrior named Shore Crossing rode in a place of honor in the procession, one of the other men taunted him, asking: "[I]f you so brave, why you not go kill the white man who killed your father?"[1] Three years earlier a white grand jury had investigated the murder. But none of the Indians would take the oath needed before they could testify, so the court dropped the charges and released the attacker, Larry Ott. At the time, Shore Crossing had done nothing to avenge his father's murder. Hearing this taunt, he made no immediate reply.

Still, given the tension and frustrations in their camp over being forced off their traditional lands by the intruding whites, the ridicule struck home. On June 14 Shore Crossing and two other young Nez Perce men rode along the river toward Ott's cabin, planning to shoot him. But Ott

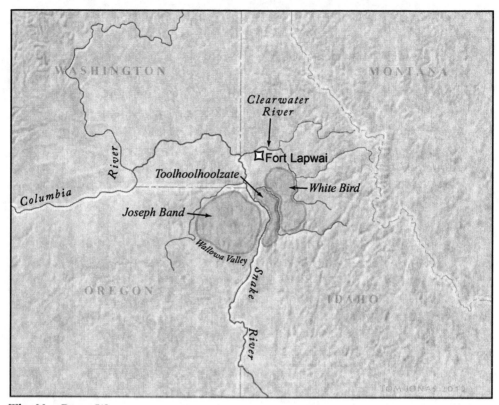

The Nez Perce War.
© 2013 University of Oklahoma Press, Norman.

had left. Angry and looking for another target, they rode on to the home
of Richard Divine, who had abused several Indians, and killed him instead. From there they raided a nearby ranch, shot three men, and then
stole some horses. Next they met Samuel Benedict, a local storekeeper
that the Indians suspected of having cheated some of his Nez Perce customers. The merchant had injured Shore Crossing earlier, so the attackers shot him. Although badly wounded, he managed to escape.[2]

Then the three young men returned to Tolo Lake and told their
friends what they had done. The news raced through the encampment
and forced the band leaders to decide what to do next. Much as the Dakota Sioux leaders did when they faced similar circumstances in June
1862, the Nez Perce chiefs hurriedly debated their few options. Perhaps

they could keep peace by surrendering the three young men to the white authorities and hope to avoid retaliation. Possibly they could flee to the new reservation. They had little time to debate: while they agonized over what to do, another group of warriors rode out of camp, attacking, robbing, and killing white settlers they found nearby. During the next four days of violence eighteen settlers died and another six lay badly wounded. Only one of the young Indians died during the attacks.[3] This rampage demonstrated the deep resentment and anger among the nontreaty bands of Nez Perces. The violent actions of the intruding pioneers and the demands of government officials that they surrender their traditional homelands directly threatened their way of life, even their survival. As had happened so often after other white-Indian violence, all-out war followed immediately after shooting began.

Previous Nez Perce history and experience included few hints of the violence and epic events that lay ahead. The origins of the Nez Perce people who lived in the Pacific Northwest remain uncertain. The tribal story about where the people in the region originated recounts how Coyote killed an evil monster, cut it to pieces, and scattered them and drops of blood across the landscape. Wherever any of them landed, a separate people grew.[4] While that gives little help in piercing the dim curtain that obscures their past, it does suggest that the many tribes of the region recognized that they shared some connections and had lived in the Northwest for eons.

The archaeological record confirms their view. It indicates that Native groups in the area had supported themselves by hunting, gathering, and fishing for thousands of years. They lived a vast region that stretched east from the Cascade Mountains to the northern Rocky Mountains and from southern Oregon and Idaho north to the Fraser River in British Columbia. Along with Salishian tribes such as the Coeur d'Alenes, Flatheads, and Spokans, the Nez Perces shared their home area with other Sahaptian-speaking groups including the Palouses, Umatillas, and Yakamas. In this large and at times beautiful homeland, the forests provided a variety of wild animals for meat and hides, the rivers contained vast amounts of salmon, the hills provided trees and bushes with seeds and berries, and the grasslands and sheltered valleys offered camas and other root crops. Yet even that apparent plenty did not always protect these people from natural disaster or human enemies.[5]

Evidence dating back as far as 500 B.C. suggests that the early groups of the inland Northwest lived in small villages, often just a few families, and hunted the herds of buffalo that had wandered west from the plains. By about 1700 their successful adaptations to the region had encouraged population growth, and by then the population is estimated to have reached about 4,500. The local communities remained small, however, with most of them containing from thirty to perhaps one hundred people. Depending on the village and the period, the people lived in A-frame long houses covered with bark or mats or in round dwellings. Each of those structures contained several families. Sometime after getting horses, the Nimiipuus (Real People), as they called themselves, added the more portable skin tepees to their dwelling choices. As in most Native societies, each settlement had a council that chose a headman to lead their discussions and serve as spokesman when dealing with outsiders. This office appears to have been hereditary at times, but only as long as the officeholder proved competent. Both the village council and anyone recognized as headman usually could only advise obedience, not require it, so the villagers enjoyed a far more democratic society than any of the white people who entered the region could have imagined. This general pattern of leadership and village organization continued well into historical times.[6]

For some generations the impact from continuing European invasions of North America did not penetrate the Nez Perce homeland. But eventually distance and isolation offered little protection from the newcomers' presence. By the early eighteenth century the horse became the first and most important new element in the lives of the northwestern tribes. Whether escaped or stolen from the Spanish after the 1680 Pueblo Revolt in New Mexico, horses brought major permanent changes to the villagers. Up to that time Nimiipuu bison hunters followed the shaggy brutes on foot, trying to frighten them into marshes and hoping that they might become mired and unable to flee. At other times they tried to drive their quarry off cliffs. Obtaining horses changed their lives dramatically. A mounted hunter could ride alongside a buffalo, put an arrow into its heart, and then chase another.[7]

Raising and using horses soon became central to the life of most Nez Perce villages, but owning these creatures brought both opportunity and challenge. Prior to becoming mounted, the men limited most of their hunting to areas west of the Rockies. Now, given their new mobility, they traveled east beyond those mountains onto the northern plains. There the increased number of bison encouraged the hunters to kill more animals. That changed women's work: they now followed the hunters, skinning the dead animals, tanning the hides, and jerking the meat. These expanded hunts, in turn, increased contacts with new tribes including the Crows and Blackfeet, who had drifted into present Montana and Wyoming by the 1750s. While the newcomers brought some chance for increased trade, they became a military threat once they got horses. After several generations the plateau people adopted many elements of what became the typical Plains culture, such as clothing, trail and hunting procedures, increased trade and raiding, and new varieties of food.[8]

By the late eighteenth century, firearms had become another important new factor in the villagers' lives. At the time, the Indians acquired these new weapons through trade or theft or as loot after a successful raid. While prized from the start, the new weapons proved almost worthless at first. Often just cheap trade goods, they needed frequent repair, which the Indian hunters rarely had the skills to carry out. Also, single-shot smoothbore muskets lacked accuracy and could not be reloaded easily by mounted hunters. Yet once these weapons became available, each tribe got its own supply. When used effectively at short range, the muskets increased serious wounds and fatalities in both hunting and raiding expeditions. Obviously, these white weapons as well as horses helped speed the changes in Nez Perce life and society.

When hunting groups combined men from several villages, new patterns of organization and leadership emerged. Hunters followed leaders who exhibited particular skills or good judgment, and over the years the position of war or hunt leader became common. As among the Plains tribes, the young men formed or joined hunting societies and warriors' lodges. These groups followed leaders who functioned alongside the usual village patterns of leadership. They, not the civil chiefs, directed and led the young men, particularly in times of emergency or when responding to threats or attacks upon the village communities. As on the central plains among the Cheyennes and Arapahos and to some extent among the Dakota villagers in Minnesota, the development of these groups diffused local power and weakened ties of village and band unity.[9] The new leaders and warrior societies further diffused village and band

structures among the Nez Perces, and this became increasingly important once the Americans arrived in the Northwest to stay.

While horses and guns brought major changes to Nimiipuu society,
epidemic disease caused the most havoc. Historical records give little evidence about when the first pathogens passed through villages far from the
coast, but smallpox appeared in 1780–81. It swept west from village tribes
along the Missouri River to the Blackfeet, Shoshonis, and then beyond to
the tribes of the plateau region, including the Nez Perces. Lacking any
immunity, all of these groups suffered major losses. Twenty years later a
second wave of the sickness moved through the villages. As in other tribes
the village shamans' ceremonies and cures failed, making the disease
even more terrifying than the disfigurement and misery that the pox inflicted. Again, the record of how many died or abandoned their homes
and came together to form new communities remains uncertain. One can
only be sure that this disaster weakened the village societies and increased
their vulnerability to the other diseases that followed. Some scholars have
speculated that the epidemics so unsettled Nez Perce society that they
turned increasingly to the teachings of prophets, which laid the foundation for their attraction to the Dreamer Religion a half-century later.[10]

By 1805, when the Nez Perces met Lewis and Clark, a few of the villagers had already dealt with white traders in southern Canada and at the
Hidatsa villages in North Dakota. These mostly fleeting contacts brought
stories that spoke of the newcomers' movements toward the northwest
and of the goods that they had to trade. The villagers first encountered
William Clark and his six companions on September 20 when the fam-
ished explorers came to Weippe Prairie, where the Indians had come to
dig camas roots. Once the white explorers got to the Nez Perce camp,
curiosity overcame most of the villagers' fear. Using clearly inadequate
sign language, the groups shared some food, tried to ask questions, and
observed each other. Soon after eating the Indian gifts of roots, berries,
and fish, almost all of the Americans became sick and were weakened by
stomach bloating, diarrhea, and fever for some days. Their stay lasted for
several weeks and remained peaceful, although the Indians stole some
small items. After receiving American flags and peace medals, the chiefs
supervised while the explorers prepared dugout canoes for their trip to
the coast. On October 7 they left.[11]

After spending a miserable winter near the Pacific the explorers started their trip home. In May 1806 Lewis and Clark returned to the Nez Perce villages. Exceptionally heavy snows forced them to remain there until June before they could recross the mountains and return to the Missouri River. Soon visits by other white explorers followed. Fur seekers from the Montreal-based Northwest Fur Company and the Hudson's Bay Company and American trappers and traders drifted through the northern Rockies and into the Northwest. During much of the next thirty years competing white parties crisscrossed the region, bringing guns, blankets, and all sorts of other trade goods to the villagers. In some ways the manufactured items improved the Indians' lives; in others they stimulated intertribal raiding and warfare, making the situation far more dangerous than before. By 1840 the actions of white trappers had denuded most of the mountain west of its fur-bearers and altered the multitribal landscape there forever.[12]

While contacts with explorers and the fur men encouraged changes in village life and economy, religious ideas triggered events that had an even greater impact on the village peoples of the Northwest. During the 1820s Hudson's Bay Company officers recruited sons of important chiefs and sent them to a mission school in Winnepeg. They returned home with some Christian ideas, and in 1830 Nez Perce leaders agreed to send two of their young men off to Canada to learn more of the new religion. At the same time stories about several of the tribesmen traveling all the way to St. Louis hoping to get religious instruction helped build American interest in the Oregon country. Garbled tales of this event persuaded a few missionary-minded Christians that they needed to bring their beliefs to the Indians of the Northwest.[13]

During the 1830s the Reverends Jason Lee, Samuel Parker, Marcus Whitman, and a few others headed west. In their enthusiastic reports to eastern supporters they made Oregon sound attractive to Americans still suffering from depression after the Panic of 1837. In the early 1840s hundreds of pioneers traveled west on what became the Oregon Trail. What began as just a handful of people within just a few years became a movement that brought several thousand settlers who pushed their way into the Indians' homeland. Before their arrival village life might have continued relatively unchanged. That possibility ended abruptly in 1840 when farmers moved into the Willamette River Valley in eastern Oregon. Even before the United States forcibly pushed its territorial claims to Oregon, the government appointed Elijah White as the subagent to Indians there. Technically he had no authority because the United States and Britain both claimed the area, but he assumed otherwise. In late 1842 he met almost two dozen Nez Perce leaders and in what seem to have been pleasant talks proposed a set of rules that he claimed would ensure continued peace. He repeated a tactic that Americans had used often when dealing with Indians. He asked the headmen to choose a single head chief who would speak for the tribe as a whole and then called for subchiefs to lead each village. The leaders knew that they had never had such a structure and that few, if any, of their fellow villagers would recognize or obey any man they named. When the agent insisted, they chose a minor chief named Lawyer to please him.[14]

In 1846 the United States and Great Britain negotiated a new northwest border at the 49th parallel, and two years later Congress established the Oregon Territory. During the 1850s generous land grants available under the Oregon Donation Act coupled with rumors of gold discoveries attracted thousands of American pioneers to the Northwest. The newcomers poured into the area and began occupying Indian land, taking advantage of several yet unratified treaties. As ever more white settlers arrived, tensions grew. In 1853 forty-seven people died in white-Indian fighting.[15] In 1854 federal authorities opened negotiations that they expected would end the violence and clarify land titles. During that December and January newly arrived territorial governor Isaac Stevens held treaty councils with tribes near the coast. When those talks ended, he had persuaded the Indians to surrender their title to 2.5 million acres of land and to accept three small reservations.

The next spring Stevens and other officials traveled east to meet Nez Perce, Cayuse, Yakama, and Palouse leaders for another round of negotiations. It took several weeks for the separate bands to appear for the meetings. Divisions among tribal chiefs also delayed the talks. In his meetings with the Nez Perces Stevens assumed that Lawyer could speak for all of the villages even though Indians rarely gave any one man that kind of authority and other chiefs had at least as many supporters as he did. In fact Lawyer, who soon became a partially acculturated Christian, had little in common with most of the tribe. While he spoke strongly in favor of signing the agreement, Looking Glass and Joseph opposed him. First they objected to selling their land at all. When Stevens insisted that they had to make way for the white settlers, they called for the new reservation to include their home territory in the Wallowa Valley. While the Indians argued about the treaty provisions, the governor learned about gold strikes near Colville and worked frantically to get the documents signed.[16]

The discussions leading up to the treaty signings demonstrated the vast gulf between what the governor proposed and what almost all of the Nez Perces wanted. Stevens promised that each family would have its own land and that the government would build flour and lumber mills and schools for the children. It would pay annuities and give everyone household and personal items. In return the Indians would give up most of their traditional homeland. Many tribal leaders objected, using religious and more general cultural arguments. One chief said that God had created each group of people and given them a particular homeland, so to sell it would be to steal from the Almighty. Another remarked that they belonged to the land and it to them. If they agreed to sell the land they would lose part of their identity. For others, the earth represented their mother, and they could not plow the land without harming her. Giving up most of their territory clearly seemed a poor choice to many. Yet when the council ended on June 11, 1855, band and village headmen signed the paper that established a Nez Perce reservation. But the agreement did not surrender any land that they considered important.[17]

Although he did not expect it, getting the Indians to put their marks on the treaties proved easier for Governor Stevens than persuading the U.S. Senate to ratify them. In his excitement over having opened much of the Pacific Northwest for pioneers, he announced that settlers could take land beyond the new reservation boundaries. That encouraged white land-seekers to move into areas still actively used by the villagers. From 1855 to 1858 pioneer encroachments caused repeated violent incidents and even some intermittent small-scale warfare, keeping tensions high east of the Cascades. During those years clear divisions among the Nez Perces emerged. Lawyer and other acculturated headmen cooperated with territorial officials, while traditionalists such as Joseph, Looking Glass, and Red Wolf became increasingly disenchanted and anti-American. Army officers commanding troops in the area temporarily averted major fighting by blocking most pioneer encroachment on tribal land, but even that effort failed to blunt rising Indian anger.[18]

In 1859 news that the Senate had ratified their treaty at last should have helped. But at about the same time rumors of gold discoveries brought more white prospectors to the area. The new town of Walla Walla served as the miners' jumping-off place, and the 1860 gold strikes at Orofino Creek in Idaho just east of the Nez Perce reservation attracted new hordes of white prospectors who crossed Indian land to the new goldfield. Supposedly the 1855 treaty kept miners off the reservation, but neither the local agent nor the army garrison commanders had any effective power to stop the miners, who increasingly moved through the area. In fact so many newcomers poured into the region that the officers took little action to stop prospectors from traveling through the ceded land or even across the reservations. They defended their inaction, saying that only the white farmers posed a threat to the Indians because they wanted to occupy the land permanently. Even if the miners caused some incidents, they would leave once the gold supply ran out.[19]

Here the officials miscalculated badly. Had the miners come alone, it might have been possible to avoid trouble, but they did not. Teamsters, saloon keepers, merchants, and a host of others flocked into the camps to serve the miners. This influx, which soon numbered at least 18,000 men, made both the government and the Indian leaders helpless. Repeated incidents of violence, robbery, and murder pitted the newcomers against the reservation people. At the same time some of the annuity goods and supplies from the government proved nearly worthless. Instead of the promised supplies, blankets, and tools that the Indians expected, shoddy material and often useless items arrived. That did nothing to diffuse anti-American anger and further divided Nez Perce society and its leaders. Lawyer and his supporters ignored the angry disapproval of many and accepted the treaty goods without any complaint.[20]

Whether they welcomed the Americans' presence and goods or objected bitterly to their changing circumstances, the Indians could do little to change the situation. As so often in the past among other groups discussed earlier, religious leaders offered alternate paths for their listeners to follow. Falling somewhere between the active leadership roles of the Red Stick prophets among the Creeks in 1812 and the only partially engaged efforts of White Crow, the Winnebago-Sauk Prophet, in 1832, the teachings of the Dreamer Prophet Smohalla during the 1850s and 1860s added another layer of friction and misunderstanding between the races.

His ideas, known as the Washani Creed, opposed both farming and mining, denounced signing papers that surrendered any Indian land to the whites, and called for a rejection of virtually all white ways. They appealed to many traditional Nez Perce opponents of Lawyer and his supporters, some of whom had cut their hair and begun farming. Their actions created disputes within the tribe resembling those that had developed among the Dakota Sioux and the Creeks earlier. Many of the traditionalists found elements of the Dreamers' teaching attractive, but others adopted only a few parts of the message. Local white officials denounced all of their tribal opponents as Dreamers while trying to depict them as heathen savages.[21]

As American physical and cultural assaults battered the northwestern tribes, territorial officials worked to extend U.S. political institutions into the new mining settlements. Edward Geary, the superintendent of Indian affairs for the Northwest, recognized that he had absolutely no power to keep the intruders off Nimiipuu lands. He hoped to prevent more white violence by getting the tribal leaders at Lapwai to accept a treaty that would move them farther from the miners and incoming settlers. This treaty, signed on April 10, 1861, opened part of Nez Perce lands north of the Snake and Clearwater Rivers to the miners. By this time the headmen seem to have accepted Lawyer's warning that any effort to force the white settlers and miners out might bring war and the loss of even more land. Whatever the other village leaders thought about his arguments made little difference. The miners had already occupied the territory, and the Indians got nothing for losing much of their remaining land because the Senate failed to ratify the treaty.[22]

Even if the new agreement had calmed the Indians' fears, it did little to end pressures from the ever-growing nearby mining communities. As thousands of newcomers pushed onto tribal lands, Nez Perce society adapted quickly. Some individuals operated ferries or worked as teamsters or guides. Others supplied livestock, food, and even forage for the miners' livestock. These increasing contacts further divided village leaders. Some called for an all-out war to exterminate the miners, while others rejected that idea. Again the headmen could not agree on any single tactic. Arguments made during the debates clearly showed the impact of white actions. Speaking against war, one of the chiefs pointed out how his village benefited from the mining. "The white men dig up and take the gold," he said. "What then? We get some of it. They buy our beef and pay for it with some of this gold." He went on to say that he would learn how to farm because the whites would buy his crops. While he admitted that earlier he had favored war, "now my eyes are open. I say peace."[23]

As many villagers adapted to the individualistic economy that threatened to engulf them, existing disagreements about how to deal with the onrushing Americans became ever more clearly defined. Lawyer and the more nearly acculturated headmen struggled to keep peace with the miners and within the tribe. Traditionalists such as Joseph, Eagle In The Light, and a few others sought to avoid the intruders and the new economic practices that they brought completely. At the same time both groups objected to the intruders' penetrating further onto Indian land and to the total lack of justice for thievery, personal injury, and loss of their land at the hands of the white invaders. As conditions worsened, the village leaders insisted that the tribe deserved better treatment because it had kept peace with Americans since the first encounter with Lewis and Clark more than a half-century earlier. Some officials agreed, but they lacked any effective power to stop the flood of miners.[24]

Having almost entirely failed to protect the Indians or to live up to assurances made during the earlier treaty councils, the United States decided to reduce the tribal land base again. It called for yet another treaty, which would acquire title to the mineral-bearing lands and at the same time move the Nez Perces out of harm's way. During early 1863 Congress appropriated money for the new talks, and in November of that year local officials told tribal leaders to prepare for another council the next spring. On May 25, 1863, the new discussions began. Calvin H. Hale, then superintendent of Indian affairs in Washington Territory, led the American delegation. Lawyer and other acculturated chiefs represented the tribe because the leaders of the traditionalist nontreaty bands had not arrived when the meetings began. The superintendent chose the lands occupied by Lawyer and other cooperative chiefs as the site for the proposed new reservation, in order to get their quick acceptance.

When they heard Hale's demand that they surrender almost nine-tenths of Nez Perce territory and that all of the bands would have to squeeze into the Lapwai Valley and the land nearby, however, even the leaders in favor of the treaty protested. They correctly feared that approving those borders would bring nothing but trouble among the bands and immediately objected. Reminding the Americans that the United States still had not paid them for land ceded in 1855, Lawyer and several other chiefs replied that the Nez Perces would sell no more land. Chief Utsinmalikin echoed Lawyer's remarks. After telling the commissioner that the Indians considered the 1855 boundary "permanent and sacred," he attacked the proposal, saying that "it does not look good, it looks crooked. . . . We have answered you, we cannot sell our country."[25] Hale could only respond weakly that the government had promised earlier to survey land for each family. Then the Nez Perces would no longer need the rest of the reservation, so the government expected to sell the excess later. At that point the meeting adjourned in confusion.

A few days after the traditionalist, nontreaty bands arrived on June 3, 1863, the council resumed. Their leaders said little in the public meetings but had no reason to support the new reservation. Hale's proposal called for them to leave their customary homeland and to move to a much smaller area then home to the acculturated northern bands. By now clear divisions separated the Nez Perce bands. Leaders of the northern groups along the Clearwater River had accepted Christianity; those in the south practiced the Dreamer Religion and other Indian religious ceremonies. Many of the acculturated people had become farmers, while their traditional relatives continued their long-practiced hunting, gathering, and fishing activities. Under Hale's proposal the southern bands would have to surrender their entire homeland, change their way of life, and move into an area dominated by their acculturated neighbors.

Most traditionalist band leaders remained opposed to any such basic changes in their lives or any surrender of their land. While the commissioners negotiated with the more acculturated upper band leaders, the chiefs of the lower bands remained aloof at first. Then fifty-three chiefs representing all of the bands met on June 5 to discuss the American demands. Lawyer and his colleagues urged acceptance of the new treaty, while others spoke against it in a heated all-night council. When it became clear that they could not agree on a unified response, the headmen of the traditional bands rejected the proposal. Then they announced that "the Nez Perce nation [was] dissolved": while the bands might remain friends, now they were "a distinct People." In their minds this declaration signaled an unwillingness to accept agreements concluded by the other Nez Perce band chiefs.[26]

Within a few hours the nontreaty bands left the council grounds and returned home. At this point the Nez Perce division over accepting or rejecting the 1863 treaty resembled that of the Sauks and Mesquakies in Illinois and the Cheyennes and Arapahos in Colorado. In both those instances the intertribal divisions stemmed primarily from basic disagreements over the location of their home territory and how to respond to the continuing white demands for them to surrender all or much of their tribal lands. In each instance the independence of every village or band leader, competition among differing groups of chiefs, disagreements over how much social and economic change to accept, and even misunderstandings about American actions divided the tribes and led to violence and warfare with the United States. Even though village leaders repeatedly rejected the idea of a single tribal spokesman, American officials refused to accept or recognize the existing diffuse Nez Perce leadership. The bureaucrats insisted that entire tribes accept decisions made by a few individuals or a single spokesman. The tribal people asserted that only those bands whose chiefs had actually signed a treaty had to observe its demands. Others simply ignored the agreements.[27]

Once the traditionalist bands left the council grounds Commissioner Hale and his companions worked quickly to persuade the rest of the village chiefs to accept the new terms. They explained that the United States could not defend them from the aggressive miners then pouring into their country and that this agreement offered them the best chance to retain some of their land. When the arm twisting ended, on June 9, 1863, Lawyer helped get the signatures of Thunder Eyes, Eagle In The Light, and a few other opposition chiefs.[28] The treaty surrendered almost ninety percent of Nez Perce land. It established a reservation centered on the territory already occupied by Lawyer's band and the other acculturated villages. Once they chose not to sign the pact, the nontreaty bands returned home with Joseph and White Bird, apparently unaware that the 1863 treaty required that they join the other Nez Perce bands on the new reservation. When officials told them that they had to relocate, they refused. In their view the treaty simply had no power over them because they had not signed it. This rejection of the new circumstances did nothing to calm the volatile situation. Thousands of miners continued to stake claims, cut timber, steal Indian cattle and horses, and bring alcohol into some of the villages. To confuse matters further, because of the Civil War the Senate ignored the treaty and took until April 1867, four years later, to ratify it. In the meantime, while the Indians failed to receive even the modest payments they expected, frontier whites acted as if the treaty had gone into effect: encroachments, violence, and disruption of village life continued.[29]

Other issues upset life for all of the Nez Perce bands whether they lived on the new reservation or not. The promised annuities from the earlier 1855 treaty trickled in slowly if at all. In fact nine years later Lawyer protested that the white bureaucrats had not fulfilled any of their commitments to the tribe. "We have no church . . . no school house . . . no doctor . . . no gunsmith . . . no blacksmith . . . I stand here . . . naked as far as these promises are fulfilled."[30] At times these pledges had not been kept because of the Civil War. Even when the goods did arrive, local officials stole most of the funds. The chiefs' complaints about whiskey peddlers went unanswered, and pioneers who cut timber on Indian land refused to pay for it. Meanwhile, no money arrived to pay for the survey of Nez Perce land into the promised twenty-acre allotments. By this time Lawyer may well have regretted his position as the recognized spokesman: his frequent complaints brought no response.

In 1867, shortly after the government ratified the now four-year-old treaty, officials in the General Land Office moved to open more of the Northwest for settlement. They decided that the 1863 agreement had surrendered all Nez Perce claims to land outside the clearly defined reservation borders. In 1867 survey crews arrived in the Wallowa Valley, the traditional homeland of Joseph's nontreaty band. The surveyors returned for the next several summers as the government prepared to sell the rich grasslands. When that happened, the Indians lost their relative isolation and in just a few years faced aggressive white settlers who brought their herds of cattle into the valley. The federal government had encouraged the newcomers to take up lands acquired by the 1863 treaty, so the cattle raisers had no reason to listen to Nez Perce complaints that they had never sold the land.[31]

While the nontreaty bands encountered increasing numbers of white pioneers, the Indians living on the reservation fared little better. Lawyer complained repeatedly about the government's failure to provide buildings, goods, and money promised by the 1863 treaty. Completely exasperated, he wrote directly to President Andrew Johnson asking for permission to visit Washington to correct the continuing problems. His request reached the capital at a time when federal officials had decided that they needed to amend the 1863 treaty. In April 1868 they brought Lawyer and three other acculturated chiefs east for meetings. Just as had happened three years earlier, this delegation failed to include anyone who represented the nontreaty bands, so once again many of the Nez Perce chiefs had no part in the discussions. Despite that, Lawyer, Timothy, and Jason signed yet another treaty. The new agreement ceded land for an army post on the reservation. In return American officials promised the Indians that the troops would help protect their timber. They offered to make additional twenty-acre land allotments for members of the nontreaty bands if the reservation lacked enough land for them. The document also pledged to pay the funds for the Nez Perce school promised earlier so that federal acculturation efforts could continue.[32]

Events during the early 1870s brought permanent changes for the Indians in the Northwest. President Ulysses Grant's Quaker or Peace Policy sought to acculturate the tribal peoples, remake them as Christian farmers, and incorporate them into the general society. Its supporters expected that this renewed effort at acculturation would open more tribal lands throughout the west for white economic development. In 1871 Congress abolished the treaty system. Now the government could avoid holding lengthy and expensive councils with tribal groups. That meant that officials heard even less of the Indians' views than earlier. That same year Old Joseph, the respected band leader, died. His son, with the same name but soon called Chief Joseph, became a civil chief and assumed much of the band leadership. While his followers mourned Joseph's passing, white stock grazers crossed the mountains and began moving into the Wallowa Valley. At first little friction between the Indians and the newcomers occurred, but in a few years the usual pattern of minor disputes and local violence developed. The government land survey and its encouragement of white cattle raisers to move into the traditional home of the largest of the nontreaty Nez Perce bands played a central role in the disputes that followed.[33]

From his earliest meetings with the Americans moving into the valley Chief Joseph explained that his father had never signed any papers selling the land to the United States. In response the officials told him that the government considered the 1863 treaty to have given up the Wallowa

Valley and assured them that ranchers could settle there. They tried to persuade the Nez Perces that the valley had plenty of room for animals belonging to both Indians and whites to graze and that they intended to remain. Despite their disagreements Joseph claimed to want friendly dealings with the pioneers and said that his band would remain at peace. As soon as he heard about the dispute the agent John Monteith met the chief to learn the band's intentions. Joseph asked him to stop the pioneers' intrusions and repeated his view that his father had never sold the valley. When Monteith replied that he lacked authority to remove the white settlers, the tensions continued.[34]

Apparently the chief's determination to remain on the land and his utter conviction that the valley still belonged to his band impressed the agent, so he wrote to his superiors that "if there is any way by which the Wallowa Valley could be kept for the Indians, I would recommend that be done."[35] A year later another council with the chief led to the same conclusion: Chief Lawyer had had no right to sign away land in 1863 belonging to all of the Nez Perce bands. Monteith, this time supported by T. B. Odeneal, superintendent of Indian affairs in Oregon, raised serious doubts about the treaty's validity. These reports brought a surprisingly quick response from Washington. In May 1873 Interior Department officials reported that the president would sign an executive order setting the valley apart for the Indians. Just when it seemed that this would settle the impasse a bureaucratic mistake compounded matters. Indian office clerks misunderstood the local boundaries and apportioned the valley in exactly the opposite manner from what both Indians and white bureaucrats had expected.[36]

The document called on the settlers and Nez Perces to exchange land rather than keep what they already occupied. This blunder left both groups dissatisfied, but the government promised to pay the pioneers for their improvements when they moved. That never happened. In fact during the next two years more newcomers entered the Wallowa Valley, so encroachments on Indian land continued. At the same time the public mood in the region became increasingly anti-Indian. Agent Monteith reflected this shift in his meetings with Joseph when the chief complained about how roughly the pioneers treated his people. As agent Thomas Forsyth had done in Illinois a half-century earlier, Monteith played down the Indians' concerns, blamed them for the ongoing troubles, and told the chief that his band should join the rest of the tribe in Idaho. Then in May 1874 news arrived that the government had reversed its decision to establish the promised new reservation in the Wallowa Valley. Now the settlers could remain, even though President Grant's executive order remained on the books.[37]

Agent Monteith made matters worse by not explaining the shift. When the Indians asked settlers to leave the land set aside for the new reservation, they refused, saying that the country now belonged to them. The Nez Perces called them liars, and tensions increased rapidly. News from other nontreaty groups brought stories of more white violence, and young men from Joseph's band began to talk about war. At the same time rumors of possible Indian violence brought troops to investigate, but they found no signs of danger. That summer Nez Perce leaders met to decide how they should deal with the white settlers. The group included Joseph, Ollokot, White Bird, Looking Glass, Red Owl, and Toohoolhoolzote, who led one of the other nontreaty bands. They asked some of the most respected warriors if they should join the Cayuses and another group in eastern Washington in an antiwhite war, but those men urged staying at peace. Despite that decision and Joseph's efforts to assure the neighboring white settlers, the pioneers asked for more protection. Two companies of troops moved into the valley.[38]

In September 1874 General Oliver O. Howard arrived to take command of the Department of the Columbia. A man with considerable experience as a commander during the Civil War and a committed Christian with a strong sense of morality, he felt personally chosen by God to work with the Indians. He had dealt with former slaves while commissioner of the Freedmen's Bureau and with the Apaches when he helped engineer a peace with Cochise just a few years earlier. Shortly after the general and the Nez Perce chief met in 1875, news that President Grant had reversed his 1873 executive order arrived. The Wallowa Valley now lay open for white occupation. When Agent Monteith explained this to Joseph, he called another council of nontreaty band leaders. After some debate the chiefs decided against war and returned home. Hoping to ensure peace, Monteith asked General Howard to send troops to the valley again, and he dispatched another two companies of cavalry. The officers of those units reported to Howard the Nez Perces' insistence that they had never given up their land. He in turn recommended that the government buy out the settlers and allow the Indians to remain, but the idea got no support in Washington.[39]

By this time regional politicians wanted to force the nontreaty bands to move onto the 1863 Idaho reservation centered at Lapwai as new rumors of Indian thievery and insolence circulated among the nervous white settlers. As often happened, however, the settlers, not the Indians, caused the next violent incident. In June 1876 some pioneers looking for lost horses came to an Indian camp and shot Wilhautyah, one of the young men there, without provocation. When Howard heard the news, he ordered troops back to the valley and sent one of his aides to Lapwai to investigate the murder. The information that he received persuaded the general that the land claims of the nontreaty bands had a solid base and that the government needed to recognize them. Still, Howard assumed that the only honest solution involved paying the Indians and then moving them to Lapwai with the rest of the Nez Perces. The answer to the question of what needed to be done if the band leaders rejected payment and an unwanted move to the reservation seemed clear. They would have no choice.[40] In the weeks that followed the shooting, Howard sent Major H. Clay Wood to meet Nez Perce leaders, who explained their claims again.

Tensions remained high while Howard waited for more direction from Washington because local civilian authorities failed to arrest the two men who had killed young Wilhautyah. Two months after the murder some of the band chiefs led their men to the settlers' cabins. They warned the frightened inhabitants to leave the valley and demanded that they turn over suspected murderers Wells McNall and Alexander Findley to them. When the settlers refused, the warriors rode off. In mid-September a local judge in the small town of Union heard their cases. He charged Findley with manslaughter but found that McNall had committed no crime. Officials encouraged the Indians to send witnesses to the trial, but they apparently refused to testify. One source suggests that they may have thought that McNall rather than Findley deserved punishment. Tribal people often refused to testify in white courts for religious reasons or because they did not understand the process and did not expect to get justice. If the witnesses were Dreamers, that would explain their refusal.[41]

In November 1876 the commission that General Howard had requested reached Lapwai. Its members included three easterners, David Jerome, A. C. Barstow, and William Stickney (none of whom had any experience in Indian affairs), and Howard and his aide Major Henry Wood. At this point Presbyterian agent Monteith and the general discussed the negative impact that the ideas of Smohalla the Dreamer Prophet had among the nontreaty Nez Perce groups. But neither of them had any clear understanding of the prophet's teachings or what influence they had on Joseph or the other chiefs. As a conservative Christian, the general objected to the Dreamers' "heathen" ideas and feared their potential for causing trouble. The agent objected to the Dreamers because they blocked his efforts to evangelize the off-reservation groups, and the other three commissioners knew nothing about these religious issues.[42]

From the start the American officials took the offensive. The nontreaty bands had to obey the 1863 treaty and move to the existing reservation, where they would receive fair payment for their land. The government's position had unexpectedly changed from just a year earlier when General Howard had suggested that the Nez Perces be allowed to remain in the Wallowa Valley. Joseph replied that the Indians wanted only a chance to remain in their traditional home area. As he had done repeatedly, he described Nez Perce beliefs about the permanent connections between the land and the people. The chief explained that those strong cultural ties meant that they could not leave the valley or sell it to the Americans. As the discussions ended, the commissioners noted the obvious tension among the Indians. In their report to Washington, they called for troops to be sent to occupy the Wallowa Valley and show the government's determination to force the nontreaty people onto the reservation.[43]

The situation deteriorated after the meeting as the United States continued to demand Nez Perce removal and band leaders refused. In fact Indian beliefs about their relationship with nature stood in direct opposition to American policy, which called for the usual three-pronged approach to acculturation: school, farm, and church. Instead of persuading the Americans, the spiritual defenses offered by Joseph and other band leaders only angered the commissioners, who denounced Indian religious beliefs as deluded "pernicious doctrines." In early 1877 the secretary of the interior accepted the general's recommendations and ordered local officials to put them into effect. The last of the Nez Perce bands had to move onto the reservation. Yet because the army had orders to keep peace and protect Indian office personnel, final authority for dealing with the bands remained in civilian hands.[44]

In May 1877 agent Monteith called the four nontreaty bands to Lapwai for yet another council. Actions at this meeting led directly to the war, as the Indians reported later. When the Nez Perces arrived, they choose Toohoolhoolzote as their spokesman. A respected older warrior and firm follower of the Dreamer teachings, he offended General Howard from the start. Unlike the diplomatic Joseph, his blunt talk and refusal to consider any compromise infuriated Howard. In fact he later described the band spokesman as an "obstinate savage" when the chief continued his insistence that the decision by some band leaders to cede their land to the whites had no relevance for his people. They had not signed that agreement and would not be bound by it. When the general described both whites and Indians as children of the national government, the chief responded that the Indians were not children and outsiders "shall not think for us."[45]

As the two men continued to talk past each other, Howard became increasingly angry. "Twenty times over I hear that the earth is your mother," he snapped. "I want to hear it no more." When the chief asked who claimed the authority to put him on the reservation, the general answered, "I am the man." When asked point-blank if he would go to the reservation, Toohoolhoolzote replied, "I am not going to the reservation."[46] Angrily Howard threatened to send the aged band spokesman to Indian Territory (present Oklahoma). Howard and Captain David Perry took the chief to the nearby guardhouse. When the two officers returned, the general asked the other band leaders if they would move to the reservation: they reluctantly agreed. As the meeting ended Howard thought that he had diffused the situation and achieved his goal, but he misread the situation entirely. He believed that his firm actions had persuaded the band leaders to cooperate, but they had just angered the Indians.[47]

As the chiefs left the council on May 14 Howard told them that they had thirty days to move their people to Lapwai. Their anger and resentment became plain. During the meetings the white spokesmen had publicly ridiculed their respected leaders and rejected their religious beliefs. Many of them considered Howard's rough and disrespectful treatment of Toohoolhoolzote and the general's threat to use soldiers to drive the villagers from their homes to be going far beyond accepted council behavior. Some described his actions as a threat of war. Some years later Yellow Wolf claimed that what the Indians saw as Howard's arrest of the chief and having armed soldiers near the council meeting grounds caused the war.[48] The day after this tense meeting with Howard the angry Indians left for home to gather their goods and animals.

In mid-June 1877 the nontreaty bands camped just a few miles from the reservation to talk and socialize one last time before moving to their new homes. By now all of the leaders seemed reconciled to their future, but anger and resentment fueled continuing talk of war. This led to the incident on June 13 when one of the young men challenged Shore Crossing to avenge his father's murder. Once he and his companions left camp the next day and began their rampage, the chiefs lost control: for several days war parties swept through the area. Their uncoordinated attacks resembled events in the Minnesota war fifteen years earlier. Armed parties repeatedly attacked individual families, farms, and small groups, shooting, burning homes and other buildings, and raping female captives, before the initial frenzy of violence ended. Then the bands moved to nearby White Bird Canyon. While they gathered, reports of the attacks and desperate calls for help reached Howard, who sent troops.

The war that followed dragged on for months as the Indians fled almost fifteen hundred miles through the northern Rockies toward Canada with army units in pursuit. Choosing to escape across the border, they followed the examples of many other tribes, beginning with the Mohawks under Joseph Brant who moved north into Canada at the end of the American Revolution. In 1862 Chief Little Crow had led Dakota Sioux north too. In the same year when the Nez Perces hoped to find safety north of the border, Sitting Bull also led hundreds of Lakota Sioux into Canada. Only a few of the Idaho refugees escaped, and most of the fugitives surrendered in early October 1877, surrounded by U.S. troops just fifty miles south of the border. There Chief Joseph sent Nelson A. Miles a message that became his famous "I Will Fight No More" speech.

The colonel told the Indians that they could return to Idaho the next spring, but his superiors overruled that promise. Rather than escorting them back to their homes in the Northwest the army sent them to Fort Leavenworth as prisoners. From there in July 1879 Office of Indian Affairs personnel supervised their transfer to Indian Territory. They lived there until 1885, when officials agreed to send several hundred of the survivors home. They returned to the Colville or Lapwai reservations that year. Once details of how badly the United States had treated the

Nez Perces were known, Joseph became a kind of public hero as Black Hawk had after his earlier defeat. His story received wide public attention, but the authorities never allowed him to return to his beloved Wallowa Valley. He died on September 21, 1904, still an exile.

The Nez Perce experiences did not mark the end of white-Indian violence in the West. Fighting against the Lakota Sioux on the northern plains continued into 1877. The next year fighting broke on the Ute Reservation in Colorado, and repeated Apache flights from their reservations in Arizona during the 1880s kept the army busy and civilians tense for another decade. By then tribal populations had plummeted, and U.S. actions had pushed all but a handful of them onto isolated western reservations. With military resistance crushed, the Indian Office personnel returned to the cultural violence that they had used for a century. Now policies to disrupt Native ceremonies and religious beliefs, to destroy tribal languages, and to coerce individual reservation residents to copy all things American came into force. Although they failed to transform many Indians into mere copies of white Americans, they did far more harm than good.

Conclusion

Hindsight is supposed to be twenty-twenty, but that claim rarely applies when one is writing history. In this case it perhaps fits even less than usual. Often the actions and decisions that led to these wars took place far removed from the hearing and sight of credible witnesses or would-be scribes. While all of the leading participants operated from self-interest, the pervasive greed, constant fraud, and bitter racial and ethnic hostility on the part of Anglo-Americans made them more to blame for these events than the Indians. Certainly the tribal people committed plenty of brutal acts and waged their own wars of aggression, but often they aimed most of their diplomatic and military actions at other tribes, not at the invading Europeans and Americans. To label the conflicts examined here "Indian Wars" diverts attention from their basic causes and begins the analysis from the wrong point of departure. They need instead to be considered wars of American aggression that were central to the territorial expansion that created the nation's present land area. In every case these conflicts resulted directly from a massive, century-long invasion of North America. That population movement brought the newcomers into areas occupied by highly militarized Native communities ready and able to defend themselves and attack their enemies. Encounters between the two led to the almost complete dispossession of indigenous peoples.

The Indians' experiences created a circumstance that stands as a polar opposite from those of other minorities in American society. Most immigrants coming to the United States looked to their new homeland in one or more of several ways: it might offer a refuge or even provide a chance for a better life. Many hoped to get some of the land and its resources for themselves. Tribal people did not share the immigrants' expectations. They already lived in established communities and had few reasons, if any, to look at their frontier neighbors favorably or to join the nearby white society. Often these conflicting desires brought the two groups into direct competition with each other. American Indians occupied much of the land and claimed its resources, while the newcomers hoped or expected to get both. As long as the relations remained peaceful, the two sides tolerated each other briefly. When open conflict broke out and the Native peoples tried to drive the invaders away, the pioneers cried "Exterminate them!"

Most of the forty wars that the United States fought against the Indians that the Census Bureau identified in 1894 shared some of the broad causes included in the following list:

Multitribal confederacy: Ohio Valley tribes
Single or joint tribal actions: Creeks, Arikaras, Sauks-Mesquakies, Dakotas, Cheyennes and Arapahos, Apaches, Nez Perces
Divided and competing tribal leadership: all but the Apaches
International border issues: Ohio Valley–British, Creeks-Spanish, Apaches–Spanish and Mexicans
Some clear religious motivation: Creeks, Sauks-Mesquakies, Nez Perces
U.S. acculturation efforts: all but Arikaras and Apaches
Trade and multitribal conflict: Arikaras
Accidental war: Sauks-Mesquakies
Neglect resulting from U.S. Civil War: Dakotas, Cheyennes and Arapahos
Questionable treaties and corruption: Sauks-Mesquakies, Dakotas, Cheyennes and Arapahos, Apaches, Nez Perces
Pioneer aggression: All of the tribes
Tribal aggression: Ohio Valley tribes, Arikaras, Cheyennes and Arapahos, Apaches
U.S. military aggression: Cheyennes and Arapahos, Apaches

Whether needy or greedy, in almost every case the invading whites demanded that the government do one of two things: either clear tribal people out of each new frontier zone or step aside so that the pioneers could do that without any outside interference. Regardless of differing local circumstances, fear, hatred, and self-interest motivated the newcomers throughout the century examined here. The Indians had counterdemands. As longtime occupants of their home territories, they expected deferential treatment. When that failed to happen, they negotiated with visiting American treaty commissioners to get much-desired and -needed goods. They also sought assurances of government protection for their land and way of life. Whatever promises the officials made, they either could not or would not fulfill them. The entire process portrayed America at its worst. It resulted from a self-righteous, immoral, and often dishonest compulsion to spread "American values" by any means, fair or foul.

For the whites, economic motivations played only one part in the process that followed. Neither they nor the Indians could escape the ethnocentrism or racism that marked their intercultural relations. The old generalization suggesting that the farther one lived from tribal people the more likely that one could feel compassion for them held considerable truth. Frontier citizens saw Indians as poor, drunken, dirty, and badly clothed vagabonds or as dangerous savages who could neither be trusted nor become civilized—hardly people they wanted as neighbors and certainly not potential members of American society. Easterners and others who had little contact with Indians could entertain more benign ideas because the Native peoples would never become their close neighbors. Whatever pious noises such people might make, they supported the government's acculturation program based on Christianity, education, and agriculture, to be carried out in near-isolation from the rest of society. Clearly aware of this ethnocentrism, tribes including the Creeks, Dakotas, Cheyennes, and Nez Perces had to deal with the "civilization" program, as eastern reformers labeled it. The more most Indians dealt with Americans and their government, the more negative their views of the whites became. Often the villagers considered their white pioneer neighbors to be selfish and greedy because they refused to share, dangerous because they destroyed the game and damaged the local environment, and dishonest and untrustworthy when they promised one thing and did something else. Broken promises brought repeated frustration and anger because Indians expected whites to live up to their pledges. Often the villagers saw Anglo-Americans as egotistical and pushy when they demanded changes from the indigenous societies.

In almost every instance U.S. officials could not or would not accept tribal customs as they dealt with tribal people. Perhaps during the early decades after Independence the easterners who served as negotiators really lacked knowledge of how the village societies functioned. Certainly they followed colonial-era British practices for negotiating treaties with the Indians. Yet earlier British officials like Sir William Johnson, who dealt with the Six Nations Iroquois in present New York, understood clearly how those tribes conducted their affairs. From the days of Lewis and Clark through most of the nineteenth century Americans tried to brush aside band and village practices; they chose a single man to serve as the tribal chief and then tried to hold him responsible for compliance with treaty demands. In some cases frontier officials had to recognize that no single man could sign for all, yet they ignored or rejected tribal practices that required all of the leaders to agree on any decision before it would be binding on them.

The policy of demanding that Indians abandon their traditional practices related to clan responsibility for retaliation when outsiders caused injury or death in their villages provides another example of American ignorance or rejection of tribal customs. Clan members had a duty to exact revenge on outsiders who harmed their clan relatives. That responsibility encouraged raiding, which in turn offered young men chances to exhibit their valor as warriors and their skill at gathering plunder for their home villages. When frontier officials demanded that the Indians stop their attacks and allow the government to make payments to "cover the blood" of the injury, they reduced or inhibited efforts to demonstrate male virtues of bravery, cunning, and leadership. Even chiefs who signed agreements to end the retaliatory raids knew that they lacked any power to enforce the promise in their own villages. When the raids continued and local agents tried to end them or to punish either the chiefs for agreeing to end the practices or the young men who had taken part in the raids, that caused bitter anger among the villagers. This occurred most among the Sauk, Mesquakie, Cheyenne, and Nez Perce peoples.

The constant demands for Indian land and resources proved a central motivation for the acculturation program. American policy makers assumed that once the villagers stopped depending on hunting, trapping, and gathering they would agree to give up most of their land. After all, sedentary farmers needed far less land than roaming hunters. This ignored the large-scale crop-raising of the Ohio Valley people, Creeks, Sauks, Mesquakies, and Nez Perces. It also overlooked the strong spiritual attachment of all the groups to their particular home areas. The Cheyenne buffalo hunters claimed certain river valleys and other parts of the central plains as their traditional territory. The Chiricahua Apaches refused to leave their Ojo Caliente Valley, and Chief Joseph's band of Nez Perces rejected calls to move from the Wallowa Valley for similar reasons. Their traditional homeland held particular and significant meanings for each of these groups. Some locations served as sites for sacred religious ceremonies. Others might be considered essential for successful gathering, fishing, or farming. Of the tribes discussed here only the Arikara people seem to have lacked these strong connections to their particular location. All of the others eventually fought to defend themselves from being forced to move from their traditional homeland.

The entire system shaping American relationships with the tribes proved creaky and ineffective. Because it required U.S. Senate approval for each pact, often months or even years passed before any agreement took effect. Before Indians received their promised goods or annuities began, pioneers pushed onto the ceded land; when tribal leaders asked for protection from the intruders, the government ignored them. Once the chiefs signed treaties, the War Department and later the Interior Department shared the responsibilities for implementing the agreement. That led to repeated disputes between civilian and military authorities over who should direct the process. During actual negotiations American officials chose not to explain the provisions in the agreement fully or failed to mention them at all. For example, negotiators such as William Henry Harrison in the Mississippi Valley or Isaac Stevens in Oregon concluded documents that had articles that Indian chiefs either failed to understand or had no idea of their content. Even when chicanery had no part in the discussions, the oral and written aspects of treaty councils had widely divergent meanings for Indians and whites.[1] Tribal chiefs complained repeatedly that Americans said one thing but did something else. The Sauk warrior Black Hawk voiced this frustration and anger when he said: "[H]ow smooth must be the language of the whites, when they can make right look like wrong, and wrong like right."[2]

It seems clear that the repeated negotiations between federal officials and village leaders did little to ease the friction between the two societies. Looking back over these wars it is hard to see how they might have been avoided. No doubt people of goodwill occasionally represented one or both sides, but their actions had little impact on the existing disputes between the invaders and the indigenous people. Ethnocentrism drove both groups. The exploding Anglo-American population brought demands for land and resource uses that left no room for many traditional Indian economic practices. White insistence that Indians abandon long-held and traditional significant areas struck directly at tribal customs and culture. The future proposed to indigenous people seemed unappealing at best. Basically they had to surrender their culture and identity. Even if some chose to do that, however, Americans seldom welcomed them into the white society. They had few options. Some fled. Others accepted some changes. When all else failed they defended their societies and homelands from repeated American cultural, economic, diplomatic, and military attacks. Because these contests pitted groups with vastly differing demographic, economic, and military resources, it comes as no surprise that the invaders won.

Notes

INTRODUCTION

1. *Report on Indians, 1890,* 637.

2. Barnes, *Perpetual War;* Divine, *Perpetual War;* and Vidal, *Perpetual War.*

3. To call this strife "Indian Wars" mislabels it, but the term remains firmly entrenched. This text uses the terms "Indian," "Native American," "tribe," "band," "tribal people," "indigenous people," and "villagers" on one side and "Americans," "Anglo-Americans," "citizens," "pioneers," "invaders," "settlers," and "whites" on the other to spare readers what often becomes the deadly repetition of the terms "whites" and "Indians."

4. Lee, "Peace Chiefs"; Grenier, *First Way of War;* Hämäläinen, *Comanche Empire;* Blackhawk, *Violence over the Land;* Calloway, *Shawnees and the War for America;* Calloway, *Scratch of a Pen.*

5. *Report on Indians, 1890,* 637–38. See also Thornton, *American Indian Holocaust,* 27–49.

6. For up-to-date comparisons, see Miller, *Skyscrapers Hide the Heavens;* and Reynolds, *Other Side of the Frontier.*

7. Nichols, *Lincoln and the Indians;* and Hatch, *Black Kettle.*

8. DiLorenzo, *Lincoln Unmasked;* Stannard, *American Holocaust;* Thornton, *American Indian Holocaust;* and Churchill, *Little Matter of Genocide.*

9. Clifton, *Being and Becoming Indian,* 6.

10. Anderson, *Conquest of Texas,* 7–11.

11. Washington to Pickering, July 1, 1796, in Washington, *Writings of George Washington,* 35:112.

12. Hurtado, *Indian Survival;* Jacoby, *Shadows at Dawn;* and Anderson, *Conquest of Texas.*

13. Silver, *Our Savage Neighbors,* xix–xxiii.

14. Knouff, "Soldiers and Violence," 171–93; and Calloway, "'We Have Always Been the Frontier.'"

15. Bloom, *American Territorial System;* Champagne, "Multidimensional Theory of Colonialism"; Cooper, *Colonialism in Question;* Ostler, *Plains Sioux;* and Whaley, *Oregon.*

16. *Congressional Globe,* 30th Cong., 2d session, 514, 678.

17. Senator James Nesmith, May 13, 1862; quoted in Nichols, *Lincoln and the Indians,* 7.

18. Utley, *Indian Frontier*; Vandervort, *Indian Wars*; and Wooster, *American Military Frontiers.*

19. Deloria, *Playing Indian.*

CHAPTER 1. THE OHIO VALLEY WAR, 1786–1795

1. Dozens of books and perhaps hundreds of articles consider aspects of this conflict. For these incidents see Faragher, *Daniel Boone,* 252–54; and Sugden, *Blue Jacket,* 74–75.

2. Faragher, *Daniel Boone,* chs. 4–6; Lofaro, *Daniel Boone,* chs. 5–7; Calloway, *Shawnees and the War,* 67–84; and Calloway, *Scratch of a Pen,* chs. 1 and 3.

3. Downes, *Council Fires,* gives a dated but still authoritative account. For a more recent discussion with an international and multigenerational approach see Skaggs and Nelson, *Sixty Year's War.* Kluger, *Seizing Destiny,* 52–83, gives a general outline, while White, *Middle Ground,* has a nuanced analysis of ethnic issues in the region.

4. Quoted in Horsman, *Expansion,* 19. See also Calloway, *American Revolution,* 282–83.

5. Calloway, *Shawnees and the War,* 79–84; and Horsman, *Expansion,* 22–23.

6. Calloway, *Crown and Calumet,* 14, 16. White, *Middle Ground,* 413–16, compares the tribal and Kentucky villagers effectively.

7. Joseph Brant, "Speech of the United Indian Nations, December 18, 1786," in *American State Papers: Indian Affairs,* 1:8–9; Sugden, *Blue Jacket,* 66–67; Horsman, *Expansion,* 23; and Prucha, *Sword of the Republic,* 18–19.

8. Continental Congress, *Journals of the Continental Congress,* 28:375–81.

9. Ibid., 32:340–41.

10. Josiah Harmar, June 15, 1788, in Smith, *St. Clair Papers,* 2:44.

11. The literature on these grisly events is extensive. Knouff, "Soldiers and Violence," gives a brief account. See also Grenier, *First Way,* chs. 4–6.

12. White, *Middle Ground,* 444–48; and Horsman, *Expansion,* 46–47.

13. St. Clair to Henry Knox, January 18, 1789, in Smith, *St. Clair Papers*, 2:108; and Horsman, *Expansion*, 47–48.

14. Quoted in Sugden, *Blue Jacket*, 87.

15. Quoted in ibid., 87.

16. Henry Knox Report, June/July 1789, in *American State Papers: Indian Affairs*, 1:12–14.

17. Jacobs, *Beginnings of the U.S. Army*, 43.

18. Smith, *St. Clair Papers*, 1:162–63.

19. Quoted in Sugden, *Blue Jacket*, 96.

20. Quoted in Sword, *President Washington's Indian War*, 85.

21. Quoted in Prucha, *Sword of the Republic*, 20.

22. Ibid., 20–22; Sugden, *Blue Jacket*, 99.

23. Smith, *St. Clair Papers*, 2:185–87.

24. Quoted in Carter, *Life and Times of Little Turtle*, 93.

25. Prucha, *Sword of the Republic*, 21–22; Sword, *Washington's War*, 116.

26. Sugden, *Blue Jacket*, 105.

27. Quoted in Sword, *President Washington's Indian War*, 119.

28. Ibid., 152.

29. Quoted in Sugden, *Blue Jacket*, 107.

30. Quoted in Sword, *President Washington's Indian War*, 122.

31. Horsman, *Matthew Elliott*, 62–63, 65–67; and Sugden, *Blue Jacket*, 107–108.

32. Sword, *President Washington's Indian War*, 126–30; Sugden, *Blue Jacket*, 110–11.

33. Sword, *President Washington's Indian War*, 136–38; Sugden, *Blue Jacket*, 113.

34. Quoted in Prucha, *Sword of the Republic*, 22.

35. Sword, *President Washington's Indian War*, 131.

36. Ibid., 131–33.

37. Horsman, *Matthew Elliott*, 64–67.

38. Eid, "American Military Leadership."

39. Many authors have discussed this campaign. My data come from Prucha, *Sword of the Republic*, 26–27; Horsman, *Matthew Elliott*, 68–69; and Sugden, *Blue Jacket*, 122–27.

40. Quoted in Sword, *President Washington's Indian War*, 204.

41. Ibid., 205–206.

42. White, *Middle Ground*, 460.

43. Horsman, *Matthew Elliott*, 69–71; Sword, *President Washington's Indian War*, 195–99.

44. Sugden, *Blue Jacket*, 133–38; Sword, *President Washington's Indian War*, 208–13.

45. White, *Middle Ground*, 457–60; Carter, *Life and Times of Little Turtle*, 114–17; Sugden, *Blue Jacket*, 130–34; and Sword, *President Washington's Indian War*, 226–31.

46. Quoted in Horsman, *Matthew Elliott*, 75.

47. Ibid., 75–91, analyzes the issues that divided tribal leaders.

48. White, *Middle Ground*, 458–60; Tanner, "The Glaize," 30–33.

49. White, *Middle Ground*, 460–61.

50. Ibid., 462–66; Horsman, *Matthew Elliott*, 86–90.

51. White, *Middle Ground*, 461–62.

52. Horsman, *Matthew Elliott*, 78–82.

53. Ibid., 84–90.

54. Quoted in ibid., 93.

55. Sword, *President Washington's Indian War*, 261–62.

56. Sugden, *Blue Jacket*, 159.

57. Gaff, *Bayonets*, 243–53, has the most detailed and up-to-date account.

58. Quoted in ibid., 325.

59. Sword, *President Washington's Indian War*, 313–19.

60. Kappler, *Indian Affairs*, 2:39–45; and Gaff, *Bayonets*, 364–67.

61. For the governor's actions see Owens, *Mr. Jefferson's Hammer*, chs. 3–4. Cave, *Prophets;* Dowd, *Spirited Resistance;* Jortner, *Gods of Prophetstown;* and Warren, *Shawnees*, examine these issues.

CHAPTER 2. THE RED STICK WAR, 1813–1814

1. Quoted in Martin, *Sacred Revolt*, 151.

2. Martin presents the religious aspects of this situation clearly (ibid.).

3. Caughey, *Alexander McGillivray;* Ethridge, *Creek Country;* and Sugden, *Tecumseh,* all address their actions among the Creeks.

4. Ethridge, *Creek Country*, 22–31; Frank, *Creeks and Southerners*, 11–25; Green, *Politics of Indian Removal*, 4–24; and Hahn, *Invention of the Creek Nation*.

5. Quoted in Green, *Politics of Indian Removal*, 25.

6. Ibid., 32–34.

7. Ethridge, *Creek Country*, 180–82. Waselkov, *Conquering Spirit*, 16–55, gives a detailed analysis of the métis and their role in Creek affairs.

8. Frank, *Creeks and Southerners*, 26–45, examines the roles of non-Indians in Creek Society. Waselkov, *Conquering Spirit*, 19–43.

9. Quoted in Saunt, *New Order*, 69.

10. Ibid., 70–75. For an earlier account see Caughey, *Alexander McGillivray*, 1–57.

11. Quoted in Green, "Alexander McGillivray," 48.

12. Saunt, *New Order*, 75–79.

13. Green, "Alexander McGillivray," 48–50. Most scholars spell this name "Hobithle," although a few use "Hopithle" instead.

14. Ibid., 50–51.

15. "Articles of Confederation," section 9, in Commager *Documents of American History*, 111–16; and Martin, *Sacred Revolt*, 83.

16. Quoted in Wright, *Creeks and Seminoles*, 136. Prucha examines these agreements briefly in *American Indian Treaties*, 36, 60–63.

17. Green, "Alexander McGillivray," 51–52.

18. McGillivray to William Panton, October 8, 1789, quoted in *Green*, "Alexander McGillivray," 54.

19. Kappler, *Indian Affairs* 2:25–29; and Green, "Alexander McGillivray," 52–55.

20. Dowd, *Spirited Resistance*, 148–57.

21. Quoted in Martin, *Sacred Revolt*, 95.

22. In chapter 2 of *Conquering Spirit*, Waselkov gives a detailed analysis of this community as it developed within Creek society by 1800.

23. Saunt, *New Order*, 153–55.

24. Ibid., 167–69; Martin, *Sacred Revolt*, 108.

25. Pound, *Benjamin Hawkins*, 162–64.

26. Dowd, *Spirited Resistance*, 149–50.

27. Quoted in Saunt, *New Order*, 216.

28. Ibid., 216–17.

29. Ibid., 218–19.

30. Quoted in Martin, *Sacred Revolt*, 120.

31. Ibid., 120–21.

32. Sugden, *Tecumseh*, 237–49; Benjamin Hawkins to William Eustis, September 21, 1811, in Hawkins, *Letters, Journals and Writings*, 2:591–92; Martin, *Sacred Revolt*, 121–22.

33. Sugden, *Tecumseh*, 242, 244.

34. Ibid., 246–47.

35. Ibid., 230–31.

36. Martin, *Sacred Revolt*, 123–24; Waselkov, *Conquering Spirit*, 88.

37. Martin, *Sacred Revolt*, 125.

38. Waselkov, *Conquering Spirit*, 88–89.

39. Quoted in Saunt, *New Order*, 250.

40. Ibid., 251–52.

41. Quoted in Waselkov, *Conquering Spirit*, 89.

42. Ibid., 91–95; Martin, *Sacred Revolt*, 127–28; and Saunt, *New Order*, 253–59.

43. Owsley, *Struggle for the* Gulf *Borderlands*, 19–21.

44. Ibid., 18–29.

45. Ibid., 26–27; Waselkov, *Conquering Spirit*, 98–100; and Saunt, *New Order*, 259–63.

46. Waselkov, *Conquering Spirit*, 116–20.

47. Saunt, *New Order*, 267–70.

48. Waselkov, *Conquering Spirit*, 269–72; and Martin, *Sacred Revolt*, 162–67.

CHAPTER 3. THE ARIKARA WAR, 1823

1. Nester, *Arikara War*, briefly discusses this conflict. An older but excellent account is Clokey, *William H. Ashley*, 90–120. For briefer analyses see Nichols, "Arikara Indians"; and Nichols, "Backdrop."

2. Ethnologists and historians have studied these. See Meyer, *Village Indians;* Lehmer, *Introduction*, 98–100, 107–10; Wedel, *Prehistoric Man*, 182–83.

3. Lehmer, *Introduction*, 136–39, 141, 172; Truteau, "Remarks," 1:295–96; and Brackenridge, *Journal*, 6:123.

4. The classic treatment of these developments is Ewers, "Indian Trade." A more recent account is Wood, "Plains Trade."

5. Nester, *Arikara War*, 57–61. For older, more detailed accounts see Chittenden, *American Fur Trade;* and Phillips and Smurr, *Fur Trade*.

6. Truteau, "Remarks"; and Nester, *Arikara War*, 62–63.

7. Ewers, "Indian Trade"; and Clokey, *William H. Ashley*, 58–60.

8. Holder, "Social Stratification."

9. Martin, "Wildlife Diseases"; and Simmons, "New Mexico's Smallpox Epidemic." See also Fenn, *Pox Americana*.

10. Truteau, "Remarks," 1:299; Fenn, *Pox Americana*, 249, 275–76.

11. October 10, 1804, *Journals of the Lewis and Clark Expedition*, 3:157; Tabeau, *Tabeau's Narrative*, 123–24.

12. Tabeau, *Tabeau's Narrative*, 126, 128–29; Selkirk, *Lord Selkirk's Diary*, 213.

13. Selkirk, *Lord Selkirk's Diary*, 213.

14. Meyer, *Village Indians*, 399–40, 42–43; and Tabeau, *Tabeau's Narrative*, 129–31.

15. Tabeau, *Tabeau's Narrative*, 69–70, 129–31.

16. Truteau, "Remarks," 1:299–300, 303, 305–308; *Journals of the Lewis and Clark Expedition*, 3:157; and Clokey, *William H. Ashley*, 94–97.

17. Meyer, *Village Indians*, 59–60.

18. Brackenridge, *Journal*, 6:123.

19. Saum, *Fur Trader and the Indian*, 46–50, 56.

20. Nichols, *General Henry Atkinson*, 107.

21. *Journals of the Lewis and Clark Expedition*, 9:78.

22. Ibid., 3:152–66.

23. Ronda, *Lewis and Clark*, 61–62.

24. Henry Dearborn to James Wilkinson, April 9, 1806, Dearborn to Thomas Jefferson, April 10, 1806, and Jefferson to the Arikaras, April 11, 1806, in *Letters of the Lewis and Clark Expedition*, 1:303–306.

25. Meyer, *Village Indians*, 48; and Nichols, "Arikara Indians," 81.

26. Oglesby, *Manuel Lisa*, 41–49; and Barry, *Beginning*, 58.

27. Oglesby, *Manuel Lisa*, 50–51; Meyer, *Village Indians*, 48; and Nichols, "Arikara Indians," 82.

28. *Letters of the Lewis and Clark Expedition*, 2:433.

29. Oglesby, *Manuel Lisa*, 74–76, 83–84.

30. Brackenridge, *Journal*, 88.

31. Bradbury, *Travels*, 128, 130; and Brackenridge, *Journal*, 113, 127.

32. Luttig, *Journal*, 64–67.

33. Oglesby, *Manuel Lisa*, 172–84; Nichols, "Arikara Indians," 85; and Sunder, *Joshua Pilcher*, 33–34.

34. Quoted in Clokey, *William H. Ashley*, 67.

35. Quoted in ibid., 73.

36. *U.S. Statutes at Large*, 2:139–46; and Clokey, *William H. Ashley*, 78–85.

37. Quoted in Clokey, *William H. Ashley*, 91.

38. Nichols, "Arikara Indians," 86; Joshua Pilcher, "Statement 18 March 1824," in Morgan, *West of William H. Ashley*, 13–14; and Morgan, *Jedediah Smith*, 50–51.

39. William Ashley to ?, June 7, 1823, in Morgan, *West of William H. Ashley*, 29–30; and anonymous to Thomas Forsyth, January 23, 1824, in Thomas Forsyth Papers.

40. Clokey, *William H. Ashley*, 94; Sunder, *Joshua Pilcher*, 41–42; and Nichols, "Backdrop," 109–10.

41. Clokey, *William H. Ashley*, 94–99; and Nichols, "Backdrop," 110–11.

42. Leavenworth, "Leavenworth's Final and Detailed Report," October 20, 1823, 202–33.

CHAPTER 4. THE BLACK HAWK WAR, 1832

1. Black Hawk, *Autobiography*, 67–69; and Trask, *Black Hawk*, 180–88.

2. Nichols, *General Henry Atkinson*, 157–65.

3. Hagan, *Sac and Fox Indians*, 7.

4. Ibid., 3–15; Callender, "Fox," 15:648–55; and Murphy, "Autonomy."

5. Thomas Forsyth to Thomas McKenney, August 28, 1824, Thomas Forsyth Papers.

6. Nichols, *Black Hawk*, 23. For a thorough discussion of the war see Jung, *Black Hawk War;* and Trask, *Black Hawk*.

7. Warren Cattle to James Bruff, September 9, 1804, in Carter and Bloom, *Territorial Papers*, 13:62.

8. Bruff to James Wilkinson, September 29, 1804, in ibid., 13:57.

9. Bruff to Wilkinson, November 5, 1804, in ibid., 13:77.

10. Nichols, *Black Hawk*, 25–26.

11. Bruff to Wilkinson, November 5, 1804, in Carter and Bloom, *Territorial Papers*, 13:76–80; Wallace, "Prelude to Disaster," 1:17–20; and Hagan, *Sac and Fox Indians*, 19–23.

12. Royce, *Indian Land Cessions*, plate 17; and Kappler, *Indian Affairs*, 2:54–56.

13. Hagan, *Sac and Fox Indians*, 21–22; Wallace, "Prelude to Disaster," 18–21; and Kappler, *Indian Affairs*, 2:54–56.

14. Kappler, *Indian Affairs*, 2:54–56.

15. Wallace, "Prelude to Disaster," 3–7.

16. Nichols, *Black Hawk*, 422–58; Hagan, *Sac and Fox Indians*, 48–59; Prucha, *Sword of the Republic*, 103–18; Horsman, "Role of the Indian," 60–77; and Gilpin, *War of 1812*.

17. Hagan, *Sac and Fox Indians*, 60–72, 84–86; Clifton, *Place of Refuge*, v.

18. Black Hawk, *Autobiography*, 29–30.

19. Hagan, *Sac and Fox Indians*, 88–89.

20. Prucha, *Great Father*, 1:135–58, for the civilization policy and ibid., 1:183–213, 243–69, for removal. See also Satz, *American Indian Policy*.

21. Hagan, *Sac and Fox Indians*, 94–97; and Nichols, *Black Hawk*, 69–72.

22. Hagan, *Sac and Fox Indians*, 97–99; and Kappler, *Indian Affairs*, 2:250–54.

23. Wallace, "Prelude to Disaster," 1:25; and Nichols, *Black Hawk*, 76–78.

24. Forsyth to Clark, May 24, 1827, and Forsyth to Taliaferro, June 15, Forsyth Papers.

25. Edwards, *History of Illinois*, 351–52.

26. Edwards to Clark, May 25, 1828, quoted in Hagan, *Sac and Fox Indians*, 107.

27. Edwards to Clark, May 29, 1828, *Edwards Papers*, 3:338; and Hagan, *Sac and Fox Indians*, 107.

28. Forsyth to Clark, May 25, 1828, Office of Indian Affairs: Letters Received, Illinois, RG 75; and Wallace, "Prelude to Disaster," 1:27.

29. Forsyth to Clark, June 10, 1828, quoted in Wallace, "Prelude to Disaster," 1:29.

30. Black Hawk, *Autobiography*, 83–84, 115, 121.

31. Forsyth to Clark, May 17, 1829, quoted in Wallace, "Prelude to Disaster," 1:30.

32. Nichols, *Black Hawk*, 91, 103; and "Minutes of an Examination of Prisoners," August 27, 1832, in Whitney, *Black Hawk War*, 2:1055–57.

33. Black Hawk, *Autobiography*, 50–51.

34. Tai-mah and Apanos-okimant to Clark, July 22, 1832, quoted in Wallace, "Prelude to Disaster," 1:42.

35. Ibid., 42.

36. Black Hawk, *Autobiography*, 59–60; and McCall, "Talks between Edmund P. Gaines and the Sauk," June 7, 1831, in Whitney, *Black Hawk War*, 2:30.

37. Quoted in Wallace, "Prelude to Disaster," 1:42.

38. Black Hawk, *Autobiography*, 51–52.

39. Ibid, 52.

40. Trask, *Black Hawk*, 80–81; and Nichols, *Black Hawk*, 92–93.

41. Wallace, "Prelude to Diaster," 1:32–33; and Nichols, *Black Hawk*, 93–94.

42. Quoted in Wallace, "Prelude to Disaster," 1:34.

43. Nichols, *Black Hawk*, 94; and Wallace, "Prelude to Diaster," 1:34–36.

44. Black Hawk, *Autobiography*, 58.

45. Wallace, "Prelude to Disaster," 1:36–37.

46. Black Hawk, *Autobiography*, 58.

47. Nichols, *Black Hawk*, 97–98.

48. Black Hawk, *Autobiography*, 61.

49. Hagan, *Sac and Fox Indians*, 123–40; and Nichols, *Black Hawk*, 98–100.

50. Wallace, "Prelude to Disaster," 1:39–41.

51. Nichols, *Black Hawk*, 116–17; and Trask, *Black Hawk*, 151–52.

52. Forsyth Report, October 1, 1832, Thomas Forsyth Papers.

53. Black Hawk, *Autobiography*, 63–65.

54. Wallace, "Prelude to Disaster," 1:41.

55. Black Hawk, *Autobiography*, 67–68.

56. Jung, *Black Hawk War*, gives a thorough account of the military operations, while Hall, *Uncommon Defense*, analyzes the uses of Indian allies during the war.

57. Hagan, *Sac and Fox Indians*, 195–97, 225–44.

CHAPTER 5. THE MINNESOTA SIOUX WAR, 1862

1. Quoted in Anderson, *Little Crow*, 232.

2. For the most complete account of the incidents that started this war see Oehler, *Great Sioux Uprising*, chs. 1–5; and Anderson and Woolworth, *Through Dakota Eyes*, 35–42.

3. Utley, *Frontiersmen in Blue*, 281; Kelsey, *Frontier Capitalist*, 137–38; and Hatch, *Black Kettle*, 97.

4. For the general history and ethnology of the Dakota Sioux tribes see Anderson, *Kinsmen;* Hickerson, *Sioux Indians*, chs. 5–7; Hurt, *Sioux Indians;* and Meyer, *History of the Santee Sioux*.

5. Anderson, *Kinsmen*, 132–43; and Meyer, *History of the Santee Sioux*, 48–49.

6. Anderson, *Kinsmen*, 58–76, lays out the developing relationships between among the Indians, traders, métis, and American officials in the region clearly. See also Hickerson, *Sioux Indians*, chs, 4–5.

7. Meyer, *History of the Santee Sioux*, 35–36; and Anderson, *Kinsmen*, 99–105.

8. Anderson, *Little Crow*, 28–29, 31; and Anderson, *Kinsmen*, 165–67.

9. See chapter 2 above.

10. Treaty of Prairie du Chien, 1825, in Kappler, *Indian Affairs*, 2:250–54.

11. Hagan, *Sac and Fox Indians*, 96–99: and Jones, *William Clark*, 281–83.

12. Treaty of Prairie du Chien, 1830, in Kappler, *Indian Affairs*, 2:305–10.

13. Hall, *Uncommon Defense*, 200–202.

14. Anderson, *Little Crow*, 26.

15. Gilman, *Henry Hastings Sibley*, 66; and Anderson, *Kinsmen*, 142–43.

16. Gilman, *Henry Hastings Sibley*, 65; and Anderson, *Kinsmen*, 167–72.

17. Satz, *American Indian Policy*, 113–15; and Prucha, *Great Father*, 2:259–69.

18. Anderson, *Kinsmen*, 151–55; and Meyer, *History of the Santee Sioux*, 56–58.

19. Kappler, *Indian Affairs*, 2:493–94.

20. Anderson, *Kinsmen*, 156–59.

21. Meyer, *History of the Santee Sioux*, 64–67; and Anderson, *Little Crow*, 46, 50–52.

22. Meyer, *History of the Santee Sioux*, 63; and Anderson, *Kinsmen*, 177–78.

23. Anderson, *Little Crow*, 53–57.

24. Kappler, *Indian Affairs*, 2:588–90; and Anderson, *Little Crow*, 59–61.

25. For a detailed look at early 1860s corruption in Minnesota, see Nichols, *Lincoln and the Indians*, 65–75; Gilman, *Henry Hastings Sibley*, 125–27; Meyer, *History of the Santee Sioux*, 78–81; and Anderson, *Kinsmen*, 187.

26. Kappler, *Indian Affairs*, 2:591–93; and Anderson, *Kinsmen*, 187–89.

27. Meyer, *History of the Santee Sioux*, 84–86; and Anderson, *Kinsmen*, 190–94.

28. Meyer, *History of the Santee Sioux*, 89–92; and Anderson, *Kinsmen*, 205–207.

29. Anderson, *Little Crow*, 76–77.

30. Anderson, *Kinsmen*, 211–12, 214–15.

31. Ibid., 214; Anderson, *Little Crow*, 80–83.

32. Meyer, *History of the Santee Sioux*, 97–101; and Anderson, *Kinsmen*, 217–21.

33. Meyer, *History of the Santee Sioux*, 101–103; and Anderson, *Kinsmen*, 226–28.

34. Anderson, *Little Crow*, 94–102.

35. Quoted in ibid., 101.

36. Quoted in ibid., 103.

37. Ibid., 106.

38. Anderson, *Kinsmen*, 231–33; Meyer, *History of the Santee Sioux*, 107–108.

39. Anderson, *Kinsmen*, 233–39.

40. Anderson, *Little Crow*, 114; Meyer, *History of the Santee Sioux*, 106–107, and Anderson, *Kinsmen*, 240–42.

41. Meyer, *History of the Santee Sioux*, 107–108; and Anderson, *Little Crow*, 114–15.

42. Anderson, *Little Crow*, 121–22.

43. Quoted in ibid, 123.

44. Quoted in Anderson, *Kinsmen*, 250. The author effectively clarifies some of the issues raised over this statement on 251.

45. Ibid., 252.

CHAPTER 6. THE CHEYENNE & ARAPAHO WAR, 1864–1865

1. Hoig, *Sand Creek Massacre*, 36–43; Hatch, *Black Kettle;* and West, *Contested Plains*, give the most thorough accounts of these events. See also U.S. Secretary of War, *Annual Report*, "Sand Creek Massacre," 32 (1867); and *Report of the Special Joint Committee*, "Condition of the Indian Tribes" (1867).

2. Hatch, *Black Kettle*, 112–16.

3. Flores, "Bison Ecology"; and Hämäläinen, "First Phase."

4. Commissioner of Indian Affairs, *Annual Report* (1853), 368. See also Berthrong, *Southern Cheyennes*, 124; Flores, "Bison Ecology," 465–86; and Hämäläinen, "Rise and Fall of Indian Horse Cultures," 842–43.

5. Grinnell, *Cheyenne Indians*, 1:337, 340–41, 345–46, 2:49; Berthrong, *Southern Cheyennes*, 70–75.

6. Hoebel, *Cheyennes*, 40, 43–45; Grinnell, *Cheyenne Indians*, 2:48–86; Powell, *People of the Sacred Mountain*, 2:188; and Mooney, *Cheyenne Indians*, 371–403, 413.

7. Kappler, *Indian Affairs*, 2:594–96.

8. Berthrong, *Southern Cheyennes*, 119–23.

9. McCann, "Grattan Massacre."

10. Adams, *General William S. Harney*, 128–33.

11. Berthrong, *Southern Cheyennes*, 132–33.

12. Hatch, *Black Kettle*, 49–50; Grinnell, *Fighting Cheyennes*, 111–12; and Hyde, *Life of George Bent*, 100.

13. Berthrong, *Southern Cheyennes*, 134–35; West, *Contested Plains*, 1–2; Commissioner of Indian Affairs, "Annual Report" (1856); and Grinnell, *Fighting Cheyennes*, 112–13.

14. Berthrong, *Southern Cheyennes*, 133–36.

15. Ibid., 139.

16. The most detailed account of this is Chalfant, *Cheyennes and Horse Soldiers*. See also West, *Contested Plains*, 2–5; Powell, *People of the Sacred Mountain*, 1:212–13; Berthrong, *Southern Cheyennes*, 139–40; and U.S. Secretary of War, *Annual Report* (1857), 96, 99.

17. Quoted in Hatch, *Black Kettle*, 67.

18. Ibid., 66–67.

19. Quoted in Berthrong, *Southern Cheyennes*, 147. For a longer discussion of this, see Commissioner of Indian Affairs, *Annual Report* (1859), 137–39.

20. Kappler, *Indian Affairs*, 2:807–11; Berthrong, *Southern Cheyennes*, 149–50; and West, *Contested Plains*, 281–83.

21. Hyde, *Life of George Bent*, 115.

22. Hatch, *Black Kettle*, 92–93, 97; and Kelsey, *Frontier Capitalist*, 118.

23. For the Minnesota attack see Utley, *Frontiersmen in Blue*, 261–80; Oehler, *Great Sioux Uprising*, chs. 4–6; and Hatch, *The Blue, the Gray, and the Red*, chs. 3 and 5.

24. Quoted in Hoig, *Peace Chiefs*, 72. See also Viola, *Diplomats in Buckskin*, 99–102.

25. Quoted in Berthrong, *Southern Cheyennes*, 168. See also Commissioner of Indian Affairs, *Annual Report* (1863), 129–30.

26. Quoted in Berthrong, *Southern Cheyennes*, 172; West, *Contested Plains*, 284–85; Grinnell, *Fighting Cheyennes*, 134–35; and Commissioner of Indian Affairs, *Annual Report* (1864), 224–25.

27. Quoted in Svaldi, *Sand Creek*, 150.

28. Berthrong, *Southern Cheyennes*, 170–73.

29. Quoted in ibid., 176.

30. Ibid., 176–80.

31. Hatch, *Black Kettle*, 115–16; and Berthrong, *Southern Cheyennes*, 186–87.

32. Quoted in Hatch, *Black Kettle*, 116.

33. Hyde, *Life of George Bent*, 129–33; and Hatch, *Black Kettle*, 117.

34. Hatch, *Black Kettle*, 117–20.

35. Hyde, *Life of George Bent*, 127.

36. Svaldi, *Sand Creek*, 149–88.

37. Ibid., 162–63; Berthrong, *Southern Cheyennes*, 190–91; and Hoig, *Sand Creek Massacre*, 59–62.

38. Quoted in Hatch, *Black Kettle*, 123–24. See also West, *Contested Plains*, 290–95.

39. Hatch, *Black Kettle*, 126–27.

40. Quoted in Lecompte, "Sand Creek," 334. Three separate federal investigations provide the gory details of the massacre and its aftermath.

41. Hatch, *Black Kettle*, 173–74, describes the tribal response to Sand Creek.

42. Ibid., 190–254; and West, *Contested Plains*, 308–16, give a complete account of events following Sand Creek.

CHAPTER 7. THE CHIRICAHUA APACHE WAR, 1861–1872

1. Many contemporary reports of these events proved inaccurate, contradictory, or incomplete. The most useful sources are Sweeney, *Cochise;* and McChristian, *Fort Bowie*. See also McChristian and Ludwig, "Eyewitness"; and Radbourne, *Mickey Free*.

2. Sweeney, *Cochise*, 144–50.

3. Ibid., 150–51; Thrapp, *Conquest*, 17; and Roberts, *Once They Moved*, 25.

4. Sweeney, *Cochise*, 152.

5. Quoted in ibid., 156.

6. Thrapp, *Conquest*, 16–18; McChristian, *Fort Bowie*, 24–25; and Sweeney, *Cochise*, 150–63.

7. Hodge, *Handbook*, 1:63; and Forbes, *Apache, Navajo and Spaniard*, xi–xxiii. Forbes posits arrivals during the 1400s. Others suggest that the Athapaskans reached the area at nearly the same time as the Spanish.

8. Goodwin, *Social Organization*, 1; Opler, *Apache Lifeway*, 1–2, 181, 462–64; Lockwood, *Apache Indians*, 1–7; and Kaut, *Western Apache Clan System*.

9. For a thorough discussion of late eighteenth century Spanish dealing with the indigenous peoples in the present American Southwest see Weber, *Spanish Frontier*, 204–35.

10. Lockwood, *Apache Indians*, 9–15, gives a somewhat disjointed account of these issues. See also Moorhead, *Apache Frontier*.

11. Quoted in Weber, *Spanish Frontier*, 206.

12. Ibid., 206, 232.

13. Moorhead, *Apache Frontier*, 115–42; and Griffen, *Utmost Good Faith*, 190–97. These two analyses provide a detailed narrative of the distrust and violence that prevented any cessation of Mexican-Apache frontier warfare and established patterns of hostilities in full operation when the United States entered the Southwest.

14. Griffen, *Utmost Good Faith*, 21–25.

15. Ibid., 23–27.

16. Griffen, "Apache Indians."

17. The most recent detailed analysis is DeLay, *War of a Thousand Deserts*, 121–24.

18. Ibid., ch. 14, traces the specific fighting in Chihuahua from 1821 to 1848. Sweeney, *Mangas Coloradas*, 44–219, examines related issues. See also Lockwood, *Apache Indians*, 30–41; and Cremony, *Life among the Apaches*, 35–46.

19. Article 11, "Treaty of Guadalupe Hidalgo," in Malloy, *Compilation of Treaties*, 519–20.

20. Kluger, *Seizing Destiny*, 492.

21. Sweeney, *Cochise*, 33.

22. Ibid., 83–86.

23. Kluger, *Seizing Destiny*, 492–93.

24. *Weekly Arizonian*, April 21, 1859.

25. Sweeney, *Cochise*, 95–118; and Sweeney, *Mangas Coloradas*, 187–362, chronicle the confusing and changing relations between the Apaches and Mexicans and relationships between and among the Indian bands and the Americans during the 1850s.

26. McChristian, *Fort Bowie*, 15–16.

27. Sweeney, *Cochise*, 119; and McChristian, *Fort Bowie*, 17.

28. Sweeney, *Cochise*, 119–20.

29. Quoted in ibid., 122.

30. Ibid., 125.

31. Quoted in ibid.

32. Ibid., 127–28.

33. Quoted in McChristian, *Fort Bowie*, 19.

34. Sheridan, *Arizona*, 67.

35. The California Volunteers have received considerable attention. The most recent treatment is Masich, *Civil War in Arizona*. See Hand, *Civil War in Apacheland;* Hunt, *Army of the Pacific;* and Hunt, *Major General James Henry General Carleton*.

36. Quoted in Ball, *In the Days of Victorio*, 46–47; and Cremony, *Life among the Apaches*, 173.

37. Quoted in Ball, *In the Days of Victorio*, 47.

38. Quoted in Sweeney, *Cochise*, 202.

39. Ibid., 199–202.

40. Quoted in Sweeney, *Mangas Coloradas*, 444.

41. Quoted in ibid., 445.

42. Quoted in ibid., 454.

43. Thrapp, *Conquest*, 21–23; and Sweeney, *Mangas Coloradas*, 445, 457.

44. Sweeney, *Cochise*, 240–59.

45. Quoted in ibid., 299.

46. Ibid., 319.

47. Ibid., 336–38.

48. Jacoby, *Shadows at Dawn*, gives the best account of the massacre.

49. Quoted in Sladen, *Making Peace with Cochise*, 17.

50. Ibid.

51. Quoted in Sweeney, *Cochise*, 357. Sladen, *Making Peace with Cochise*, gives a firsthand account.

52. Sweeney, *Cochise*, 358–65. For Howard's version see *My Life and Experiences*.

CHAPTER 8. NEZ PERCE WAR, 1877

1. McWhorter, *Hear Me*, 190.

2. Ibid., 191–93; Josephy, *Nez Perce Indians*, 512–15; and West, *Last Indian War*, 124–25.

3. McWhorter, *Hear Me*, 207–26, includes narratives from both whites and Indians. See also Josephy, *Nez Perce Indians*, 516–20; and West, *Last Indian War*, 126–30.

4. Aoki, *Nez Perce Texts*, 27–29; and Aoki and Walker, *Nez Perce Oral Narratives*, 103.

5. Josephy, *Nez Perce Country*, 2–3. See also Ames and Maschner, *Peoples of the Northwest Coast*.

6. Walker, *American Indians of Idaho*, 70–79, briefly treats tribal organization. See also Josephy, *Nez Perce Country*, 6–20; and Lavender, *"Let Me Be Free,"* 10–20.

7. Haines, *The Nez Percés*, 17–25; Josephy, *Nez Perce Indians*, 27–37; Lavender, *"Let Me Be Free,"* 21–24; and West, *Last Indian War*, 16–19.

8. Ewers, *Blackfeet*.

9. Walker, *American Indians of Idaho*, 128–39.

10. Boyd, *Coming of the Spirit of Pestilence*, 21–60; Fenn, *Pox Americana*, 273; Meyer, *Village Indians*, 27.

11. Ronda, *Lewis and Clark*, 157–62; and *Journals of the Lewis and Clark Expedition*, 5:222–48.

12. Josephy, *Nez Perce Indians*, 40–119, treats the issues effectively.

13. For Oregon missionary activity see ibid.; Cebula, *Plateau Indians;* Drury, *Henry Harmon Spalding;* Drury, *Marcus and Narcissa Whitman;* and West, *Last Indian War*, 49–51.

14. West, *Last Indian War*, 30–32.

15. Richards, *Isaac Stevens*, 193.

16. Ibid., 198–224; and West, *Last Indian War*, 61–67.

17. "Treaty with the Nez Perces, 1855," in Kappler, *Indian Affairs*, 2:702–706; West, *Last Indian War*, 63–67; and Lavender, *"Let Me Be Free,"* 152–54.

18. Ibid., 158–69; West, *Last Indian War*, 70–74.

19. McWhorter, *Hear Me*, 97–100; West, *Last Indian War*, 75–81.

20. West, *Last Indian War*, 80.

21. Josephy, *Nez Perce Indians*, 434–36; Ruby and Brown, *Dreamer Prophets,* 29–49; and Mooney, *Ghost Dance Religion*, 721.

22. Deloria and DeMallie, *Documents of American Indian Diplomacy*, 2:1341–43.

23. Quoted in Josephy, *Nez Perce Indians*, 404.

24. Ibid., 409–10; and Lavender, *"Let Me Be Free,"* 171–80.

25. Quoted in Josephy, *Nez Perce Indians*, 422. See also West, *Last Indian War*, 89–91.

26. West, *Last Indian War*, 92–93.

27. Nichols, *Black Hawk*, 68–70; and Berthrong, *Southern Cheyennes*, 149–50.

28. Josephy, *Nez Perce Indians*, 415–28; and McWhorter, *Hear Me*, 106–11.

29. Josephy, *Nez Perce Indians*, 431–37; West, *Last Indian War*, 98–99.

30. Quoted in Josephy, *Nez Perce Indians*, 436.

31. Ibid., 447–53.

32. "Nez Perce Treaty of 1868," in Kappler, *Indian Affairs*, 2:1024–25.

33. Prucha, *Great Father*, 1:488–533; and West, *Last Indian War*, 104–107.

34. Josephy, *Nez Perce Indians*, 453–55.

35. Quoted in ibid., 455.

36. Ibid., 455–57; and West, *Last Indian War*, 105–107.

37. Josephy, *Nez Perce Indians*, 461–63.

38. Ibid., 462–64.

39. Crook, *General George Crook*, 169; and Josephy, *Nez Perce Indians*, 467–68.

40. Josephy, *Nez Perce Indians*, 469–74.

41. Ibid., 475–83; and West, *Last Indian War*, 110–11.

42. Josephy, *Nez Perce Indians,* 485–86.

43. *Report of Civil and Military Commission to Nez Perce Indians.* See also West, *Last Indian War,* 114.

44. West, *Last Indian War,* 114–15.

45. Quoted in ibid., 117.

46. Quoted in Howard, *Nez Perce Joseph,* 52–53, 58–59; and Howard, "Young Joseph."

47. Howard, *My Life and Experiences,* 256; and Josephy, *Nez Perce Indians,* 503–504.

48. McWhorter, *Yellow Wolf,* 41.

CONCLUSION

1. DeMallie, " 'Touching the Pen.' "

2. Black Hawk, *Autobiography,* 52.

Bibliography

ARCHIVAL AND MANUSCRIPT COLLECTIONS

Office of Indian Affairs: Letters Received. Illinois. Record Group 75. National Archives.

Thomas Forsyth Papers. Draper Collection. State Historical Society of Wisconsin.

U.S. GOVERNMENT DOCUMENTS

American State Papers: Indian Affairs. 2 vols. Washington, D.C.: Gales & Seaton, 1832–34.

American State Papers: Military Affairs. 7 vols. Washington, D.C.: Gales & Seaton, 1834–61.

Carter, Clarence E., and John Porter Bloom, eds. *The Territorial Papers of the United States.* 28 vols. Washington, D.C.: Government Printing Office, 1934–75.

Commissioner of Indian Affairs. *Annual Report.* 1849–69. Washington, D.C.: Government Printing Office, 1850–70.

Congressional Globe, 30th Cong., 2d session. Washington, D.C.: Blair & Rives, 1833–73.

Continental Congress. *Journals of the Continental Congress.* 34 vols. Washington, D.C.: Government Printing Office, 1904–37.

Kappler, Charles J., comp. and ed. *Indian Affairs: Laws and Treaties.* 7 vols. Washington, D.C.: Government Printing Office, 1904–41.

Malloy, William M., comp. *Compilation of Treaties in Force: Prepared under Resolution of the Senate, of February 11, 1904*. Washington, D.C.: Government Printing Office, 1904.

Report of Civil and Military Commission to Nez Perce Indians. 1876. House Executive Document 1, pt. 5. vol. 1. 45th Cong., 2d sess. 8: 607–13. Washington, D.C.: Government Printing Office, 1876.

Report of the Special Joint Committee. "Condition of the Indian Tribes." Sen. Report 156, 39th Cong., 2d sess., 1867. Washington, D.C.: Government Printing Office, 1868.

Report on Indians Taxed and Indians Not Taxed in the United States (except Alaska) at the Eleventh Census: 1890. Washington, D.C.: Government Printing Office, 1894.

Royce, Charles C. *Indian Land Cessions in the United States*. Bureau of American Ethnology, Report No. 18, part 2. Washington, D.C.: Government Printing Office, 1904.

United States. Secretary of War. *Annual Report*. Washington, D.C.: Government Printing Office, 1865–70.

———. *Annual Report*. "Sand Creek Massacre." Senate Ex. Doc. 26. 39th Cong., 2d session. Washington, D.C.: Government Printing Office, 1867.

U.S. Statutes at Large (1816). Vol. 3. Boston: Little, Brown & Co., 1850.

PUBLISHED PRIMARY SOURCES

Anderson, Gary C., and Alan Woolworth, eds. *Through Dakota Eyes: Narrative Accounts of the Minnesota Indian War of 1862*. St. Paul: Minnesota Historical Society Press, 1988.

Aoki, Haruo. *Nez Perce Texts*. University of California Publications in Linguistics, Vol. 90. Berkeley: University of California Press, 1979.

Aoki, Haruo, and Deward E. Walker, Jr. *Nez Perce Oral Narratives*. University of California Publications in Linguistics, Vol. 104. Berkeley: University of California Press, 1989.

Ball, Eve, ed. *In the Days of Victorio: Recollections of a Warm Spring Apache*. Tucson: University of Arizona Press, 1970.

Basso, Keith, ed. *Western Apache Raiding and Warfare*. Tucson: University of Arizona Press, 1993.

Beal, Merrill D. *"I Will Fight No More Forever": Chief Joseph and the Nez Perce War* (1963). Reprinted, Seattle: University of Washington Press, 1982.

Bent, George. *Life of George Bent Written from His Letters*. By George E. Hyde. Edited by Savoie Lottinville. Norman: University of Oklahoma Press, 1968.

Berghold, Rev. Alexander. *The Indians' Revenge or Days of Horror: Some Appalling Events in the History of the Sioux*. 1891. Edited by Don Heinrich Tolzmann. Roseville, Minn.: Edinborough Press, 2007.

Bishop, Harriet E. *Dakota War Whoop: or, Indian Massacres and War in Minnesota, of 1862–3.* St. Paul: The author, 1864.

Black Hawk. *Autobiography.* Edited by Roger L. Nichols. Ames: Iowa State University Press, 1999.

Brackenridge, Henry M. *Journal of a Voyage Up the River Missouri: Performed in Eighteen Hundred and Eleven.* Early Western Travels, Vol. 6. Edited by Reuben G. Thwaites. 32 vols. Cleveland: Arthur H. Clark, 1904–1907.

Bradbury, John. *Travels in the Interior of America in the Years 1809, 1810, and 1811.* Early Western Travels, Vol. 5. Edited by Reuben G. Thwaites. 32 vols. Cleveland: Arthur H. Clark, 1904–1907.

Bryant, Charles S., and Abel B. V. Murch. *A History of the Great Massacre by the Sioux Indians in Minnesota: Including the Personal Narratives of Many Who Escaped* (1864). Reprinted, Millwood, N.Y.: Kraus, 1973.

Commager, Henry Steele, ed. *Documents of American History.* 5th ed. New York: Appleton-Century-Crofts, 1949.

Cremony, John C. *Life among the Apaches* (1868). Reprinted, Lincoln: University of Nebraska Press, 1983.

Crook, George. *General George Crook: His Autobiography* (1946). Edited by Martin F. Schmitt. Reprinted, Norman: University of Oklahoma Press, 1986.

Deloria, Vine, Jr., and Raymond J. DeMallie, eds. *Documents of American Indian Diplomacy: Treaties, Agreements, and Conventions, 1775–1979.* 2 vols. Norman: University of Oklahoma Press, 1999.

Edwards, Ninian W. *The Edwards Papers.* Edited by E. B. Washburne. Chicago Historical Society Collections. 3 vols. Chicago: Chicago Historical Society, 1884.

———. *History of Illinois from 1778 to 1833 and Life and Times of Ninian Edwards.* New York: Arno Press, 1975.

Hand, George. *The Civil War in Apacheland: Sergeant George Hand's Diary, California, Arizona, West Texas, New Mexico, 1861–1864.* Edited by Neil C. Carmony. Silver City, N.Mex.: High Lonesome Books, 1996.

Hawkins, Benjamin. *The Collected Works of Benjamin Hawkins, 1796–1810.* Edited by Thomas Foster. Tuscaloosa: University of Alabama Press, 2003.

———. *The Letters, Journals, and Writings of Benjamin Hawkins, 1796–1816.* Edited by C. L. Grant. 2 vols. Savannah, Ga.: Beehive Press, 1980.

Howard, Oliver Otis. *Famous Indian Chiefs I Have Known.* Lincoln: University of Nebraska Press, 1989.

———. *My Life and Experiences among Our Hostile Indians.* Hartford, Conn.: A. D. Worthington & Co., 1907.

———. *Nez Perce Joseph: An Account of His Ancestors, His Lands, His Confederates, His Enemies, His Murders, His War, His Pursuit and Capture.* Boston: Lee & Shepard, 1881.

The Journals of the Lewis and Clark Expedition. Edited by Gary E. Moulton. 13 vols. Lincoln: University of Nebraska Press, 1983–2001.

Knopf, Richard C. *Anthony Wayne, A Name in Arms: Soldier, Diplomat, Defender of Expansion Westward of a Nation—The Wayne-Knox-Pickering-McHenry Correspondence.* Pittsburgh: University of Pittsburgh Press, 1959.

Leavenworth, Henry. "Leavenworth's Final and Detailed Report." In *Official Correspondence of the Leavenworth Expedition of 1823 into South Dakota for the Conquest of the Ree Indians,* edited by Doane Robinson, 202–33. South Dakota Historical Collections, Vol. 1. Pierre: South Dakota State Historical Society, 1902.

Lee, Lorenzo Porter. *History of the Spirit Lake Massacre* (1857). Reprinted, Fairfield, Wash.: Ye Galleon Press, 1967.

Letters of the Lewis and Clark Expedition with Related Documents, 1782–1854. 2d ed. Edited by Donald Jackson. Urbana: University of Illinois Press, 1978.

Luttig, John C. *Journal of a Fur Trading Expedition on the Upper Missouri, 1812–1813* (1920). Edited by Stella Drumm. Reprinted, New York: Argosy-Antiquarian, 1964.

McChristian, Douglas C., and Larry L. Ludwig, eds. "Eyewitness to the Bascom Affair: An Account by Sergeant Daniel Robinson, Seventh Infantry." *Journal of Arizona History* 42:3 (Autumn 2001): 277–300.

McWhorter, Lucullus Virgil. *Yellow Wolf: His Own Story* (1948). Rev. ed. Minneapolis: Ross & Haines, 1970.

Morgan, Dale L., ed. *The West of William H. Ashley.* Denver: Old West Publishing Co., 1964.

Powell, Peter J. *People of the Sacred Mountain: A History of the Northern Cheyenne Chiefs and Warrior Societies, 1869–1879.* 2 vols. San Francisco: Harper & Row, 1981.

Selkirk, Thomas D. *Lord Selkirk's Diary, 1803–1804: A Journal of His Travels in North America and the Northeastern United States.* Edited by Patrick C. White. Publications of the Champlain Society, No. 34. Toronto: Champlain Society, 1958.

Sladen, Joseph A. *Making Peace with Cochise: The 1872 Journal of Captain Joseph Alton Sladen.* Edited by Edwin R. Sweeney. Norman: University of Oklahoma Press, 1997.

Smith, William Henry. *The St. Clair Papers: The Life and Public Services of Arthur St. Clair . . . with His Correspondence and Other Papers* (1882). 2 vols. Reprinted, Freeport, N.Y.: Books for Libraries Press, 1970.

Tabeau, Pierre-Antoine. *Tabeau's Narrative of Loisels' Expedition to the Upper Missouri.* Edited by Annie H. Abel. Norman: University of Oklahoma Press, 1939.

Truteau, Jean-Baptiste. "Remarks on the Manners of the Indians Living High Up the Missouri." In *Before Lewis and Clark: Documents Illustrating the History of the Missouri, 1785–1804,* edited by Abraham Nasatir, 1:259–311. 2 vols. St. Louis: St. Louis Historical Documents Foundation, 1952.

Washington, George. *The Writings of George Washington from the Original Manuscript Sources, 1745–1799.* Edited by John C. Fitzpatrick. 39 vols. Washington, D.C.: Government Printing Office, 1931–1944.

Weekly Arizonian. 1859.

Whipple, Henry Benjamin. *Lights and Shadows of a Long Episcopate: Being Reminiscences and Recollections of the Right Reverend Henry Benjamin Whipple, D.D., LL.D.* New York: Macmillan, 1912.

Whitney, Ellen M. comp. and ed. *The Black Hawk War, 1831–1832.* 2 vols. in 4 parts. Collections of the Illinois Historical Library, Vols. 35–38. Springfield: Illinois State Historical Society, 1970–78.

Wynkoop, Edward W. *The Tall Chief: The Unfinished Autobiography of Edward W. Wynkoop, 1856–1866.* Edited by Christopher B. Gerboth. Denver: Colorado Historical Society, 1993.

BOOKS

Adams, George Rollie. *General William S. Harney: Prince of Dragoons.* Lincoln: University of Nebraska Press, 2001.

Ames, Kenneth M., and Herbert D. G. Maschner. *Peoples of the Northwest Coast: Their Archaeology and Prehistory.* London: Thames & Hudson, 1999.

Anderson, Fred, and Andrew R. L. Cayton. *The Dominion of War: Empire and Liberty in North America, 1500–2000.* New York: Viking, 2005.

Anderson, Gary C. *The Conquest of Texas: Ethnic Cleansing in the Promised Land.* Norman: University of Oklahoma Press, 2005.

———. *Kinsmen of Another Kind: Dakota-White Relations in the Upper Mississippi Valley, 1650–1862.* Lincoln: University of Nebraska Press, 1984.

———. *Little Crow: Spokesman for the Sioux.* St. Paul: Minnesota Historical Society Press, 1986.

Barnes, Harry Elmer. *Perpetual War for Perpetual Peace.* Caldwell, Idaho: Caxton Printers, 1953.

Barry, Louise. *The Beginning of the West: Annals of the Kansas Gateway to the American West, 1550–1854.* Topeka: Kansas Historical Society, 1972.

Berthrong, Donald J. *The Southern Cheyennes.* Norman: University of Oklahoma Press, 1963.

Blackhawk, Ned. *Violence over the Land: Indians and Empires in the Early American West.* Cambridge, Mass.: Harvard University Press, 2006.

Bloom, John Porter, ed. *The American Territorial System.* Athens: Ohio University Press, 1973.

Boyd, Robert T. *The Coming of the Spirit of Pestilence: Introduced Infectious Diseases and Population Decline among Northwest Coast Indians, 1774–1874.* Vancouver, B.C.: University of Vancouver Press, 1999.

Calloway, Colin. *The American Revolution in Indian Country: Crises and Diversity in Native American Communities.* New York: Cambridge University Press, 1995.

———. *Crown and Calumet: British Indian Relations, 1783–1815.* Norman: University of Oklahoma Press, 1986.

————. *The Scratch of a Pen: 1763 and the Transformation of North America.* New York: Oxford University Press, 2006.

————. *The Shawnees and the War for America.* New York: Penguin Library of American Indian History, 2007.

Carpenter, John A. *Sword and Olive Branch: Oliver Otis Howard.* Pittsburgh: University of Pittsburgh Press, 1964.

Carter, Harvey Lewis. *The Life and Times of Little Turtle: First Sagamore of the Wabash.* Urbana: University of Illinois Press, 1987.

Caughey, John W. *Alexander McGillivray of the Creeks.* Norman: University of Oklahoma Press, 1938.

Cave, Alfred A. *Prophets of the Great Spirit: Native American Revitalization Movements in Eastern North America.* Lincoln: University of Nebraska Press, 2006.

Cebula, Larry. *Plateau Indians and the Quest for Spiritual Power, 1700–1850.* Lincoln: University of Nebraska Press, 2003.

Chalfant, William Y. *Cheyennes and Horse Soldiers: The 1857 Expedition and the Battle of Solomon's Fork.* Norman: University of Oklahoma Press, 1989.

Chittenden, Hiram Martin. *The American Fur Trade of the Far West.* 3 vols. New York: F. P. Harper, 1902.

Churchill, Ward. *A Little Matter of Genocide.* San Francisco: City Light Books, 1998.

Clifton, James A. *Being and Becoming Indian: Biographical Studies of North American Frontiers.* Chicago: Dorsey Press, 1989.

Clokey, Richard M. *William H. Ashley: Enterprise and Politics in the Trans-Mississippi West.* Norman: University of Oklahoma Press, 1980.

Collins, Charles. *An Apache Nightmare.* Norman: University of Oklahoma Press, 1999.

Cooper, Frederick. *Colonialism in Question: Theory, Knowledge, History.* Berkeley: University of California Press, 2005.

Craig, Reginald S. *The Fighting Parson: The Biography of Colonel John M. Chivington.* Los Angeles: Westernlore Press, 1959.

Cremony, John R. *Life among the Apaches* (1868). Reprinted, Glorieta, N.Mex.: Rio Grande Press, 1969.

DeLay, Brian. *War of a Thousand Deserts: Indian Raids and the U.S.-Mexican War.* New Haven: Yale University Press, 2008.

Deloria, Philip J. *Playing Indian.* New Haven: Yale University Press, 1998.

DiLorenzo, Thomas J. *Lincoln Unmasked: What You're Not Supposed to Know about Dishonest Abe.* New York: Crown Forum, 2006.

Divine, Robert A. *Perpetual War for Perpetual Peace.* College Station: Texas A&M University Press, 2000,

Dowd, Gregory Evans. *A Spirited Resistance: The North American Indian Struggle for Unity, 1745–1815.* Baltimore: Johns Hopkins University Press, 1992.

————. *War under Heaven: Pontiac, the Indian Nations, and the British Empire.* Baltimore: John Hopkins University Press, 2002.

Downes, Randolph C. *Council Fires on the Upper Ohio: A Narrative of Indian Affairs in the Upper Ohio Valley until 1795*. Pittsburgh: University of Pittsburgh Press, 1940.

Drury, Clifford M. *Henry Harmon Spalding: Pioneer of Old Oregon*. Caldwell, Idaho: Caxton Printers, 1936.

———. *Marcus and Narcissa Whitman and the Opening of Old Oregon*. Glendale, Calif.: Arthur H. Clark, 1973.

DuVal, Kathleen. *The Native Ground: Indians and Colonists in the Heart of the Continent*. Philadelphia: University of Pennsylvania Press, 2006.

Edmunds, R. David. ed. *American Indian Leaders: Studies in Diversity*. Lincoln: University of Nebraska Press, 1980.

Edwards, Ninian W. *History of Illinois from 1778 to 1833 and Life and Times of Ninian Edwards*. Springfield: Illinois State Journal, 1870.

Ethridge, Robbie F. *Creek Country: The Creek Indians and Their World*. Chapel Hill: University of North Carolina Press, 2003.

Ewers, John C. *The Blackfeet: Raiders of the Northwestern Plains*. Norman: University of Oklahoma Press, 1958.

Faragher, John Mack. *Daniel Boone: The Life and Legend of an American Pioneer*. New York: Henry Holt, 1992.

Fenn, Elizabeth A. *Pox Americana: The Great Smallpox Epidemic of 1775–82*. New York: Hill & Wang, 2001.

Forbes, Jack D. *Apache, Navajo and Spaniard*. Norman: University of Oklahoma Press, 1971.

Fowler, Loretta. *Arapaho Politics, 1851–1978*. Lincoln: University of Nebraska Press, 1982.

Frank, Andrew. *Creeks and Southerners: Biculturalism on the Early American Frontier*. Lincoln: University of Nebraska Press, 2005.

Frantz, John B., and William Pencak, eds. *Beyond Philadelphia: The American Revolution in the Pennsylvania Hinterland*. University Park: Pennsylvania State University Press, 1998.

Gaff, Alan D. *Bayonets in the Wilderness: Anthony Wayne's Legion in the Old Northwest*. Norman: University of Oklahoma Press, 2004.

Gilman, Rhoda R. *Henry Hastings Sibley: Divided Heart*. St. Paul: Minnesota Historical Society Press, 2004.

Gilpin, Alec R. *The War of 1812 and the Old Northwest*. East Lansing: Michigan State University Press, 1958.

Goodwin, Grenville. *The Social Organization of the Western Apache*. Tucson: University of Arizona Press, 1969.

Green, Michael D. *The Politics of Indian Removal: Creek Government and Society in Crisis*. Lincoln: University of Nebraska Press, 1982.

Grenier, John. *The First Way of War: American War Making on the Frontier, 1607–1814*. New York: Cambridge University Press, 2005.

Griffen, William B. *Utmost Good Faith: Patterns of Apache-Mexican Hostilities in Northern Chihuahua Border Warfare, 1821–1848.* Albuquerque: University of New Mexico Press, 1988.

Grinnell, George Bird. *The Cheyenne Indians.* 2 vols. New York: Cooper Square, 1923.

———. *The Fighting Cheyennes.* New York: Charles Scribner's Sons, 1915. Reprinted, Norman: University of Oklahoma Press, 1956.

Hagan, William T. *The Sac and Fox Indians.* Norman: University of Oklahoma Press, 1958.

Hahn, Steven C. *The Invention of the Creek Nation, 1670–1763.* Lincoln: University of Nebraska Press, 2004.

Haines, Francis. *The Nez Percés: Tribesmen of the Columbia Plateau.* Norman: University of Oklahoma Press, 1955.

Hall, John W. *Uncommon Defense: Indian Allies in the Black Hawk War.* Cambridge, Mass.: Harvard University Press, 2009.

Hämäläinen, Pekka. *Comanche Empire.* New Haven: Yale University Press, 2008.

Hatch, Thom. *Black Kettle: The Cheyenne Chief Who Sought Peace But Found War.* New York: John Wiley & Sons, 2004.

———. *The Blue, the Gray and the Red: Indian Campaigns of the Civil War.* Mechanicsburg, Pa.: Stackpole, 2003.

Hickerson, Harold. *The Chippewa and Their Neighbors: A Study in Ethnohistory.* New York: Holt, Rinehart & Winston, 1970.

———. *Sioux Indians: Mdewakanton Band of Sioux Indians.* Vol. 1. New York: Garland Publishing Co., 1974.

Hinderaker, Eric. *Elusive Empires: Constructing Colonialism in the Ohio Valley, 1763–1800.* New York: Cambridge University Press, 1997.

Hodge, Frederick W., ed. *Handbook of American Indians North of Mexico.* 2 vols. Washington, D.C.: Government Printing Office, 1912.

Hoebel, E. Adamson. *The Cheyennes: Indians of the Great Plains.* New York: Holt, Rinehart & Winston, 1978.

Hoig, Stan. *Peace Chiefs of the Southern Cheyennes.* Norman: University of Oklahoma Press, 1980.

———. *The Sand Creek Massacre.* Norman: University of Oklahoma Press, 1961.

Horsman, Reginald. *Expansion and American Indian Policy, 1783–1812.* East Lansing: Michigan State University Press, 1967.

———. *Matthew Elliott: British Indian Agent.* Detroit: Wayne State University Press, 1964.

Huebner, Andrew J. *The Warrior Image: Soldiers in American Culture from the Second World War to the Vietnam Era.* Chapel Hill: University of North Carolina Press, 2008.

Hunt, Aurora. *The Army of the Pacific.* Glendale, Calif.: Arthur Clark Co., 1951.

———. *Major General James Henry Carleton, 1814–1873: Western Frontier Dragoon.* Glendale, Calif.: Arthur H. Clark, 1958.

Hurt, Douglas. *The Ohio Frontier: Crucible of the Old Northwest, 1720–1830* (1830). Bloomington: Indiana University Press, 1996.

Hurt, Wesley R. *Sioux Indians*. 4 vols. New York: Garland Pub., Inc., 1974.

Hurtado, Albert L. *Indian Survival on the California Frontier*. New Haven: Yale University Press, 1988.

Hyde, George E. *Life of George Bent Written from His Letters*. Edited by Savoie Lottinville. Norman: University of Oklahoma Press, 1968.

Jacobs, James Ripley. *The Beginnings of the U.S. Army, 1783–1812*. Princeton: Princeton University Press, 1947.

Jacoby, Karl. *Shadows at Dawn: An Apache Massacre and the Violence of History*. New York: Penguin Press, 2008.

Jones, Landon Y. *William Clark and the Shaping of the West*. New York: Hill & Wang, 2004.

Jortner, Adam. *The Gods of Prophetstown: The Battle of Tippecanoe and the Holy War for the American Frontier*. New York: Oxford University Press, 2012.

Josephy, Alvin M. *Nez Perce Country*. Lincoln: University of Nebraska Press, 2007.

———. *The Nez Perce Indians and the Opening of the Northwest*. New Haven: Yale University Press, 1965.

Jung, Patrick J. *The Black Hawk War of 1832*. Norman: University of Oklahoma Press, 2007.

Kaut, Charles R. *The Western Apache Clan System: Its Origins and Development*. Albuquerque: University of New Mexico Press, 1957.

Kelsey, Harry J., Jr. *Frontier Capitalist: The Life of John Evans*. Denver: State Historical Society of Colorado, 1969.

Kluger, Richard. *Seizing Destiny: How America Grew from Sea to Shining Sea*. New York: Vintage Books, 2008.

Lavender, David. *"Let Me Be Free": The Nez Perce Tragedy*. New York: Harper Collins, 1992.

Lehmer, Donald J. *Introduction to Middle Missouri Archeology*. Anthropological Papers, No. 1. Washington, D.C.: National Park Service, 1971.

Lockwood, Frank C. *The Apache Indians*. New York: Macmillan, 1938.

Lofaro, Michael A. *Daniel Boone: An American Life*. Lexington: University Press of Kentucky, 2003.

Mann, Barbara Alice. *George Washington's War on Native America*. Lincoln: University of Nebraska Press, 2008.

Martin, Joel W. *Sacred Revolt: The Muskogees' Struggle for a New World*. Boston: Beacon Press, 1991.

Masich, Andrew E. *The Civil War in Arizona: The Story of the California Volunteers, 1861–1865*. Norman: University of Oklahoma Press, 2008.

McChristian, Douglas C. *Fort Bowie, Arizona: Combat Post of the Southwest, 1858–1894*. Norman: University of Oklahoma Press, 2005.

McWhorter, L. V. *Hear Me, My Chiefs! Nez Perce History and Legend*. Caldwell, Idaho: Caxton Printers, 1952.

Meyer, Roy W. *History of the Santee Sioux: United States Indian Policy on Trial.* Lincoln: University of Nebraska Press, 1967.

————. *The Village Indians of the Upper Missouri: The Mandans, Hidatsas, and Arikaras.* Lincoln: University of Nebraska Press, 1977.

Miller, J. R. *Skyscrapers Hide the Heavens: A History of Indian-White Relations in Canada.* 3d ed. Toronto: University of Toronto Press, 2000.

Mooney, James. *The Ghost Dance Religion and the Sioux Outbreak of 1890.* Fourteenth Annual Report of the Bureau of American Ethnology, Part 2. Washington, D.C.: Government Printing Office. 1896.

Moorhead, Max L. *The Apache Frontier: Jacobo Ugarte and Spanish-Indian Relations in Northern New Spain, 1769–1791.* Norman: University of Oklahoma Press, 1968.

Morgan, Dale L. *Jedediah Smith and the Opening of the West.* Indianapolis: Bobbs-Merrill, 1953.

Moses, A. Dirk. *Empire, Colony, Genocide: Conquest, Occupation, and Subaltern Resistance in World History.* New York: Berghahn Books, 2008.

Nester, William R. *The Arikara War: The First Plains Indian War, 1823.* Missoula, Mont.: Mountain Press Publishing Co., 2001.

Nichols, David A. *Lincoln and the Indians: Civil War Policy and Politics.* Columbia: University of Missouri Press, 1978.

Nichols, Roger L. *Black Hawk and the Warrior's Path.* Arlington Heights, Ill.: Harlan Davidson, 1992.

————. *General Henry Atkinson: A Western Military Career.* Norman: University of Oklahoma Press, 1965.

Oehler, C. M. *The Great Sioux Uprising.* New York: Oxford University Press, 1959.

Oglesby, Richard Edward. *Manuel Lisa and the Opening of the Missouri Fur Trade.* Norman: University of Oklahoma Press, 1963.

Opler, Morris. *An Apache Lifeway.* Chicago: University of Chicago Press, 1965.

Ostler, Jeffrey. *The Plains Sioux and U.S. Colonialism from Lewis and Clark to Wounded Knee.* Cambridge: Cambridge University Press, 2004.

Owens, Robert M. *Mr. Jefferson's Hammer: William Henry Harrison and the Origins of American Indian Policy.* Norman: University of Oklahoma Press, 2007.

Owsley, Frank Lawrence, Jr. *Struggle for the Gulf Borderlands: The Creek War and the Battle for New Orleans, 1812–1815.* Tuscaloosa: University of Alabama Press, 1981.

Perdue, Theda. *"Mixed Blood" Indians: Racial Construction in the Early South.* Athens: University of Georgia Press, 2003.

Phillips, George H. *Chiefs and Challengers: Indian Resistance and Cooperation in Southern California.* Berkeley: University of California Press, 1975.

Phillips, Paul C., and J. W. Smurr. *The Fur Trade.* 2 vols. Norman: University of Oklahoma Press, 1961.

Pound, Merritt B. *Benjamin Hawkins: Indian Agent.* Athens: University of Georgia Press, 1951.

Prucha, Francis Paul. *American Indian Treaties: The History of a Political Anomaly.* Berkeley: University of California Press, 1994.

————. *The Great Father: The United States Government and the Indians.* 2 vols. Lincoln: University of Nebraska Press, 1984.

————. *The Sword of the Republic: The United States Army on the Frontier, 1783–1846* (1969). Bloomington: Indiana University Press, 1977.

Radbourne, Allan. *Mickey Free: Apache Captive, Interpreter, and Indian Scout.* Tucson: Arizona Historical Society, 2005.

Reynolds, Henry. *The Other Side of the Frontier: Aboriginal Resistance to the European Invasion of Australia.* Rev. ed. Sydney: University of New South Wales Press, 2007.

Richards, Kent D. *Isaac Stevens: Young Man in a Hurry.* Provo: Brigham Young University Press, 1979.

Roberts, David. *Once They Moved Like the Wind: Cochise, Geronimo, and the Apache Wars.* New York: Simon & Schuster, 1993.

Rollings, Willard H. *The Osage: An Ethnohistorical Study of Hegemony on the Prairie-Plains.* Columbia: University of Missouri Press, 1992.

Ronda, James P. *Lewis and Clark among the Indians.* Lincoln: University of Nebraska Press, 1984.

Ruby, Robert H., and John A. Brown. *Dreamer Prophets of the Columbia Plateau: Smohalla and Skolaskin.* Norman: University of Oklahoma Press, 1989.

————. *John Slocum and the Indian Shaker Church.* Norman University of Oklahoma Press, 1996.

Satz, Ronald N. *American Indian Policy in the Jacksonian Era.* Lincoln: University of Nebraska Press, 1975.

Saum, Lewis O. *The Fur Trader and the Indian.* Seattle: University of Washington Press, 1965.

Saunt, Claudio. *A New Order of Things: Property, Power, and the Transformation of the Creek Indians, 1733–1816.* New York: Cambridge University Press, 1999.

Sheridan, Thomas E. *Arizona: A History.* Tucson: University of Arizona Press, 1995.

Silver, Peter. *Our Savage Neighbors: How Indian War Transformed Early America.* New York: W. W. Norton & Co., 2008.

Skaggs, David Curtis, and Larry L. Nelson, eds. *The Sixty Year's War for the Great Lakes, 1754–1814.* East Lansing: Michigan State University Press, 2001.

Stannard, David E. *American Holocaust: The Conquest of the New World.* New York: Oxford University Press, 1992.

Steele, Ian K. *Warpaths: Invasions of North America.* New York: Oxford University Press, 1994.

Sugden, John. *Blue Jacket: Warrior of the Shawnees.* Lincoln: University of Nebraska Press, 2000.

————. *Tecumseh: A Life.* New York: Henry Holt, 1997.

Sunder, John. *Joshua Pilcher: Fur Trader and Indian Agent.* Norman: University of Oklahoma Press, 1968.

Svaldi, David. *Sand Creek and the Rhetoric of Extermination: A Case Study in Indian-White Relations.* Lanham, Md.: University Press of America, 1989.

Sweeney, Edwin R. *Cochise: Chiricahua Apache Chief.* Norman: University of Oklahoma Press, 1991.

———. *Mangas Coloradas: Chief of the Chiricahua Apaches.* Norman: University of Oklahoma Press, 1998.

Sword, Wiley. *President Washington's Indian War: The Struggle for the Old Northwest, 1790–1795.* Norman: University of Oklahoma Press, 1985.

Thornton, Russell. *American Indian Holocaust and Survival: A Population History since 1492.* Norman: University of Oklahoma Press, 1987.

Thrapp, Dan L. *The Conquest of Apacheria.* Norman: University of Oklahoma Press, 1967.

Trask, Kerry A. *Black Hawk: The Battle for the Heart of America.* New York: Henry Holt, 2006.

Utley, Robert M. *Frontier Regulars: The United States Army and the Indian, 1866–1891.* New York: Macmillan, 1973.

———. *Frontiersmen in Blue: The United States Army and the Indian, 1848–1865.* New York: Macmillan, 1967.

———. *The Indian Frontier of the American West, 1846–1890.* Albuquerque: University of New Mexico Press, 1983.

Vandervort, Bruce. *Indian Wars of Mexico, Canada and the United States, 1812–1900.* New York: Routledge, 2006.

Vidal, Gore. *Perpetual War for Perpetual Peace: How We Got to Be So Hated.* New York: Thunder's Mouth Press/Nation Books, 2002.

Viola, Herman. *Diplomats in Buckskin: A History of Indian Delegations in Washington City.* Washington, D.C.: Smithsonian Institution Press, 1981.

Walker, Deward E. *American Indians of Idaho.* Moscow: University Press of Idaho, 1978.

Warren, Stephen. *The Shawnees and Their Neighbors, 1795–1870.* Urbana: University of Illinois Press, 2005.

Waselkov, Gregory A. *A Conquering Spirit: Fort Mims and the Redstick War, 1813–14.* Tuscaloosa: University of Alabama Press, 2006.

Weber, David J. *The Spanish Frontier in North America.* New Haven: Yale University Press, 1992.

Wedel, Waldo. *Prehistoric Man on the Great Plains.* Norman: University of Oklahoma Press, 1961.

West, Elliott. *The Contested Plains: Indians, Goldseekers, and the Rush to Colorado.* Lawrence: University Press of Kansas, 1998.

———. *The Last Indian War: The Nez Perce Story.* New York: Oxford University Press, 2009.

Whaley, Gray H. *Oregon and the Collapse of Illahee.* Chapel Hill: University of North Carolina Press, 2010.

White, Richard. *The Middle Ground: Indians, Empires, and Republics in the Great Lakes Region, 1650–1815*. New York: Cambridge University Press, 1991.

Wood, W. Raymond, and Margot Liberty, eds. *Anthropology on the Great Plains*. Lincoln: University of Nebraska Press, 1980.

Wooster, Robert. *The American Military Frontiers: The United States Army in the West, 1783–1900*. Albuquerque: University of New Mexico Press, 2009.

———. *The Military and United States Indian Policy, 1865–1903*. New Haven: Yale University Press, 1988.

Wright, J. Leitch, Jr. *Creeks and Seminoles: The Destruction and Regeneration of the Muscogulge People*. Lincoln: University of Nebraska Press, 1986.

ARTICLES AND BOOK CHAPTERS

Anderson, Gary C. "As Red Men Viewed It: Three Indian Accounts of the Uprising." *Minnesota History* 38 (September 1962): 126–49.

Callender, Charles. "Fox." In *Handbook of North American Indians: Northeast*, edited by Bruce G. Trigger, 15:636–47. 20 vols. Washington, D.C.: Government Printing Office, 1978.

———. "Sauk." In *Handbook of North American Indians: Northeast*, edited by Bruce G. Trigger, 15:648–55. 20 vols. Washington, D.C.: Government Printing Office, 1978.

Calloway, Colin G. "'We Have Always Been the Frontier': The American Revolution in Shawnee Country." *American Indian Quarterly* 16, no. 1 (Winter 1992): 39–51.

Champagne, Duane. "A Multidimensional Theory of Colonialism: The Native North American Experience." *Journal of American Studies of Turkey* 3 (1996): 3–14.

Clifton, James A. *A Place of Refuge for All Time: The Migration of American Potawatomi into Upper Canada, 1835–1845*. Mercury Series. Ottawa: National Museum of Man, 1975.

Cramer, Harry G., III. "Tom Jeffords—Indian Agent." *Journal of Arizona History* 17, no. 2 (Summer 1976): 265–97.

DeMallie, Raymond J. "'Touching the Pen': Plains Indian Treaty Councils in Ethnohistorical Perspective." In *Ethnicity on the Great Plains*, edited by Frederick C. Luebke, 38–53. Lincoln: University of Nebraska Press, 1980.

Eid, Leroy V. "American Military Leadership: St. Clair's 1791 Defeat." *Journal of Military History* 57, no. 1 (January 1993): 71–88.

Ewers, John C. "The Indian Trade of the Upper Missouri before Lewis and Clark." In *Indian Life on the Upper Missouri*. edited by John C. Ewers, 14–33. Norman: University of Oklahoma Press, 1954. Reprint, 1968.

Flores, Dan. "Bison Ecology and Bison Diplomacy: The Southern Plains from 1800 to 1850." *Journal of American History* 77, no. 2 (September 1991): 465–85.

Green, Michael D. "Alexander McGillivray." In *American Indian Leaders: Studies in Diversity*, edited by R. David Edmunds, 41–63. Lincoln: University of Nebraska Press, 1980.

Griffen, William H. "Apache Indians and the Northern Mexican Peace Establishments." In *Southwestern Culture History: Collected Papers in Honor of Albert Schroeder*, edited by Charles H. Lange, 183–95. Albuquerque: Archaeological Society of New Mexico, 1985.

Hämäläinen, Pekka. "The First Phase of Destruction: Killing the Southern Plains Buffalo, 1790–1840." *Great Plains Quarterly* 21, no. 2 (Spring 2001): 101–14.

—————. "The Rise and Fall of Plains Indian Horse Cultures." *Journal of American History* 90, no. 3 (December 2003): 833–62.

Holder, Preston. "Social Stratification among the Arikara." *Ethnohistory* 5, no. 3 (October 1958): 212–16.

Horsman, Reginald. "The Role of the Indian in the War." In *After Tippecanoe: Some Aspects of the War of 1812*, edited by Philip P. Mason, 60–77. East Lansing: Michigan State University Press, 1963.

Howard, Oliver Otis. "Young Joseph." *North American Review* 128 (April 1879): 412–33.

Isern, Thomas D. "The Controversial Career of Edward W. Wynkoop." *Colorado Magazine* 40, no. 1 (Winter–Spring 1979): 1–18.

Kane, Lucile M. "The Sioux Treaties and the Traders." *Minnesota History* 32 (June 1951): 65–80.

Kelsey, Harry "Background to Sand Creek." *Colorado Magazine* 45, no. 4 (Fall 1968): 279–300.

Knouff, Gregory. "Soldiers and Violence on the Pennsylvania Frontier." In *Beyond Philadelphia: The American Revolution in the Pennsylvania Hinterland*, edited by John B. Frantz and William Penack, 171–93, 245–51. University Park: Pennsylvania State University Press, 1998.

Lecompte, Janet. "Sand Creek." *Colorado Magazine* 41, no. 4 (Fall 1964): 314–35.

Lee, Wayne E. "Peace Chiefs and Blood Revenge: Patterns of Restraint in Native American Warfare, 1500–1800." *Journal of Military History* 71, no. 3 (July 2007): 701–41.

Martin, Calvin. "Wildlife Diseases as a Factor in the Depopulation of the North American Indian." *Western Historical Quarterly* 7, no. 1 (January 1976): 47–62.

McCann, Lloyd E. "The Grattan Massacre." *Nebraska History* 37, no. 1 (Spring 1956): 1–26.

Mooney, James. "The Cheyenne Indians." In *American Anthropological Association Memoirs* 6, 357–442. Washington, D.C.: Government Printing Office, 1907.

Murphy, Lucy Eldersveld. "Autonomy and the Economic Roles of Indian Women of the Fox-Wisconsin Riverway Region, 1763–1832." In *Negotiators of Change: Historical Perspectives on Native American Women*, edited by Nancy Shoemaker, 72–89. New York: Routledge, 1995.

Nichols, Roger L. "The Arikara Indians and the Missouri Trade: A Quest for Survival." *Great Plains Quarterly* 2, no. 2 (Summer 1982): 77–93.

———. "Backdrop for Disaster: Causes of the Arikara War of 1823." *South Dakota History* 14, no. 2 (Summer 1984): 93–113.

Simmons, Marc. "New Mexico's Smallpox Epidemic of 1780–1781." *New Mexico Historical Review* 41, no. 4 (October 1966): 310–26.

Tanner, Helen Hornbeck. "The Glaize in 1792: A Composite Indian Community." *Ethnohistory* 25, no. 1 (Winter 1978): 15–39.

Trennery, Walter N. "The Shooting of Little Crow: Heroism or Murder?" *Minnesota History* 38 (September 1962): 150–53.

Wallace, Anthony F. C. "Prelude to Disaster: The Course of Indian-White Relations Which Led to the Black Hawk War of 1832." In *The Black Hawk War, 1831–1832*, edited by Ellen M. Whitney, 1:1–51. 2 vols. Springfield: Illinois Historical Library, 1970–78.

Wood, W. Raymond. "Plains Trade in Prehistoric and Protohistoric Intertribal Relations." In *Anthropology on the Great Plains,* edited by W. Raymond Wood and Margot Liberty, 98–109. Lincoln: University of Nebraska Press, 1980.

Index

CPSIA information c
Printed in the USA
LVOW12s09312501

370883LV00

6 143828